INDONESIA AND MALAYSIA

SCANDINAVIAN INSTITUTE OF ASIAN STUDIES

STUDIES ON ASIAN TOPICS

1. THE METHOD OF HOLDING THE THREE ONES
Poul Andersen
2. CATALOGUE OF CHINESE MANUSCRIPTS IN DANISH ARCHIVES
Erik Baark
3. INDIA-CHINA COMPARATIVE RESEARCH
Erik Baark and Jon Sigurdson (Editors)
4. THE KAMMU YEAR
Kristina Lindell et al.
5. INDONESIA AND MALAYSIA
Thommy Svensson and Per Sørensen (Editors)

STUDIES ON ASIAN TOPICS NO. 5

INDONESIA AND MALAYSIA
Scandinavian studies in contemporary society

Edited by
THOMMY SVENSSON and PER SØRENSEN

CURZON PRESS

SCANDINAVIAN INSTITUTE OF ASIAN STUDIES
Kejsergade 2, DK-1155 Copenhagen K

First published 1983

Curzon Press Ltd : London and Malmö

ISBN 0 7007 0152 4
ISSN 0142 6028

Printed in Great Britain by
Biddles Ltd, Guildford, Surrey

CONTENTS

CONTRIBUTORS

Lien Pekih Aass, Jakata

Svein Aass, Norwegian Foreign Service, Jakarta

Sven Cederroth, Department of Social Anthropology, University of Gothenburg

Ingela Gerdin, Department of Social Anthropology, University of Gothenburg

Elisabet Lind, The Ethnographical Museum, Stockholm

Magnus Lindgren, Department of Social Anthropology, University of Gothenburg (died in 1978)

Wil Lundström-Burghoorn, Department of Social Anthropology, University of Gothenburg

Ingrid Rudie, Institute of Social Anthropology, University of Oslo

Thommy Svensson, Department of History, University of Gothenburg

Per Sørensen, Scandinavian Institute of Asian Studies, Copenhagen

Lars Vikør, Gjettum, Norway

FOREWORD

In 1845, the corvette *Galathea* of the Royal Danish Navy was sent on a round-the-world trip under Commodore Steen Bille. In his written instructions it was explicitly mentioned that he, after a visit to Batavia, should show the flag in the waters of Bali and Lombok in appreciation and recognition of the work of Mads Lange in Badung. The Dutch in Batavia had in 1844 named Mads Lange as their agent on Bali. However, at the time of the visit of the *Galathea* in 1846, the Dutch were making preparations for their venture against the independent rulers of Bali. They were accordingly not interested in having the Danish flag flying in the waters of Bali, and eventually succeeded in manipulating Commodore Bille from anchoring outside Badung. Mads Lange was thus deprived of the honour planned for him by the Danish government.

Born in 1807, Mads Lange left Denmark for good with three brothers, in 1833. He started trading from Lombok, but moved in 1839 to Badung on Bali. He was much liked and respected by the local population, and so revered by the Dutch that they, in 1927, erected a stately monument over his grave near Kuta. So he managed, in 1849, to settle the dispute between the Dutch and the local rajahs, after they had defeated the Dutch in 1848. In 1856, he had decided to return to Denmark, but died before he ever got away. A letter to the Rajah of Tambanan announcing his departure was never sent and is now in the National Museum in Copenhagen, which also holds many other gifts donated by Mads Lange, including a still untranslated manuscript said to be a history of Bali.[1]

With his first wife - a Balinese woman - Mads Lange had a son, who later came to work with the famous 'white Rajah' Brook of Borneo. With his second wife - a Chinese - he had a daughter, Cecilie. She was mainly raised in Singapore and abroad, and in 1870 met and married Sultan Abu Bakar of Johore. Their son, Ibrahim, succeeded his father as Sultan of Johore, while a daughter was married to the Sultan of Pahang. In other words, Mads Lange and his family came to influence heavily the trade and nineteenth-century history of the countries which are the subject of this volume, and the preceding conference which inspired it.

From 3 to 5 June, 1977, a symposium on Indonesia and Malaysia was held in Kungälv near Gothenburg, in Sweden. Besides the two excellent papers on Lombok, much new evidence, along with important research results were presented. It has been with great satisfaction that the Scandinavian

Foreword

Institute of Asian Studies has supported, within its limited means, both the research through grants (see Graph 1, Introduction), and the conference, as well as the publication of this volume. The thirteen papers read at the conference, and those appearing here, reflect but a fraction of the research which has been or is being carried out under these auspices. It is, therefore, our fervent hope that it shall be possible in the not too distant future, to further stimulate and support new research - as in the case of the Lampang Field Project,[2] - by the realization of a field project or field station in the Malaysian-Indonesian sphere.

On behalf of the Scandinavian Institute of Asian Studies, it is a pleasure for me to thank all of those who have contributed to the success of the conference, and to this publication.

Per Sørensen

1 Catalogue of Oriental Manuscripts, IV:2(85-87), 1977.

2 The Lampang Field Station. A Scandinavian Research Center in Thailand, 1969-1974. Reports. The Scandinavian Institute of Asian Studies, Special Publication No. 5.

INTRODUCTION

The publication of a book of scholarly essays about Indonesia and Malaysia is a remarkable event in Scandinavian academic life. It could not have happened a hundred, fifty or twenty years ago, hardly even in the 1960s.

Asian studies have of course been carried out in the Scandinavian countries for several centuries. But until quite recently Southeast Asia stood outside the scholarly interest. In the beginning, the Christian tradition - as elsewhere in Europe - put the areas of the Old Testament in the main focus. Islam and its countries of origin became an important tributary stream.[1]

Following the separation of language studies from theology, fields of study were initiated in the eighteenth and nineteenth centuries by the establishment of chairs in various West Asian languages and literatures at Scandinavian seats of higher learning - in Turkology, Egyptology, Assyriology, Iranian and Semitic Studies. Later on the fields of interest spread eastward as evidenced by chairs, first in Indology, then in Sinology and last in Japanology. But the world of Southeast Asia, until recently, has remained largely untouched.[2]

Apart from the universities, however, Scandinavians had direct contacts with Asia already in the seventeenth and eighteenth centuries, and here Southeast Asia received more attention. For instance, some of the pupils of the renowned Swedish botanist of the eighteenth century, Carolus Linnaeus, travelled through Southeast Asia between the years 1744 and 1788. Their diaries and letters, and the scientific descriptions they made of the areas visited, are still valuable sources of information about Southeast Asia in the eighteenth century.[3]

The Danish and Swedish East Asiatic Companies have also maintained contacts with the Far East for a long time, contacts that were not only strictly commercial. Their records report on many events in Asia and also contain a number of Asian manuscripts and original letters from local potentates. Unlike most of those found in, for instance, Dutch collections, these are often preserved in their original, untranslated form and are still largely unused in scientific research.

Although none of the Scandinavian countries became big colonial powers, practical collaboration with Asia was intensified in the nineteenth and twentieth centuries, in the areas of international relations, business, and missionary activity. All of these activities left their own internal traditions of knowledge, as well as collections of material on Asia. One can name, in this connection, the quite extensive collection of Old Javanese and other Indonesian manuscripts held by the Royal Library in Copenhagen.[4]

Scholarly activities on the one hand, and practical contacts on the other, produced two traditions of learning up to World War II, still largely independent of each other. One was *theoretical* and academic. It was founded on the study of written sources and inscriptions and concerned with historically related problems. In the field of Indonesian and Malaysian studies this tradition is represented by the philological works of Kurt Wulff,[5] but also by the research of the Danish economic historian, Kristof Glamann.[6] The academic tradition, however, from the standpoint of volume, remained for a long time limited.

The other tradition was founded on the *practical* activities in Asia, in business undertakings, on travellers' direct contacts and observations on-the-spot, on collections of material objects, and on the study of contemporary conditions. These activities have, for instance, resulted in the ethnographical collections at the National Museum in Copenhagen and the Ethnographical Museum in Stockholm.[7] But to this tradition belong also naturalists' works,[8] journalistic and travellers' accounts,[9] memoirs,[10] and even a few examples of fiction.[11] Until quite recently these studies achieved a much greater volume than those at the universities.

The modern social sciences find most of their roots in the practical tradition; especially social anthropology with its strong emphasis on extensive field-work.[12] But studies of Southeast Asia within these new scientific fields of inquiry arose only after World War II - a development that is strongly associated with the name of Prof. Karl Gustav Izikowitz, whose research and teaching at the University of Gothenburg in the 1950s, 1960s and early 1970s laid a foundation for Southeast Asian anthropology in Scandinavia.[13]

The newly-created scholarly interest after World War II focused in the beginning almost entirely on mainland Southeast Asia, and especially on Thailand where it could be built on old Danish contacts.[14] In addition to Prof. Izikowitz' researches among the hill peasants in Indochina, and more than ten Danish botanical expeditions to Thailand in the 1950s and 1960s, scholarly studies were initiated in other fields of research.[15] Archaeological studies were launched by two Thai-Danish expeditions, one in 1960-2, and the other in 1965-6.[16] Language studies, initiated by Kurt Wulff during the inter-war period, by his work in historical linguistics, was continued by Prof. Søren Egerod's research on Thai dialectology.[17]

These activities provided the foundation for further intensification and deepening of Scandinavian research through the establishment by the Scandinavian Institute of Asian Studies (SIAS) of a field station in Lampang, located in northern Thailand, during the five years, 1969-1974.[18]

Southeast Asian studies had, however, been neglected for the most part at the Scandinavian universities, and for still another decade Thai studies remained the only exception.

It was not until the end of the 1960s that the organisational and economic conditions for work with the Southeast Asian countries on a larger scale were created by the erection of the Research Councils, the appropriation of some scientific funds, and the foundation of the Scandinavian Institute of Asian Studies in Copenhagen in 1967.

The prerequisites were now met for the emergence of Indonesian and Malaysian studies at the Universities. And once these were created, the research field grew very rapidly during the 1970s. This development is clearly reflected in the volume of research grants given. As an example, Graph 1 shows the position held by Indonesian and Malaysian studies in the scholarship programme of SIAS during the 1970s.

Slowly at first, more rapidly later on during the latter half of the 1970s, Scandinavian academic research on Indonesia and Malaysia gained in interest and importance, foremost in the field of social anthropology,[19] but also in other sectors of the social sciences,[20] modern history,[21] and linguistics.[22]

Today, Southeast Asian studies have not yet been permanently institutionalized in the universities, but are made possible primarily by means of temporary grants to smaller and clearly defined research projects. This, in combination with the - in a broad sense - utilitarian objectives that came to characterize the policy of the funding authorities, has strongly influenced the nature of research, so that the social sciences and the study of contemporary problems heavily dominate the scene (Table 1).

As research accelerated, a need for strengthened contacts among the scholars and a co-ordination of the activities, arose. Accordingly, in June 1977, SIAS arranged the first Scandinavian Conference on Indonesian and Malaysian Studies in Kungälv, north of Gothenburg in Sweden. It assembled some 50 participants to discuss practical research problems

Graph 1. Number of scholarships given to Indonesian and Malaysian studies by the Scandinavian Institute of Asian Studies for the academic years 1972/3 - 1979/80. Percentage of the total number of scholarships given for research on Asia.

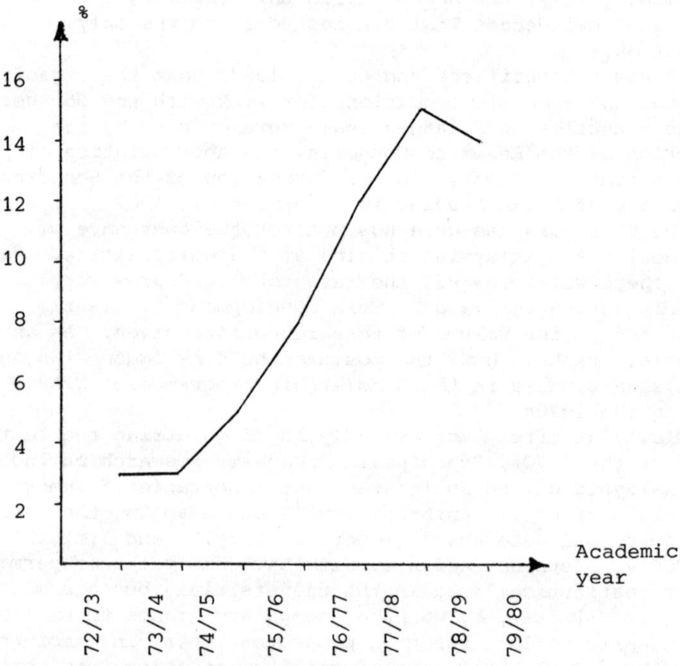

(trend: moving averages, sums of 2's)

Source: Newsletter of the Scandinavian Institute of Asian Studies (Copenhagen), 6-13 (1973-1979).

Table 1. Current research on Indonesia and Malaysia in the Scandinavian countries in 1980. Number of active researchers. Approximate figures.

Country/primary discipline	*Primary focus*		*Total*
	Indonesia	*Malaysia*	
Sweden	11	4	15
Social anthropology & ethnology	6	1	7
History	4	–	4
Political science & economics	1	3	4
Language	–	–	–
Norway	6	2	8
Social anthropology & ethnology	1	2	3
History	1	–	1
Political science & economics	2	–	2
Language	2	–	2
Denmark	4	3	7
Social anthropology & ethnology	2	3	5
History	1	–	1
Political science & economics	1	–	1
Language	–	–	–
TOTAL	21	9	30

Sources: SIAS's *'scholars lists'* and *Newsletter; Asienstudier i Norden 1979*. Copenhagen 1980, mimeo., and the author's own information.

and to take inventory regarding the status and content of the studies being carried out.

Thirteen papers were presented at the conference.[23] Six of these - in somewhat revised form - constitute the groundwork of this book, supplemented by a few additional contributions by scholars who lacked the opportunity to contribute on that occasion.

The essays of the book can be broadly divided into three groups, representing different lines of research.

The first group is represented by the articles of Elisabet Lind and Lars Vikør. Both of them have studied at the University of Leiden - the centre for cultural studies on Indonesia in Europe - and their research falls into a well-established tradition at this seat of learning, where the analysis of systems of ideas and language development occupies a prominent position.

In her article *The Rhetoric of Sukarno,* Elisabet Lind deals with the problem of how popular, anti-colonial leaders disseminated their ideas to a people still heavily stamped by traditional world-views. She analyses the rhetoric contained in the speeches of Indonesia's former, charismatic president and how the rhetoric fits into the pattern of the Javanese symbolic structure: the conceptions of social justice, history, kingship, power and social organization.

The author demonstrates how Sukarno established contact with the Javanese way of thinking by modelling his speeches after the formalized structure of *wayang* - the traditional puppet-theatre - and how his use of acronyms fits into the traditional pattern of transforming foreign words and concepts into Javanese ones.

In *Language Policy and Planning in Indonesia and Malaysia* Lars Vikør treats in an historical perspective the development of the present-day Indonesian language, *Bahasa Indonesia,* and the attempts made by the authorities to plan and direct its development. He also compares the Indonesian scene and the Malaysian, with their differing backgrounds, and discusses the attempts at linguistic co-operation between the two countries, especially the spelling reform of 1972.

The author concludes that the major problem is not that of bilingualism, but one of socio-lingualism. It is not that most Indonesians have another language as a native tongue, but instead the sharp line of demarcation between the popular languages and the abstract, rational and westernized official language.

The second group of essays - dealing exclusively with Indonesia - falls within a new and still largely unexplored field in Indonesian historiography: agrarian developments at the local level in an historical perspective. In this respect, the articles follow a recent trend in international research to shift attention from cultural and political studies toward social and economic ones. Instead of studying individuals and ideas, the focus is here put on the behaviour of collectives of people, class relations and the search for structural explanations.

Taken together these articles take issue with the broad generalizations hitherto made with regard to agrarian and class relations in rural areas. They underline the big regional variations and complex patterns of change, and emphasize the need for further concrete, local studies.

In *Peasants and Politics in Early Twentieth-Century West Java* Thommy Svensson studies the conditions of the politization of rural Java. The author presents a local case-study of the communist-oriented, popular organization *Sarekat Rakyat* in Priangan in the 1920s, focusing on the question of why rural mass politics played a bigger role in this area than elsewhere in Java.

The conclusion - based on materials mainly in Dutch archives - is that Priangan possessed a unique agro-economic system, which - in contrast to the communalistic patterns in most other areas - was based on individualistic structures. This was a condition for the concentration of land in the hands of a few and a corresponding proletarization of large parts of the rural population. Rich villagers emerged and became the local leaders of the Sarekat Rakyat, and they mobilized poorer sections of the population through ties of patronage.

The author argues that this structure of mobilization at the local level transformed the anti-colonial strategy of the national Communist Party beyond recognition. The findings indicate that there is a strong need for further local studies of the political movements in Java.

Since the 1960s Clifford Geertz' well-known theory of involution has dominated the conceptualization of rural Java and other parts of 'Inner Indonesia'.[24] The following two articles take issue with the 'geertzian' picture.

In their study *Rural Change in Suharto's Indonesia* Lien Pekih Aass and Svein Aass present data from field-work in East Java in 1973-4 that was made in the same area as Geertz and his associates studied in the 1950s. The authors demonstrate that dramatic changes have taken place during the past twenty years.

Firstly, they analyse traditional labour relations and the land tenure pattern, the division of labour, wages and income patterns. Then they turn to changes in the methods of production, focusing on harvesting methods. They point at the shift from the old *bawon*-system, which was designed to give all villagers a share of the products of the land, to the *tebasan* system introduced in the early 1970s. And they demonstrate how the new practices eliminate job opportunities for a significant number of villagers. In this way they can conclude that the once egalitarian community has turned into one increasingly based on the opposition between landowners and landless peasants.

Ingela Gerdin's *Land and Labour in West Lombok* combines data from her own anthropological fieldwork in 1972-3 and 1975-6 with written, historical source-material.

She analyses the major changes in property and labour relations that have taken place since pre-colonial times in West Lombok. On this basis she refutes the 'geertzian picture'. The author demonstrates that the changes have not meant an increasing complexity of forms - which would have been in line with Geertz' theory - but instead that a shift has taken place from one form of land tenure to another: share-cropping arrangements have been replaced by the use of day-labourers. Instead of niches in an egalitarian way being created for everyone, land and labour have become commodities and the producers have been separated from the means of production.

A different way to approach new perspectives and interpretations is represented by Magnus Lindgren. The article is called *The Problem of Kinship* and it is a theoretical and conceptual discussion. It is based on a Marxist method, with which Lindgren scrutinizes existing research on descent in the New Guinea Highlands. Here he treats the more general problem of the role of kinship in primitive societies and the interrelationships between kinship, ideology and relations of production. He concludes that descent can be seen as an ideology, which legitimizes and hides inequality and exploitation.

The third group of essays is anthropological and deals with various concrete aspects of village life: marriage-patterns, naming and address customs, and neighbourhood co-operation. Methodologically these articles differ from the structurally-oriented ones of the second group in that they concentrate on ideas and customs and attempt on this foundation, to interpret the rationale behind common peoples' behaviour.

In the first essay, *Marrying the Ancestors,* Sven Cederroth treats the problem of how traditional cosmology and traditional institutions in a rapidly changing social system are manipulated by élite-groups in order to maintain their positions.

Based on field-work made in 1972-3 and 1975-6 the author focuses on the nobility in the religiously syncretic village Suren in North Lombok. Having pointed at the diminishing influence of the nobility and its loss of material privileges, he studies the marriage strategies of the noble families. Treating the various marriage-institutions in the village in detail, he concludes that these were consciously used by the noble families as instruments to maintain their alleged superiority.

Wil Lundström-Burghoorn in a shorter essay entitled *Names, Naming and Address Customs in Minahasa,* points at the importance of language and the spoken word. Based on field-work in 1974-5 she discusses the practices used when addressing people in the northernmost peninsula of Sulawesi and the factors conditioning the address customs. The author emphasizes that names and terms of address are much more than ethnographical details and curiosities of little value, and, accordingly, deserve greater attention than they usually get in anthropological research.

Finally, Ingrid Rudie's essay *Controversial Reciprocity: On Social Change and Role Negotiation in a Kelantan Malay Community* is based on field-work carried out in Malaysia in the 1960s. It treats the changing patterns of neighbourhood co-operation both in agriculture and ceremonial undertakings.

Originally there existed a system of exchange of labour and goods between neighbours that worked outside regular market transactions. It functioned in such a way that in the long run every participant got roughly so much out of the exchange as he or she put into it. Due to external developments and a transformed, more differentiated social system, the exchange, however, has gradually become less equal, or come to be regarded as such by the villagers.

This has had the result that villagers increasingly refuse to participate. The author discusses these changes and how the process has been perceived by the inhabitants, mainly focusing on cognitive aspects.

Scandinavian scholarly studies relating to Indonesia and Malaysia have only to a limited extent been influenced by established traditions of research in the field. As a result, other scientific conditions and norms have prevailed, and theoretical and methodological impulses from entirely different neighbouring disciplines have been able to gain a greater prominence, thus giving Scandinavian research a special profile.

In a larger perspective, this 'privilege of backwardness' might constitute a condition for the emergence of an intellectual milieu which can more readily contribute to innovation by leading to the consideration of new problems, attended by fresh analysis.

Thommy Svensson

NOTES

1 See *Holmberg, Å.*, Tema: Sydöstasien. En introduktion (in: Historisk Tidskrift, 1977:3).

2 *Asienstudier i Norden 1979* (Copenhagen 1980, mimeo.), p.1.

3 See e.g. *Osbeck, Per*, Dagbok öfwer Ostindisk Resa Åren 1750, 1751, 1752 (Stockholm 1757, facsimile edition in 1969), which was translated into both English and German.

4 *Naerssen, F.H. van & Pigeaud, Th.G.Th. & Voorhoeve, P.*, Catalogue of Indonesian Manuscripts. Part 1-2. Copenhagen 1975-7. (The Royal Library, Copenhagen. Catalogue of oriental manuscripts, xylographs etc. in Danish collections, vol. 4:1-2).

5 *Wulff, K.*, Den oldjavanske Wirataparwa og dens sanskritoriginal. Copenhagen 1916. *Wulff, K.*, Über das Verhältnis des malayo-polynesischen zum indo-chinesischen. Copenhagen 1942.

6 *Glamann, K.*, Dutch-Asiatic Trade, 1620-1740. Copenhagen & The Hague 1958.

7 In contrast to the Indonesian collection at e.g. the Ethnographical Museum in Gothenburg that to a larger extent rests on modern anthropological work.

8 E.g. *Bergman, Sten*, Stenålder och grön urskog. Stockholm 1954. (Further references can be found in the bibliography.)

9 E.g.*Krarup Nielsen, Aage*, Merdeka. Strejftog i Indonesien. Copenhagen 1953. *Karabuda, B.*, Amok. Stockholm 1971. The journalistic tradition has successfully been continued on a more scientific level by Einar von Bredow, see e.g. *Bredow, E. von*, Sydöstasien - sken och verklighet. Stockholm 1968.

10 See especially the many books by *Eric Lundqvist*, among others 'Dajak' (1938), 'Sawah' (1947), 'Vildarna finns i väst' (1951), 'Öarna och morgondagen' (1961), 'Mitt Indonesien' (1972), but also for instance *Bock, C.*, Hoved-jaegere på Borneo. Beretning om en reise opover Mahakkan og nedover Barito samt reiseskildringer fra Sumatra. Kristiania 1883. *Ascanius, O.A.*, Blandt Asiens urbefolkning. Copenhagen 1939; *Wöller, Johan*, Rejsen til Insulinde. Copenhagen 1939.

11 E.g. *Lundqvist, E.*, Dullah och hans kvinnor. Stockholm 1966.

12 Otto Christian Dahl is a good example of how practical work directly has given impulses to scholarly activity, although the example is taken from a field of research only indirectly related to the subject of this book. During his life in Madagascar between 1929 and 1957 Dahl combined missionary work with studies of the

Malayo-polynesian languages. See e.g. *Dahl, O.Chr.,* Proto-Austronesian. Copenhagen 1973.

13 E.g. *Izikowitz, K.G.,* Lamet. Hill Peasants in French Indo-China. Gothenburg 1951.

14 See *Thai-Danish Relations. 30 Cycles of Friendship.* Publ. by The Royal Danish Ministry of Education, Copenhagen 1981.

15 *Newsletter of the Scandinavian Institute of Asian Studies,* no. 3 (1970), p.2.

16 *Archaeological Excavations in Thailand,* vol. 1-3. Copenhagen 1967-1969. See also *Sørensen, Per,* The Ongbah Cave and Its Fifth Drum (in: Early Southeast Asia. Essays in Archaeology, History and Historical Geography, ed. by A.B. Smith & W. Watson, London 1979), pp. 78-97, where further references can be found.

17 *Wulff, K.,* Chinesisch und Tai. Sprachvergleichende Untersuchungen. Copenhagen 1934; and *Egerod, S.,* Studies in Thai Dialectology (in: Acta Orientalia, no. 26 (1961), pp. 43-91).

18 *The Lampang Field Station: A Scandinavian Research Center in Thailand 1969-1974. Reports.* Ed by S. Egerod and P. Sørensen. Copenhagen 1976.

19 See e.g. *Elmberg, John-Erik,* Balance and Circulation. Aspects of Tradition and Change among the Mejprat of Irian Barat. Stockholm 1968. *Lind, Elisabet,* The Ideal Equilibrium. Balanced Opposition in Javanese Symbolic Structure. Unpubl. thesis, University of Stockholm 1974. *Cederroth, Sven,* Symbols of a Sasak Community in Northern Lombok, and *Gerdin, Ingela,* Ruinous Feasting. Changed Effects of the 'Big Feast' among the Balinese in Lombok (both in: Ethnos, no. 1-4:1975). *Lundström-Burghoorn, Wil,* Minahasa Civilisation. A Tradition of Change. Gothenburg 1981. (Further references can be found in the bibliography.)

20 See e.g. *Indonesia 1980: politikk, økonomi, kultur.* En artikkelsamling. Ed. by Jan-Petter Myklebust. Bergen 1980. *Aass, Svein,* The Relevance of Chayanov's Macro-Theory to the Case of Java (in: Peasants and History: Essays in the Honour of Daniel Thorner, Calcutta 1980). *Törnquist, Olle,* Outline of a Communist Shadow-Play. Problems of a Communist Strategy. The Case of Indonesia. Summary of an Ongoing Project. (Publications of AKUT, University of Uppsala, May 1980).

21 See e.g. the issue on Indonesia in *Historisk Tidskrift,* 1977:3. *Svensson, Thommy,* Peasants and Politics in Twentieth-Century Java. Research Program. (Publ. of

The South-East Asian History Project, Department of History, University of Gothenburg, January 1978.)

22 See e.g. *Hiorth, Finngeir,* Active/Passive and Non-Substantival ke-an Forms in Bahasa Indonesia; and, The Prefix Ter- in Bahasa Indonesia (in: Review of Indonesian and Malayan Affairs, no. 8:2 (1974) and no. 9:1 (1975). *Vikør, Lars,* Language Policy, Language Planning and Spelling Reform in Indonesia and Malaysia. Unpubl. thesis, University of Leiden 1977.

23 *Aass, L.P. & Aass, S.,* Communal Rights and Rural Change with Particular Reference to Harvesting Methods. A Case Study of a Javanese Village. *Andersson, B. & Dryselius, L. & Olsson, I. & Svensson, Th.,* The 1965 Indonesian coup. A source-critical analysis (in Swedish, later published in Historisk Tidskrift, 1977:3, pp. 289-320). *Cederroth, S.,* Religious reform movements in Lombok (in Swedish, later published in Historisk Tidskrift, 1977:3, pp. 350-373). *Clemmesen, J.,* Aspects of Change among the Proto-Malay Jakun. *Gerdin, I.,* Control and Conflict in the Balinese State of Lombok. *Hiorth, F.,* East-Timor: past and present (in Norwegian). *Hoadley, M.C.,* Man, Land, and Ruler. Cirebon-Priangan Administration of ca. 1700. *Lind, E.,* The Rhetoric of Sukarno. *Lundström-Burghoorn, W.,* Names, Naming and Address Customs in Minahasa. *Nyberg, T.,* The study of Buddhism in Southeast Asia (in Swedish). *Rudie, I.,* Controversial reciprocity. On occupational differentiation and role negotiation in a local Kelantan society (in Norwegian). *Svensson, Th.,* The problem of local leadership in Indonesian communism, 1923-5 (in Swedish, later published in Historisk Tidskrift, 1977:3, pp. 321-339). *Törnquist, O.,* The bourgeoisie and the revolutionary strategy in the 'Third World'. The case of PKI and Indonesia (in Swedish).

24 *Geertz, C.,* Agricultural Involution. The Processes of Ecological Change in Indonesia. Berkeley 1963.

SELECTED BIBLIOGRAPHY

Aass, S., The Agrarian Question in Indonesia. Unpubl. Thesis, University of Oslo 1974.

Aass, S., The Relevance of Chayanov's Macro-Theory to the Case of Java (in: Peasants and History: Essays in the Honour of Daniel Thorner, Calcutta 1980).

Andersson, B. & Dryselius, L. & Olsson, I. & Svensson, Th., Kupphändelserna i Indonesien 1965. En källkritisk analys (in: Historisk Tidskrift, 1977:3, pp. 289-320).

Andersson, B. & Svensson, Th., Forskning och politik i Sovjetunionen. En fallstudie av sovjetisk orientalistik 1948-1970 (in Historisk Tidskrift, 1978:4, pp. 374-416).

Archaeological Excavations in Thailand, vol. 1-3. Copenhagen 1967-9.

Ascanius, O.A., Blandt Asiens urbefolkning. Copenhagen 1939.

Asienstudier i Norden 1979. Copenhagen 1979, mimeo.

*Bache, E., Solskinsøen Bali.*Copenhagen 1932.

Bergman, S., Stenålder och grön urskog. Stockholm 1954.

Bergman, S., Through Primitive New Guinea. London 1957.

Bergman, S., My Father Is a Cannibal. London 1961.

Blomberg, R., Tropisk urskog. Stockholm 1940.

Bock, C., Hoved-jaegere paa Borneo. Beretning om en reise opover Mahakkam og nedover Barito samt reiseskildringer fra Sumatra. Kristiania 1883.

Bock, C., Reis in Oost- en Zuid-Borneo van Koetei naar Bandjermassin ondernemen op last der Indische regeering in 1879 en 1880, dl. 1-2. 's-Gravenhage 1881-7.

Boeg, P., Fra besaettelse til borgerkrig i Indonesien (in: Økonomi og politik, 32, 1958, pp. 45-72).

Bolling, F.A., Oost-Indisch reisboek (Copenhagen 1678) (in: Bijdragen tot de Taal-, Land - en Volkenkunde, 68, 1913).

Bredow, E. von, Sydöstasien - sken och verklighet. Stockholm 1968.

Bredow, E. von, Omvälvningen i Indonesien (in: Världspolitikens dagsfrågor, 1969:3).

Bredow, E. von, Asiatisk loggbok. Stockholm 1971.

Bredow, E. von, Suhartos Indonesien (in: Världspolitikens dagsfrågor, 1978:11).

Bylin, G., Vad händer i Indonesien? Göteborg, 1967.

Cederroth, S., Symbols of a Sasak Community in Northern Lombok (in: Ethnos, 1975:1-4).

Cederroth, S., Religiösa reformrörelser på Lombok (in: Historisk Tidskrift, 1977:3, pp. 350-73).

Bibliography

Cederroth, S., Religionen som inte finns. . . (in: Rapport från SIDA, 1980:8).

Dahl, O.Chr., Proto-Austronesian. Copenhagen 1973.

Egerod, S., Studies in Thai Dialectology (in: Acta Orientalia, 26, 1961, pp. 43-91).

Elmberg, J.E., Islands of Tomorrow. London 1956.

Elmberg, J.E., Balance and Circulation. Aspects of Tradition and Change among the Mejprat of Irian Barat. Stockholm 1968.

Ekeberg, C.G., Capitaine C.G. Ekebergs ostindiska resa åren 1770 och 1771. Stockholm 1971. (Fasc.)

Eskelund, K., Brune tömmermaend. Rejsen gennem Indonesien. Copenhagen 1953.

Eskelund, K., Indonesian Adventure. London 1954.

Geertz, C., Agricultural Involution. The Processes of Ecological Change in Indonesia. Berkeley 1963.

Gerdin, I., Ruinous Feasting. Changed Effects of the 'Big Feast' among the Balinese in Lombok (in: Ethnos, 1975:1-4).

Gerdin, I., Frågor kring kontroll av människor och jord på det förkoloniala Lombok under 1800-talet. Ett försök till problemfixering (in: Historisk Tidskrift, 1977:3, pp. 340-9).

Gillsäter, S., We ended in Bali. London 1961.

Glamann, K., Dutch-Asiatic Trade, 1620-1740. Copenhagen & The Hague 1958.

Hendriksen, A., Insulindes perle. Copenhagen 1945.

Hiorth, F., Active/Passive and Non-Substantival ke-an Forms in Bahasa Indonesia (in: Review of Indonesian and Malayan Affairs, 8:2, 1974).

Hiorth, F., The Prefix Ter- in Bahasa Indonesia (in: Review of Indonesian and Malayan Affairs, 9:1, 1975).

Hiorth, F., Indonesia de siste ti år (in: Samtiden, 1975:7, pp. 409-20).

Holmberg, Å., Tema: Sydöstasien. En Introduktion (in: Historisk Tidskrift, 1977:3, pp. 283-8).

Indonesia 1980: politikk, økonomi, kultur. En artikkelsamling. Ed. by J-P. Myklebust. Bergen 1980.

Izikowitz, K.G., Lamet. Hill Peasants in French Indo-China. Gothenburg 1951.

Jensen, P.E., Indonesien. Copenhagen 1971.

Jerndal, J., Indonesien (in: Världspolitikens dagsfrågor, 1958:5).

Kamstrup, H.I., Femten aar paa Sumatra. Erindringer fra mit planter- og jaegerliv. Kristiania 1899.

Karabuda, B., Amok. Ett politiskt reportage från Indonesien. Stockholm 1971.

Kaudern, W., I Celebes obygder, del 1-2. Stockholm 1921.
Klausen, A.M., Basket-work Ornamentation among the Dayaks. Oslo 1957.
Krarup Nielsen, A., Perler og palmer. Copenhagen 1931.
Krarup Nielsen, A., Merdeka. Strejftog i Indonesien. Copenhagen 1953.
The Lampang Field Station: A Scandinavian Research Center in Thailand 1969-1974. Reports. Ed. by S. Egerod & P. Sørensen. Copenhagen 1976.
Linck, O., Sumatra. Copenhagen & Oslo 1927.
Lind, E., The Ideal Equilibrium. Balanced Opposition in Javanese Symbolic Structure. Unpubl. thesis, University of Stockholm 1974.
Lindberg, B., Sumatra. Reseskildringar. Helsingfors 1910.
Ljunglöf, L., Indonesien under Sukarno (in: Världspolitikens dagsfrågor, 1962:8).
Lundqvist, E., Dajak. Stockholm 1938.
Lundqvist, E., Sawah. Stockholm 1947.
Lundqvist, E., Vildarna finns i väst. Stockholm 1951.
Lundqvist, E., Djungeltagen. Stockholm 1953.
Lundqvist, E., Balilegender. Stockholm 1955.
Lundqvist, E., Rani. Stockholm 1955.
Lundqvist, E., Öarna och morgondagen. Stockholm 1961.
Lundqvist, E., Glädjens blomster. Stockholm 1965.
Lundqvist, E., Dullah och hans kvinnor. Stockholm 1966.
Lundqvist, E., Mitt Indonesien. Stockholm 1972.
Lundqvist, E. & Lundaahl, R., Bali. Stockholm 1957.
Lundström-Burghoorn, W., Minahasa Civilization. A Tradition of Change. Gothenburg 1981.
Mjöberg, E., Borneo, dess land och folk (in: Ymer, 1926).
Mjöberg, E., Borneo, huvudjägarnas land. Stockholm 1927.
Mjöberg, E., I tropikernas villande urskogar. Äventyr och upplevelser i Nederländska Indien. Stockholm 1928.
Mjöberg, E., De tusen templens ö. Studier och upplevelser på Bali. Stockholm 1929.
Naerssen, F.H. van & Pigeaud, Th.G.Th. & Voorhoeve, P., Catalogue of Indonesian Manuscripts. Part 1-2. Copenhagen 1975-7. (The Royal Library, Copenhagen. Catalogue of Oriental Manuscripts, Xylographs etc. in Danish Collections, vol. 4:1-2.)
Newsletter of the Scandinavian Institute of Asian Studies, 6-13 (1973-9).
Osbeck, P., Dagbok öfwer Ostindisk Resa Åren 1750, 1751, 1752. Stockholm 1757.
Petersen, H., Singkeh. Copenhagen 1944.
Rudi, I., Modernisering, verdidebatt og lokalt lederskap (in: Tidskrift for Samfunnsforskning, 1968).

Sandvad, J., Bergene braender. Copenhagen 1941.

Sjögren, Ch., Holländska Indien. Orienterande handbok för svenska affärsmän. Stockholm 1922.

Skjerdal, K., Steinalder i atomtiden. Oslo 1977.

Svensson, Th., En studie av bondemobilisering i Priangan, västra Java, 1923-5 (in: Historisk Tidskrift, 1977:3, pp. 321-39).

Svensson, Th., Peasants and Politics in Twentieth-Century Java. Research Program. (Publications of the South-East Asian History Project, Department of History, University of Gothenburg, January 1978.)

Svensson, Th., On the Sources of Indonesia's Colonial Economy. Some Aspects on the Present State of Historical Statistics (in: Newsletter of the Scandinavian Institute of Asian Studies, 13, 1979).

Sydostasien. Ed. by S. Egerod & K. Glamann & P. Mohr. Copenhagen 1971.

Sørensen, P., The Ongbah Cave and Its Fifth Drum (in: Early Southeast Asia. Essays in Archaeology, History and Historical Geography, ed. by A.B. Smith & W. Watson, London 1979, pp. 78-97).

Thai-Danish Relations. 30 Cycles of Friendship. Copenhagen 1981. (Publ. by The Royal Danish Ministry of Education.)

Theilade, H., Krama. Billeder fra Java. Copenhagen 1942.

Tirén, S., En nedtystad massaker (in: Kommentar, 1969:7).

Toreson, A., Ostindisk resa 1674-1683 (ed. by O.G. Sundberg). Stockholm 1948.

Toussieng, P., Mahakam. Copenhagen 1941.

Törnquist, O., Indonesien (in: Kommentar, 1975:11-12).

Törnquist, O., Outline of a Communist Shadow-Play. Problems of a Communist Strategy. The Case of Indonesia. Summary of an Ongoing Project. (Publications of AKUT, University of Uppsala, May 1980.)

Vikør, L., Politiske og økonomiske problem i Indonesia (in: Syn og Segn, 1976:6).

Vikør, L., Språkpolitikk på fem kontinent. Oslo 1977.

Vikør, L., Language Policy, Language Planning and Spelling Reform in Indonesia and Malaysia. Unpubl. thesis, University of Leiden 1977.

Wagner, U., Colonialism and Iban Warfare. Stockholm 1972.

Wickbom, T.G., Gul Monsun. Sydöstasiatiska strövtåg. Stockholm 1962.

Wulff, K., Den oldjavanske Wirātaparwa og dens sanskritoriginal. Copenhagen 1916.

Wulff, K., Chinesisch und Tai. Sprachvergleichende Untersuchungen. Copenhagen 1934.

Bibliography

Wulff, K., Über das Verhältnis des malayo-polynesischen zum indochinesischen. Copenhagen 1942.

Wöller, J., Rejsen til Insulinde. Copenhagen 1939.

Øverås, A., Indonesia. Øriket under ekvator. Oslo 1959.

THE RHETORIC OF SUKARNO

Elisabet Lind

INTRODUCTION

Among the often controversial opinions about Sukarno, the first and former president of the Republic of Indonesia, there is one on which writers commonly agree: that Sukarno was a charismatic leader. It should perhaps be pointed out that *charisma,* following the current definition, is to be understood as a quality that the followers of a leader believe him to possess rather than as a personal quality *per se.* What concerns us here is the process of validation of charisma. Ann Ruth Willner and Dorothy Willner, in discussing charismatic leadership in newly independent states, draw a link between politics and myth. 'Recent events in a people's politics', they suggest, 'particularly those marking a major transition or extraordinary occurrence in public life, can become endowed with the quality of myth if they fit or can be fitted into the pattern of a traditional myth of body of myths'.[1] They further suggest that when an assimilation occurs between a historical event or a particular individual with similar mythical ones then 'the event or individual [becomes endowed] with the aura or sanction of the myth itself'.[2]

If one accepts this interpretation of the interplay between politics and myth in newly independent states with its reference to charismatic leaders then it is of interest to inquire into a local case in order to find out the particular structural system of ideas that makes the local case a variation on the general theme. This brings us back to Sukarno and the process of validation of charisma.

The first point to be discussed is how aspects of the local, structural system of ideas were brought to bear on Sukarno endowing him with the quality of charisma and the second and main point is the strategy of Sukarno's rhetoric or in other words how the process of the validation of his charisma may be observed in his speeches.

1. THE BACKGROUND

The local, structural system of ideas which form the base for much of Indonesian political thinking has up to the present day been predominantly Javanese. This is to be explained by the fact that the Javanese have played a dominant role in Indonesian political life particularly during the period of Guided Democracy (1959-65). The ethnic Javanese making a part of the Indonesian political élite, have largely been drawn from the traditional Javanese élite, the *priyai*, who having had a Dutch education, came from a background where traditional values still were, and still remain, strong.[3] Although as Herbert Feith has pointed out[4] 'Indonesian history isn't the history of Java and it is certainly not the history of the ethnic Javanese. . .' the impact made by the ethnic Javanese on the rest of Indonesia can hardly be overestimated. This is partly due to the fact that they constitute the largest ethnic group in Indonesia and partly to the long-established tradition of highly organized kingdoms, the power of which at periods reached beyond the island of Java. Also it was in Java that the Dutch colonial government settled and it was here that the early resistance movement against the colonial regime started. Feith[5] further states that 'the fact that the *prijaji* Javanese have emerged in a position of political preponderance under Guided Democracy can hardly be seen as a natural consequence of "decolonization", or of the resilience of their culture'. Still 'the pattern of traditional myth or body of myths' into which the political events during the Sukarno period was fitted was, as I will show below, predominantly Javanese as was the way in which Sukarno himself clothed his political message in traditional Javanese terms.

1.1 Sukarno identified as The Just Ruler, Ratu Adil

In Java messianic movements have a documented tradition of some odd two hundred years. These movements, most of which have had a fairly short duration, are connected with a prophecy allegedly made by a historical figure, Jayabaya, who in the mid-twelfth century, foretold the future history of Java. The prophecy contains *inter alia* a foretelling of the appearance of a Just Ruler, *Eurocakra* or *Ratu Adil*, who will liberate Java from foreign dominance, restore peace and order and create a prosperous society.[6] During the nineteenth century the most well-known Ratu Adil movement was the one led by Prince Dipanagara, the hero of the Java war (1825-30), and in the first two decades of the twentieth century the steadily more widely spreading belief in a Ratu Adil was channelled by Sarekat Islam (The Muslim Society) whose rapidly growing membership consisted not only of fervent Muslims *(santri)* but of non-Muslims *(abangan)* as well, and whose leader, Tjokroaminoto, was believed to be a

Ratu Adil. 'Sarekat Islam', says Bernhard Dahm, 'should grow to the biggest Ratu Adil movement that ever existed on Java'.[7] The mystical appeal that Sarekat Islam had on the masses did not last however; it was checked by Tjokroaminoto who officially declared that the eagerly awaited Ratu Adil was not to appear in the shape of an individual but in the shape of socialism. The one who was to take up the fallen mantle of Tjokroaminoto was Sukarno, whom people, when he became the leader of the Nationalist Party and came to stand as the foremost symbol for the independence movement, should identify as a Ratu Adil. Sukarno was thus a late link in a long tradition. But of importance is the fact that the people's belief in his being a Ratu Adil remained steadfast through the whole period of the fight for independence; a fact which illustrates the charismatic appeal he had to people.[8] How then did Sukarno, himself, view the belief in the appearance of a Ratu Adil? He fully realized that the social conditions of the people under Dutch rule favoured the spreading of such a belief. In his famous defence speech before the Dutch judges in 1930 he gives an explanation of why the belief in Jayabaya's prophecy still was so strong, of why the people believed in and constantly hoped for the appearance of a Ratu Adil. 'There is only one explanation', he says, 'and that is that the suffering people incessantly hope and wait for help like a man in darkness every hour, every minute, every second waits and wonders when, when will the sun finally rise?'[9] But like Tjokroaminoto before him, he did not see Ratu Adil as an individual, but rather as a social condition and one under which the people should experience social justice and live in harmony and prosperity:

> Friends, I suggest: if we are looking for democracy it had better not be Western democracy, but *permusjawaratan* [deliberation among representatives] that brings life, that is politic-economic democracy that is capable of creating social prosperity. The Indonesian people have for a long time talked about this matter. What is meant by Ratu Adil? What is meant by the idea of Ratu Adil is social justice. The people want to live in harmony. The people who felt that there was a shortage of food and clothing created under the leadership of Ratu Adil a new world in which justice prevailed. Because of this if we truly understand and love the Indonesian people let us accept this principle of social justice that is not just only political equality, friends, but

> also in the economic field we have to create equality which means the best possible harmony.[10]

Sukarno thus identifies Ratu Adil as a condition of social justice, a concept which in the original text is rendered in Dutch. When he interprets it he uses the word *sejahtera*, here translated as prosperity/harmony. *Sejahtera* means peaceful and prosperous and is synonymous with *selamet*, a peaceful condition 'without any disturbances'.[11] Sukarno also says that the Indonesian people earlier 'under the leadership of Ratu Adil *[created]* a new world in which justice prevailed,' i.e. a world in which there was an abundance of food and clothing and which was prosperous and peaceful, and this, it is implied, will once more be the goal of the Indonesian nation. Although Sukarno states that social justice means political as well as economic equality the example he gives of a just world (society) is one cast in traditional Javanese terms. He refers back to a feudal society the peace and prosperity of which depended on the leadership of a Just Ruler, Ratu Adil. This view of social justice comes very close to the ideal view of a traditional Javanese kingdom as it is expressed in the standard introduction of wayang (shadow puppet) play, a piece of text that all Javanese, having watched *wayang* performances from their early infancy, know more or less by heart. In such an introduction the country in which the play is set is praised as the ideal country:

> This country is *panjang punjung pasir wukir loh jinawi gemah ripah karta tur raharja*. It is *Panjang* (long) because one can speak at length about it, *punjung* (elevated) because its power is strong and influential, . . . *loh* (fertile) because everything that is planted yields plenty, *jinawi* (cheap) because all things are cheap to buy, *gemah* (prosperous) because merchants can travel day and night without interruption since they encounter no danger on the roads, *ripah* (populous) because foreigners have thronged into the country, the roofs of their houses touch so that open spaces look crowded because of the prosperous condition of the country, *karta* (prosperous) because the farmers peacefully work on their land; buffalos, cows, chickens and ducks do not have to be tethered and tied; during daytime they roam around freely and at night they return by themselves, *raharja* (peaceful) because all enemies are far away, and the ministers are famous for the unequalled way in which they carry on their duties, having

> unsurpassed insight and knowledge in administrative task, always having in their minds to increase the excellence of the king. This country, great is its torch, spreading its radiance over the world, high is its smoke, its fame spreads afar, not only the island of Java has submitted, but numerous foreign kingdoms having submitted willingly impressed by the perfection of this country. . . . And now the names of the king should be mentioned . . . [Here follows an enumeration of all the names together with an interpretation of their meaning]. . . . As for the character of the king, he gives clothes to those who lack a dress to put on, he feeds those who starve, gives water to those whose wells are dry, supplies walking-sticks to those who stumble, he gives sunshades to those who suffer from the heat and umbrellas to those who get caught in the rain, he cures those who are ill, he hands out the just amount of gifts and fines, he is just in his punishments, never partial. . . . If one should sum up all the excellent qualities of the king it would take the whole night.[12]

By phrasing social justice in terms of general prosperity, peacefulness, a condition without any disturbances, and in terms of a society in which food and clothes are cheap, Sukarno easily evokes the mood of the *wayang* play in which a prosperous and peaceful country is pictured, a country the blessings of which are due to the beneficial influences of the ruler. Thus, the goal set by Sukarno, social prosperity, does not in itself imply a structural change as it appears to be reachable within the traditional structural framework.

One more aspect that should be brought up in connection with Sukarno's concept of social prosperity is the Javanese view of history 'as a series of recurrent cycles' rather than 'as a linear movement through time', the latter view corresponding more closely to the Western view of history. According to the former view history oscillates, as it were, between epochs of order, called *jaman mas* 'the golden age' and those of disorder, called *jaman edan* 'the made age', the two types of epochs constantly alternating.[13] That Sukarno's view of history closely corresponds to the traditional Javanese view is borne out by a passage in his defence speech of 1930 in which he explains the strategy used by the Nationalist Party (PNI) to reinforce the, at the time, steadily growing nationalism. 'PNI', Sukarno says 'arouses and brings to life the people's awareness of their "glorious past", their "dark ages", and the "promise of a brightly beckoning future"'. He elaborates on these three themes and describes Indonesia's, particularly Java's, great past, the miserable condition of the Indonesian people at the time and the hope of recapturing the greatness of the past in the future. The miserable conditions under which the Indonesian people suffered were the reason for their belief in the appearance of a Ratu Adil, a 'Just Ruler'.[14] Anderson[15] remarks that 'Sukarno's *Socialisme à la Indonesia* is much closer in every way to the *Djaman Mas* (Golden Age) than it is to Marx's classless society. It is a *restoration* above all: the old order re-emerging in technical, modern dress; the golden age at a much higher level of average income per capita, but with the older verities and structures scarcely altered.'

If one accepts the above interpretation of Sukarno's concept of social prosperity as a condition prevailing during a period of order under the leadership of a 'Just Ruler' then the question arises as to the traditional conception of Javanese kingship and how far this still was valid in Indonesian political thinking during Sukarno's period of incumbency?

1.2 The conceptual framework of the traditional Javanese kingship

In what he calls 'The Doctrine of the Exemplary Center' Clifford Geertz has aptly summed up the essence of Javanese kingship as 'the notion that the king's court and capital, and at their axis the king himself, form at once an image of divine order and a paradigm for social order'.[16]

The traditional Javanese state was highly centripetal. As the capital just as elsewhere in South-East Asia, was viewed as a microcosmic replica of macrocosm,[17] so the king himself was the worldly embodiment of the universal ruler, a belief which is expressed in the name *Paku Buwana* 'The Nail of the Universe', still carried by the Susuhunan of Surakarta (Central Java). The centripetal orientation recurred in the administrative structure of the state which was arranged in concentric circles with the king, court and capital in the centre.[18] The king moreover was the sole source of power, the top administrators 'merely reflected the light which radiated from the Sultan . . .' 'The closer their "blood" or formal relation to the Sultan, the more intense the light they could reflect from him to others', Selosoemardjan states, speaking about the top administrators of the Yogya Principality.[19]

If the capital symbolized the unity of the state which is borne out both by the use of the same term, *nagara*, for state as well as capital, and by a passage in the famous chronicle Nāgara-Kertāgama in which the whole country is said to be a copy of the capital,[20] the king symbolized the unity of the state. This may be inferred from the direct correlation that existed between a ruler's general character and behaviour and the situation in the realm. The beneficial influence of an excellent ruler spread through the country and created peace and prosperity. Conversely flaws in his character or a misstep on his part had disasterous consequences for the whole society, which then faced a complete collapse.[21]

The traditional king, then, was not only identified with the centre, but at the same time he was believed to represent the unity of the state. The centre representing the unity of diverse and even opposed phenomena is a basic element in the Javanese symbolic structure at different levels of abstraction. A common illustration of this is the way in which various concepts, elements, objects, etc. are arranged in a scheme of five (sometimes nine) in such a way that four entities are placed in the four cardinal directions (in the case of nine, eight entities are placed in the four cardinal directions and in their intermediate sections) and the fifth (ninth) is placed in the centre. The centre is believed to have absorbed the different qualities of all the other entities, to represent the totality of them all.[22]

The conception of the centre as a unity of diverse elements thus permeates the whole traditional Javanese symbolic structure. Anderson's analysis of the Javanese conception of power is relevant in this context. As he brings up important aspects of the Javanese power complex, the understanding of which is essential for an appraisal as to how far the Javanese tradition has continued into Indonesian politics, I will here give the main points of his argumentation. Anderson contrasts the Javanese concept of power to the (modern) Western concept, which he sees as directly opposed to the Javanese. The Javanese conception of power, he argues, is that of something concrete. Power in the Javanese view is almost substantial and Anderson defines it as the 'divine energy,which animates the universe'. Power, furthermore, is homogeneous as it derives from one source, divine energy, and it is identical in quality whoever possesses it. The third point is that as the universe is fixed in size, so the amount of power that exists within it remains constant. Applied to the distribution of power the ultimate consequence of this view is 'that concentration of power in one place or in one person requires a proportional diminution elsewhere'. Lastly, power in itself is considered to be neither good nor evil, hence, according to the Javanese there is no such thing as legitimate or illegitimate power, power is a thing in itself.[23]

If one accepts this interpretation of the Javanese conception of power a correlation between power and centre lies close at hand in so far as power implies concentration of divine energy in a way similar to the notion of the centre as a point into which diverse entities are absorbed and concentrated.

Acquisition of power is traditionally achieved through meditation and various ways of practising asceticism, *tapa*. Absolute concentration is needed in order to succeed, should it slacken or the tapa be interrupted the possibility to achieve one's goal is forfeited as examples in the *wayang* literature show.[24] The goal, the acquisition of supernatural power, is the prerequisite for political power. Possession of supernatural power deriving from a great amount of divine energy in an individual is particularly important for a ruler. This divine energy is called *wahyu kedaton* or *cahya nurbuwah,* 'a substance which graced kingship'.[25] The outward sign of this substance was the radiance, *teja* or *cahya* that the one possessing it gives off. Loss of power, first visible in the disappearance of the radiance, follows on the loss of *wahyu* which, as it were, becomes focused in the new ruler.[26] When the substance wahyu moves from one individual to another if often has a meteorlike appearance, 'a dazzling blue, green or white ball of light *(andaru, pulung)*, streaking through the night sky'.[27] Unusual meterological phenomena such as thunder and lightning from a clear sky in broad daylight also may mark the transference of wahyu. Such a thing happened when the present Vice-President of the Republic of Indonesia, Sultan Hamengkubuwono IX, returned to Indonesia to meet his dying father. Interestingly enough it happened first when father and son left the train at the railway station in Yogyakarta (the capital of the Principality) and after that the old Sultan had given his son a sacred dagger *(kris)* that a ruling Sultan never may part from. The burst of thunder from the clear sky, says Selosoemardjan, 'made a deep impression upon Jogjakarta's people, and it created the belief that the young Crown Prince must be endowed with exceptional qualities'.[28]

The view that the possession of wahyu was *the* criterion of a ruler regardless of whether his claims to sovereignty were legitimate or not, lay the way open to usurpation but, as Moertono points out, speaking about the change of incumbents, the incumbency itself was never questioned.[29]

A final point to be brought up is the traditional king's inactivity in political matters. Political and administrative tasks were the prime minister's obligation while the king's function was mainly symbolic and ritual. The king's mere presence guaranteed the welfare of the country, welfare meaning not only prosperity but that all matters went smoothly according to a fixed pattern in which no disturbances occurred. The king only intervened if something happened that disturbed this order, for example the outbreak of a plague epidemic, and then not in person but represented by a sacred heirloom which was carried in a procession that circumambulated the city of Yogyakarta.[30]

The king's ritual function was to display his greatness, a sign of his possession of wahyu. The further his authority extended the greater was the king and his kingdom. Ritual glorification of the king therefore was viewed as a matter of utmost importance. In the *wayang* theatre which formed part of this ritual glorification a point is made, as we have seen above, of how foreign kings, impressed by the perfection of the Javanese kingdom, voluntarily submit to its authority. The greatness of the Javanese kingdom is also metaphorically expressed in the standard introduction of a *wayang* play in which its influence on foreign kingdoms is described as a great torch, whose radiance illuminates the whole world and whose smoke, rises high (see also Moertono). The importance of ritual at the court far exceeded the more practical task of governing the country. The traditional Javanese state was a 'Theatre State' as Clifford Geertz aptly puts it.[31]

> Spectacle was what the state was for; its central task was less to govern - a job that the villagers largely accomplished for and among themselves - than to display in liturgical form of the dominant themes of the Javanese culture. The capital was a stage upon which the priests and nobles, headed by the king, presented an endless sacred pageant with respect to which the ordinary man was at once spectator, spear carrier and, through the tribute and service he was obliged to render, sponsor.

To sum up then: the traditional Javanese kingdom was structurally as well as symbolically a highly centripetal state. The king, viewed as the worldly embodiment of the universal ruler, represented the centre of the state. The Javanese conception of centre is that of a focal point into which diverse entities become absorbed and the king therefore was believed to personify the unity of the state. The king's role was symbolic and ritual. The beneficial influence that radiated from him guaranteed the country's welfare and that no disturbances occurred in the patterned order. The glorification of the king was an important ritual theme, the more splendid the ceremonial activities around him, the greater and more far reaching became his authority. The ceremonial activities served the purpose of 'showing of force' to use, in the context, an anachronistic expression. The state, to paraphrase Geertz, could be likened to a huge stage on which the play about the glory of the king and the splendour of the kingdom continually was performed.

To what extent did the traditional symbolic structure influence the political thinking during the Sukarno period? That the belief in a Ratu Adil, 'A Just Ruler', played a role is, as we have seen above, well documented in the literature dealing with the Indonesian independence movement. Attention has also been drawn to other themes, particularly in Sukarno's political thinking, which correspond to themes in the traditional symbolic structure. Geertz, for example, has brought up the *Panca Sila* concept, Sukarno's Five Principles which have become the ideological foundation of the Indonesian state. Sukarno's uniting of the five principles into one principle, the *gotong royong* principle, (the latter expression is commonly used by farmers for mutual co-operation) Geertz sees as a 'metaphoric reworking' of the traditional concept of the centre as the unity. The reworking is a complex one uniting, in Geertz' view the 'exemplary centre' which belongs to the 'great tradition' with the 'little tradition' of the farm sphere, and added to this are the modern concepts of nationalism, democracy, etc., which Sukarno, so to say, grafts on the old stock of the traditional concept of five, and so moulds it all 'into one luminous image'.[32] Sukarno's use of the concept unity is also discussed by Benedict Anderson. He makes the observation that Sukarno in his speeches again and again calls for unity and refers this back to the traditional conception of power as a concentration of diverse entities in the one who possesses power. Unity is essential since it implies concentration, hence power, and dispersion results in loss of power. Sukarno's call for unity shows a certain anxiety which, for a correct understanding thereof should be viewed within the traditional framework of power as a concentration of diverse entities while dispersion of them invariably results in the loss of power.[33] Sukarno's syncretistic view of himself when he claims to be neither a nationalist, a Muslim nor a Marxist but 'a mixture of all those -isms,' and later his plans to form a NASAKOM cabinet, including the main political parties oriented towards nationalism (*Nas*ionalisme), religion (*A*gama) and communism (*Kom*unisme) respectively, point in the same direction.[34] These few examples show that some of the main aspects of the symbolic structure, existing in the traditional Javanese kingdom have remained valid in modern Indonesian policy making.

2. SUKARNO'S RHETORIC AND THE WAYANG PLAY

It is now time to turn to Sukarno's strategy as it is revealed in his speeches or differently put, to look into how Sukarno's charisma was validated through his rhetoric. Sukarno, as we have seen above, reworked with great dexterity traditional Javanese symbols and metaphors and fitted them into a modern political framework. Like most other ethnic Javanese (Sukarno was of a mixed Balinese-Javanese extraction and brought up in East Java) Sukarno was familiar with the wayang theatre, having watched wayang performances from his early childhood on.[35] Bernhard Dahm, in particular, has drawn attention to Sukarno's use of the Bratayuda theme, i.e. the battle between two cousin groups, the hundred Kurawa brothers and the five Pandawa brothers in the Mahabharata epos, as a metaphor for the Dutch-Indonesian relationship during the period of Indonesia's fight for independence.[36] This metaphor like the Panca Sila metaphor and the Ratu Adil symbol are all drawn from the body of traditional Javanese myth. In the highly literate traditional Javanese society mythical themes were incorporated into various literary genre such as *kidung,* songs, composed in 'little metres', *kakawin,* literature composed in 'big metres' (the latter genre containing such works as the Ramayana kakawin, the Bharata-yuddha, both based on Hindu epics, and Arjunawiwaha), and *babad,* chronicles, to mention some of the more important genre.[37] It is however noteworthy that the whole mythical complex is embodied in the wayang theatre which served as a philosophical foundation for the traditional way of life.[38] Moreover wayang performances were rhetoric and the *dhalang* (puppeteer) an orator. Given the many allusions to the wayang theatre in Sukarno's speeches, the question must be put whether wayang as a whole, the structure of the play, its philosophy and its rhetoric has not influenced Sukarno's speech strategy to a greater extent than has commonly been acknowledged? A comparison of the role of the dhalang, his rhetoric, various components of the wayang play such as play structure, and message, with Sukarno's role, rhetoric, and political message will, I hope, provide an answer. The next step, thus, will be to outline those aspects of the wayang theatre which just have been mentioned and to compare them to Sukarno's rhetorical strategy to see if my suggestion holds true.

2.1 The dhalang as a mediator

The wayang theatre has perhaps been the most important vehicle for spreading myth among the people. Myth should here be understood in its widest sense, i.e. including established values which, clothed in the metaphors of myth, in this way were disseminated to all layers of the population. The dhalang, in the traditional society, acted as a mediator between the ruling class and the common people rendering the ethics set by the former in terms understandable to the latter, at the same time acting as an educator, and he mediated between the common people and the ruling class by acting as a barometer of the people's current mood in the clown scenes. The clown scenes are remarkable in that they are the only anachronistic scenes in a wayang play, the clown dialogue may and mostly does contain comments and criticism on the current economical and political situation.[39]

The message that the dhalang mediates through the wayang play is that of a 'just and prosperous society', the peacefulness, order and prosperity of which depends on the excellent qualities of the king (see the introduction to a wayang play cited above). The society pictured is one of a strict hierarchical order. Within the framework of this order special codes of conduct are prescribed for members of each social level, and correct behaviour equals keeping within the rules set for the particular level to which an individual belongs.[40] In the traditional wayang play, however, common people to not occur, the roles include gods, kings and members of their courts, to which a prime minister also belongs; priests, giants and demons from overseas and clown-servants complete the list. The clown-servants form a marginal group being neither of the people nor belonging to the nobles. They act as the people's mouthpiece, they have godlike qualities (they do not die) and one clown-servant character in particular, Semar, at times shows his power which exceeds that of all the classified gods. The puppets in a wayang play represent models of behaviour on a scale which ranges from refined *(alus)*, to crude *(kasar)*. The concept alus is a fairly complex one. It connotes a quality of self-restraint, expressed in bodily movements, in a voice never raised, and in the ability to control one's emotions; it means the ability to master the different levels of the Javanese language, which is a status language, and it also connotes physical beauty which is viewed as the outward appearance of inward perfection. Conversely kasar connotes the opposite of these qualities: clumsy and unrestrained bodily movements, lack of self-control, expressed in a loud voice and in a raucous laughter, it connotes the inability to master the intricacies of the Javanese language and it connotes an ugly physical appearance, the outward expression of a crude character. The heroes (and heroines) of the wayang play are, not surprisingly, classified as alus characters while giants and demons, their opposites, are classified as kasar. The ideal model, then set up for the Javanese from their early childhood is the alus character of the wayang play.

A wayang play lasts for nine hours, the dhalang is the sole performer accompanied by a *gamelan* orchestra and singers. Not only is a skilful handling of the puppets necessary but a complete mastering of the different levels of the Javanese language and an ability to modulate the voice so that it will fit the alus as well as the kasar characters of the play. It stands to reason that such a difficult task could hardly be accomplished if the dramatic structure of the play was not highly standardized and the language did not follow a restricted code.

A wayang play is divided into three parts, each part lasting for three hours. Each part contains a number of standard scenes which have fixed names. Each scene in turn 'is made up of certain standard dramatic elements, or building blocks: Two types of narration, dialogue, and songs (in addition to puppet movements . . .)'.[41] The language used is a mixture 'of Sanskrit, old-Javanese (Kawi), special forms of palace address, and colloquial language. . . . Foreign or contemporary words may not be inserted except in clown scenes'.[42] Fixed phrases are used in the narration as well as in the dialogues; in the latter such phrases illustrate the ceremonial politeness characteristic for alus behaviour. The songs (Suluk) are sung in an archaic language not understood by the public and not even by the dhalang, who learns it by heart. They express a hero's state of mind, emotions and set the general mood of a particular situation.[43] The plays are set in the never-never land of a distant mythical past. The plot describes a circular motion, beginning with a description of a kingdom, pictured as 'a just and prosperous society,' from there moving on to a conflict developed between this kingdom and a foreign kingdom (thus an equal power), it describes the development and solution of the conflict which is solved through a series of battles and the final victory of the first kingdom, which in the end re-emerges as the 'just and prosperous' kingdom it was in the beginning of the play.

The nine-hour-long play begins at 9 pm and ends at dawn, the climax of the conflict occurs at midnight and the final victory coincides with the sunrise. The sunrise corresponds to the wind direction, East, which in the Javanese symbolic structures carries a number of good connotations, East being associated with the rice-goddess Dewi Sri, the provider of the staple food rice, the basis of life.

In summary: The dramatic structure of a wayang play is fixed and contains a number of standard scenes which follow upon each other in a given order. The language follows a formal code except in the clown scenes, the only scenes in which the code is evaluative.[44] The songs, which are unintelligible, set the mood of a particular situation and have mainly a motif value. Conflicts between competing kingdoms are solved in battle, never through diplomacy.[45] The plot describes a circular motion, the 'just and prosperous society' re-emerges in full power at dawn, a time of day that in itself carries prosperous connotations. Finally the ideal model of behaviour, the alus character, identified with the we-group while the crude (kasar) character is identified with a they-group, the outsiders; in the play such a character often comes from overseas *(sabrangan)*.

The message of 'a just and prosperous society' is handed on by the dhalang every time he performs. Given the fixed structural form of the message together with the fact that wayang performances traditionally were, and still to a great extent are, given at ritual occasions, the play and its message come closer to ritual than to entertainment. The formal code of the language used in the play also brings it closer to ritual language, and as in a ritual a single phrase may evoke the proper emotive response and, so to say, function as a cue to the following sequences, the very use of 'wayang language' triggers off the same effect. The dhalang may be viewed as the traditional mediator of the political message of the ruling class to the common people, and as the mouthpiece of the people in the clown scenes he also functioned as a mediator in the other direction, although perhaps to a lesser extent. This brings us over to Sukarno's role as mediator, his political message and his strategy for bringing it across.

2.2 Structural similarities in the rhetoric of the dhalang and in the rhetoric of Sukarno

Like the dhalang Sukarno had a political message to mediate but unlike the former Sukarno's message was his own, a message from The Great Leader of the Revolution *(Pemimpin Besar Revolusi)* to the Indonesian People. Sukarno as the first president of the newly independent Republic of Indonesia was faced with the task of mediating between the modern, internationally oriented élite and the traditional, locally oriented rural masses as well as more or less traditionally oriented town dwellers in the minor towns. Another problem with which he had to cope was to render modern political concepts intelligible to a largely uneducated population. The wayang rhetoric lay close at hand as it was well known not only to Sukarno himself, and a number of people in his political entourage, but to a majority of the Indonesian people as well since roughly two-thirds of the population, i.e., the Javanese, Sundanese (of West Java) and the Balinese have been raised in the wayang tradition. If Sukarno's political message could be modelled on the rhetoric of the dhalang and on the structure of the wayang play it would be correctly decoded by the people, whose support was essential first in the fight for independence and later in the building of the new nation.

Sukarno's message that the Republic was going to cope with the social, economic, and political problems of a young state was simplified into the promise of building a 'just and prosperous society'. This phrase Sukarno reiterates up to the end of his political life. In his 'Political Manifesto', the speech of 17 August 1959, some weeks after he had dissolved the Constituent Assembly and reintroduced the 1945 constitution, Sukarno mentions that he has installed a National Planning Board which 'would plan a blueprint for a just and prosperous society . . .'

'In this blueprint by the National Planning Board "order, peacefulness, prosperity, no disturbances, low prices, fertility; everything that is planted yields plenty, all things are cheap to buy", must clearly be expressed'. (Tata-tentrem-karta-rahardja, gemah-ripah, loh-djinawi, subur kang sarwa tinandur, murah kang sarwa tinuku, itulah harus djelas tampak nanti dalam pola Dewan Perantjang Nasional itu!').[46] Sukarno's citation is, not surprisingly, taken from the standard introduction of a wayang play. The goal to be reached, the 'just and prosperous society', however, lies far away. It will be reached through the Revolution. However, in the period between the proclamation of the Republic in 1945 and Sukarno's Political Manifesto of 1959 the Indonesian Nation has deviated from the revolutionary aim which was stated in 1945. But, says Sukarno, 'inner changes, the awareness of having deviated in this way, will automatically cause changes and improvements in the external sphere'.[47] In the same speech Sukarno likens the present situation to purgatory, but this he views as a necessary purifying process for the ultimate achievement of 'the happiness of Paradise *[existing in]* the just and prosperous society'.[48]

Already in his defence speech before the Dutch judges in 1930 Sukarno displays a concept of time which is cyclical. The Nationalist Party, (PNI) Sukarno said, aimed at strengthening the Indonesian nationalism. This should be done in three steps: 'first, we show the people that the life they led long ago was a good life; second, we intensify the people's realization that their life today is a dismal one; third, we turn their gaze to the bright and shining rays of a future day and show them how to reach that future full of promise'.[49]

We have seen above that in the Javanese view history oscillates between two epochs, the *jaman mas* 'the golden age' and the *jaman edan* 'the mad age'. Sukarno's description of the present-day situation fits the epoch jaman edan. But it may also allude to the second part of a wayang play before the turning point of the battle. In the beginning of this part the hero of the play, who does not appear before the second part, has caused a cosmic upheaval by meditating intensively. His goal is to achieve supernatural power which, once he possesses it, guarantees the final victory of his kingdom.[50] The awareness that, according to Sukarno, 'automatically will cause changes and improvements in the external sphere' comes close to the view that a goal set will be reached only through a concentrated and steadfast will which, pursued without any deviation *automatically* brings the goal about. That the spirit is a weapon, 'which, if conscious and aroused . . . is more powerful than . . . a thousand armadas and a thousand armies, fully equipped and armed' Sukarno pointed out already in 1930.[51] In 1951 speaking at the Gajah Mada university of Yogyakarta he admonishes the people to 'think in terms of a spirit-will-deed'. In the same speech he calls for a will concentrated on a single purpose: 'Can the will-to-struggle of a nation be called up so that it is prepared to move, to toil, to labour, and to wrestle, to sacrifice, to suffer, to be ready to spring into a sea of fire in order to achieve its objective? The history of the world has proved that such things are possible'.[52] And as late as 1965 two and a half months before the abortive coup he states that 'the main criterion for a revolutionary is oneness between words and deed.'[53] The concentrated will of an individual is important but more important is the collective will of the people that lies behind their acts.[54]

> A leader's task is to bring the group . . . the class . . . the nation he leads to act. Why does a man become a leader if not to bring the men to act? But an act is an effect, the effect of desire, the effect of will. There is no action without desire, there is no action without will. Therefore 'to bring men to act' implies that the will must first be activated. And if this truth is related to questions concerning the life of a nation or a society, then it means that the leader must above all activate the collective will, must shake, awaken, move, intensify the collective will. For what? To give birth to collective action, to bring about a collective deed.

The collective will and deed may like the *gotong royong*, 'mutual co-operation', principle in the Panca Sila concept be viewed as the unity of all individual wills which have their focal point in the centre personified by the ruler/leader. Sukarno is like a magnet absorbing all individual wills into one thereby increasing his own power on which ultimately, speaking in wayang terms, the prosperity of the nation depends.

In the sphere of foreign policy Sukarno saw the fighting against neocolonialism and imperialism, concepts reduced by Sukarno to the acronym NEKOLIM, as an important task. The imperialism of the Old Established Forces (OLDEFO), i.e., the Western powers threatened the New Emerging Forces (NEFO), i.e. the newly independent states in Africa and Asia. The OLDEFO were also a threat to the Indonesian revolution and to the NEFO nations in general who had to unite against the OLDEFO.[55] The Indonesian revolution reached far beyond the boundaries of the Indonesian nation. 'It was the obligation of Indonesia to carry the message of the Revolution and to bear the responsibility of revolution, throughout the world. The Indonesian Revolution "like an eagle spreads its wings to cross the seven seas and the five continents and becomes the beacon of mankind's struggles."'[56] Due to its progressiveness, overtly expressed through its revolution, Indonesia serves as an example for the New Emerging Forces. Its revolution becomes a *beacon* that may be observed from afar, calling on the New Emerging Forces to follow in its footsteps. Here again Sukarno's words sound like an echo of the wayang: 'This country, great is its torch, spreading its radiance over the world, high is its smoke, its fame spreads afar, not only the island of Java has submitted, but numerous foreign kingdoms have submitted willingly impressed by the perfection of this country. . . .'

However, there are more structural similarities between the wayang and Sukarno's dividing the world in friends (the NEFO nations) and foes (the OLDEFO nations). The wayang scene is divided into two sides which are complementary but opposed to each other. The two sides do not only stand for left and right but also carry the connotation of male-female, old-young, night-day, evil-good, etc. In the most well-known plays the left side is represented by the hundred *Kurawa* brothers and the right side by the five *Pandawa* brothers of the Mahabharata epos. The conflict between them concerns the rule over the kingdom Ngastina to which both sides have a claim. The Kurawa forfeit their right, however, due to their use of ruses and strategems and have therefore become associated with evil. Conversely the Pandawa have become associated with good. Traditionally there existed an ambiguity between the two opposite sides, not only were they complementary but on the shadow of the wayang screen the shadows cast by the puppets changed place as the puppets of the left became the shadows to the right and vice versa. This of course still is the case but the old ambiguity 'has tended to be devalued towards a commonplace morality play between Good and Evil'.[57] The Kurawa may then easily be identified with foes and the Pandawa with friends or less strongly put: the Kurawa stand for 'they' and the Pandawa for 'we'. Bernhard Dham, in his analysis of Sukarno's role in the Indonesian independence movement has observed that Sukarno, in order to awaken a conscious nationalism and a will to fight for independence among the Indonesian people metaphorically talked about the fight as the Bratayuda fight between the Kurawa and the Pandawa, the Kurawa being identified with the Dutch as well as those who were against independence, and the Pandawa being identified with the Indonesians and/or those pro independence.[58]

The division of the world into NEFO and OLDEFO nations, i.e., in friends and foes, in 'we' and 'they', in good and evil, is but a later reiteration of the same theme. And as in the wayang a conflict is solved in battle and never through diplomacy, so the OLDEFO, being the enemies of the NEFO and hence of the Indonesian revolution, had to be completely destroyed.[59]

To summarize: my suggestion is that Sukarno developed his political strategy closely following the structure of the wayang play. Although one single speech does not contain the whole structural sequence of a wayang play, a great many contain one or more. Direct quotations from the wayang particularly on the theme of 'a just and prosperous society' are quite frequent. In other cases, not brought up here, the mere mentioning of the name of a wayang figure to the listener familiar with the wayang world connotes all that the particular figure represents. Metaphors like 'the spirit is a weapon . . . more powerful than . . . a thousand armadas . . .' evokes the picture of the meditating wayang hero whose strong will and whose concentration on a single goal automatically results in the goal's achievement.

2.3 The use of acronyms

This, then,was part of Sukarno's message mediated from above to below. I will next turn to Sukarno's particular way of mediating modern, political concepts to a public largely unfamiliar with them, but before that something should be said about the mediation the other way round, from the common people to the élite.

In the traditional society the dhalang acted as a mediator between the common people and the ruling class by letting the clowns in the play comment on the current situation. Dhalangs in Surakarta and Yogyakarta could still during the late period of Sukarno's presidency let the clowns complain about inflation and high rice prices as I myself have witnessed. Did Sukarno like the dhalang mediate the people's message? That Sukarno regarded himself as the mouthpiece of the people is fairly clear. He carried the title 'The Bearer of the Message of the People's Suffering',[60] and as such he acted during the independence movement.[61] In 1957, speaking about forming a *Gotong Royong* Cabinet, Sukarno states:[62]

> I am not taking sides. I am only expressing what is in the heart of hearts of our society, what was in the heart of hearts of our youth when, on October 28, 1928, they took the pledge of 'One Nation, One Country, One Language'; what was in the heart of hearts of us all when we made the Proclamation of 17 August, 1945.

But this again refers back to an earlier period of Sukarno's political life when he voiced the Indonesian People's need and will, conveying the message in wayang metaphors to the presumably puzzled Dutch.

As late as 1963, in his National Day Speech, which mainly deals with the economic situation, Sukarno still maintains that he is the People's voice:[63]

> I am now paying full attention to the voice of the People with regard to the way in which *Dekon* [Sukarno's Economic Declaration in March the same year] is being implemented. I have often said - I said this in Manila, too - that I am merely the mouthpiece of the People. After a while when I am fully convinced as to the true voice of the common people then, God willing, my own tongue shall utter that cry from their hearts.

No doubt Sukarno was aware of the fact that the goal set, the 'just and prosperous society', was not even within reach for a number of years. The problem of *sandang-pangan,* food and clothing for the people, still was not solved, and this had been one of the basic tasks. If Sukarno felt the need of the people he, on the other hand, seems to have been unable to pass from thought to act with regard to essential problems. Earlier in the same speech he, as it were, takes refuge in his being a revolutionary, as if thereby all problems would *automatically* be solved:[64]

> As the Great Leader of the Revolution, I devote very great attention to this economic 'point'. But let me be frank: I am not an economist. I am not an expert in economic techniques. I am not an expert in the techniques of trade. I am a revolutionary, and I am just a revolutionary in economic matters.

Herein lies Sukarno's weakness or rather the weak point in the traditional, symbolic structure on which he based his political strategy. Sukarno's reaction to practical problems fits into the role of the traditional, Javanese ruler, whose noninterference in state matters I have mentioned above. Expressed in symbolic terms: the beneficial influence of the Great Leader of the Revolution, as earlier that of the traditional ruler, spread to the people and guaranteed the prosperity of the society, and no practical measures had to be taken to bring it about.

Sukarno's speeches were given in Indonesian, the official language, but an Indonesian interspersed with Javanese expressions and sentences, and with French, for example, 'le désir d'etre ensemble', and 'l'eploitation de l'homme par l'homme.' Sometimes he combines foreign words with Indonesian, for example, Tahun Vivere Pericoloso 'A Year of Living Dangerously', the title of his National Day Speech, 1964. Like the dhalang Sukarno uses a great deal of redundancy to get his message across.

In the wayang rhetoric the formal speech code is norm and the evaluative an exception, used only in the clown scenes. No such clearcut division exists in Sukarno's rhetoric. The formal code, I suggest, is explicit in Sukarno's use of wayang vocabulary and implicit when, as often, the public identifies a problem, or a situation posed, as one belonging to the wayang sphere.

Writers on Sukarno have called attention to the abundant use of acronyms in his rhetoric. To mention just a few examples:

Indonesian acronyms

AMPERA	*Am*anat *P*enderitaan *Rak*jat, 'Message of the Suffering of the People'
DJAREK	*Dja*lan *Re*volusi *K*ita, 'The Way of Our Revolution'
BERDIKARI	*Berdi*ri di atas *Ka*ki Sendi*ri*, 'To Stand on One's own Feet'

Mixed acronyms

DWIKORA	*Dwi Ko*mando *Ra*kjat, 'The People's Dual Command'
TAVIP	*Ta*hun *Vi*vere *P*ericoloso, 'A Year of Living Dangerously'

Acronyms of Indonesianized words

MANIPOL	*Mani*festo *Pol*itik, 'The Political Manifesto'
NASAKOM	*Nas*ionalisme, *A*gama, *Kom*unisme, 'Nationalism, Religion, Communism'
NEKOLIM	*Ne*okolonialisme, *Kol*onialisme, *Im*perialisme, 'Neocolonialism, Colonialism, Imperialism'
RESOPIM	*Re*volusi, *So*cialisme Indonesia, *Pi*mpinan Nasional, 'Revolution, Indonesian Socialism, National Leadership'

Acronyms of foreign European words

CONEFO	*Con*ference of the *N*ew *E*merging *F*orces

GANEFO	*G*ames of the *N*ew *E*merging *Fo*rces
OLDEFO	*Old E*stablished *Fo*rces

The acronyms contain concepts coined by Sukarno. The Indonesian acronyms in particular render, in compressed form, Sukarno's revolutionary programme. The acronyms became the slogans of the day, people wrote them on walls, on roofs, and some, like RESOPIM, were made the theme of popular songs. Sukarno's acronyms may easily be pushed aside as empty slogans,[65] but they become much more interesting if they are placed in a traditional context. Benedict Anderson has drawn attention to the way in which Koranic texts were taught in Muslim schools *(pesantren)* in Indonesia. Whole passages were memorized by rote and acquired something like the quality of an incantation. 'Islam', says Anderson, 'had forbidden the continued use *[sic!]* of Shivaitic and Tantric *mantra;* Java answered by turning the Koran into a book of *mantra*'.[66] In the same article[67] Anderson makes an apt analysis of Sukarno's acronyms. While the string of words that an acronym is made from 'are used syntactically to convey an idea or an appearance' the acronym, he claims, 'has become a *mantra* in which the overt meaning is of no importance'. The similarity between the Koranic texts, that were memorized but not understood, and the acronyms lies, then, in the transformation of the original meaning into a new esoteric meaning, which is grasped intuitively.

A direct parallel occurs in the wayang. Yudistira, the oldest of the five Pandawa, possesses a sacred heirloom called *Kalimasada,* which he uses as a magic weapon. Kalimasada consists of an unintelligible piece of text and its power lies precisely in the fact that it cannot be understood. The name in fact is a Javanese corruption of *Kalimat Sahadat,* the Muslim profession of faith.[68] The original meaning has been lost, that which remains is the vague notion of something powerful, hidden in the words, it has, in other words, been turned into a mantra. The songs *(suluk)* sung by the dhalang to set the mood of the scene to follow have had their meaning transformed in a similar way. Unintelligible to the dhalang as well as to the public their meaning is grasped intuitively.

Sukarno's acronyms, then, fit into a traditional pattern of transforming foreign words and concepts into Javanese ones while in the process of transformation they acquire a new esoteric meaning.

3. *CONCLUSION*

I have argued that in validating his charisma Sukarno modelled his speeches on the Javanese wayang play, its structure, and its rhetoric. This lay close at hand as in the traditional Javanese society the wayang play served as a vehicle for disseminating political messages. President Suharto, who lacks Sukarno's charismatic appeal and who is a less skilled orator, continues to use wayang for political purposes. Within the framework of *Repelita* (Rencana Pembangunan Lima Tahun) 'The Five Year Development Programme', that was started in 1969, Suharto summoned dhalangs from Java, Madura, Sumatra (those were exiled Javanese), and Bali to Jakarta for a briefing. In his speech to the dhalangs he echoes Sukarno. The dhalangs, he was convinced, wanted to take part in the Indonesian People's fight for achieving 'a just and prosperous society.' In order to reach this goal the consciousness of the Indonesian People had to be awakened. The dhalangs task must be to stimulate and arouse the People's consciousness. He concludes:

> I am convinced that you Dalangs without changes in your presentation of the *lakons* [plays] and without altering the structure of the *pakem* [the outline of the plot] will be able to insert that which should be forwarded to the people. This could be done in the jokes or wherever you want to insert it. The important thing is that [the message] should be understood by as many as possible.
>
> (Saja jakin bahwa Ki Dalang, dengan tidak merubah dari pementasan lakon2 dengan tidak menjimpan daripada ketentuan PAKEM dsb. itu bisa menjelipkan apa jang harus disampaikan kepada rakjat ini. Apakah dalam lelutjonnja, atau dalam apanja sehingga akan banjak dimengerti.)[69]

NOTES

This paper was originally written for a conference on rhetoric held at the Memorial University of Newfoundland in September 1976.

1 *Willner, A.R. & D.*, The Rise and Role of Charismatic Leaders (in: Annals of the American Academy of Political and Social Science, March 1965), p. 83.

2 Ibid., p. 83.

3 *Benda, H.J.*, Decolonization in Indonesia: The Problem of Continuity and Change (in: American Historical Review, 70:4, 1965), pp. 1069, 1072f. See also the dialogue between *Benda, H.J.*, Democracy in Indonesia (in: Journal of Asian Studies, 23:3, 1964, pp. 449-56) and *Feith, H.*, History, Theory, and Indonesian Politics (in: Journal of Asian Studies, 24:2, 1965, pp. 305-12).

4 *Feith, H.*, History . . ., p. 307.

5 Ibid., p. 307.

6 *Dahm, B.*, Soekarno en de strijd om Indonesië's onafhankelijkheid (The Netherlands 1964), p. 19-27, see also note 7, and 8, p. 316.

7 Ibid., p. 31, see also pp. 27-32, and *Legge, J.D.*, Sukarno: A Political Biography (London 1972), p. 45.

8 *Dahm, B.*, Soekarno . . ., pp. 35, 157f, 201.

9 Indonesia menggugat, cited in Ibid., p. 121.

10 Sukarno's Panca Sila speech given before the Investigating Committee for Indonesia's Independence on 1 June 1945, two and a half months before the proclamation of the Republic of Indonesia. *(Tudjuh Bahan Pokok Indoktrinasi Republik Indonesia*, 3rd ed., n.pl., n.y., p. 36. English translation in *Feith, H. and Castles, L. (eds.)*, Indonesian Political Thinking 1945-65 (Ithaca & London 1970) p. 47; my own translation differs slightly from that of the latter.)

11 *Poerwadarminta, W.J.S.*, Kamus Umum Bahasa Indonesia (3rd ed. Djakarta 1961), p. 824.

12 *Soemosapoetro, S.R.M.*, Lampahan: Donorodjo. Serat Tutunan Tjaking Pakeliran Padalangan Ringgit Durwa (n.pl. 1963?), pp. 6f.

13 *Anderson, B.R.O'G.*, The Idea of Power in Javanese Culture (in: Culture and Politics in Indonesia, ed. by C. Holt, Ithaca & London 1972), pp. 19ff, and *Dahm, B.*, Soekarno . . ., pp. 21f.

14 *Feith, H. & Castles, L. (eds.)*, Indonesian . . ., pp. 30f, and *Dahm, B.*, Soekarno . . ., p. 121.

15 *Anderson, B.R.O'G.*, The Language of Indonesian Politics (in: Indonesia, 1, 1966), p. 114.

16 *Geertz, C.*, Islam Observed (New Haven & London 1968), p. 36.

Notes to Chapter 1

17 *Heine-Geldern, R.,* Conceptions of State and Kingship in Southeast Asia (Ithaca 1956), p. 3.
18 *Selosoemardjan,* Social Changes in Jogjakarta (Ithaca 1962), pp. 25f.
19 Ibid., p. 21, and *Moertono, S.,* State and Statecraft in Old Java: A Study of the Later Mataram Period 16th to 19th Century (Ithaca 1968), p. 5.
20 *Pigeaud, Th.,* Java in the 14th Century. A Study in Cultural History (The Hague 1960), p. 14, (The Hague 1963), p. 21, canto 17, stanza 3. Although Pigeaud translates *nagari* as 'one town', the following lines make it clear that the poet Prapanca, when mentioning the Royal compound, refers to the capital.
21 A number of such situations are recorded in myths and chronicles, see for example *Babad Tanah Djawi,* ed. by Meinsma ('s-Gravenhage 1941), pp. 7f.
22 Javanese books on mantic practices invariably contain such schemes, see for example *Kitab Primbon Betaldjemur Adammakna* (Ngajogjakarta 1961), p. 6.
23 *Anderson, B.R.O'G.,* The Idea . . ., pp. 4-8.
24 See for example the *Murwakala Lakon* (Leiden University Library: ms. LOr. 6431), p. 3, see also pp. 4-27.
25 *Moertono, S.,* State . . ., p. 56.
26 *Anderson, B.R.O'G.,* The Idea . . ., pp. 16f.
27 *Moertono, S.,* State . . ., p. 56.
28 *Selosoemardjan,* Social . . ., p. 23.
29 *Moertono, S.,* State . . ., p. 58.
30 Ibid., p. 37f., and *Tirtakoesoema, S.R.,* De viering van de garebeg Moeloed Dal 1863 in Jogjakarta (in: Djåwå, 12, 1932, pp. 41-9).
31 *Geertz, C.,* Islam . . ., p. 38.
32 *Geertz, C.,* Ideology as a Cultural System (in: Ideology and Discontent, ed. by D.E. Apter, London 1964), pp. 65f.
33 *Anderson, B.R.O'G.,* The Idea . . ., p. 23.
34 Ibid., p. 15, and *Dahm, B.,* Soekarno . . ., p. 184.
35 *Dahm, B.,* Soekarno . . ., pp. 36-40.
36 Ibid., pp. 59, 74, 95ff, 104f.
37 *Uhlenbeck, E.M.,* A Critical Survey of the Languages of Java and Madoera ('s-Gravenhage 1964), pp. 126-35.
38 *Moertono, S.,* State . . ., pp. 36, 38ff, 59ff.
39 *Brandon, J.R. (ed.),* On Thrones of Gold. Three Javanese Shadow Plays (Cambridge, Mass. 1970), p. 79.
40 *Anderson, B.R.O'G.,* Mythology and the Tolerance of the Javanese (Ithaca 1965), pp. 7f.
41 *Brandon, J.R. (ed.),* On Thrones . . ., p. 29.
42 Ibid., pp. 31f.
43 Ibid., p. 30.

44 See *Comaroff, J.*, Talking Politics: Oratory and Authority in a Tswana Chiefdom (in: Political Language and Oratory in Traditional Society, ed. by M. Bloch, London . . . 1975), pp. 152-5 on formal and evaluative codes.
45 *Brandon, J.R.*, Theatre in Southeast Asia (Cambridge, Mass. 1967), p. 118.
46 *Bahan-Bahan Pokok Indoktrinasi* (3rd ed., n.pl. 1965), pp. 146f.
47 'Perobahan-perobahan batin, kesadaran tentang penjelewengan ini, dengan sendirinja nanti akan membawa perobahan-perobahan dan perbaikan dialam lahir', ibid., p. 110f.
48 Ibid., p. 133.
49 *Feith, H. & Castles, L. (eds.)*, Indonesian . . . ., p. 30.
50 *Brandon, J.R. (ed.)*, On Thrones . . ., pp. 23f.
51 *Feith, H. & Castles, L.*, Indonesian . . ., p. 115.
52 Ibid., pp. 61f.
53 Ibid., p. 121.
54 Ibid., p. 59.
55 *Weatherbee, D.E.*, Ideology in Indonesia: Sukarno's Indonesian Revolution (New Haven 1966), pp. 23-7. *Legge, J.D.*, Sukarno . . ., pp. 343ff.
56 *Weatherbee, D.E.*, Ideology . . ., p. 58, including a quotation from Sukarno 1965.
57 *Anderson, B.R.O'G.*, Mythology . . . ., p. 6.
58 *Dahm, B.*, Soekarno . . ., pp. 86-123.
59 *Weatherbee, D.E.*, Ideology . . ., pp. 59-82.
60 *Legge, J.D.*, Sukarno . . ., p. 315.
61 *Dahm, B.*, Soekarno . . ., pp. 121, 157.
62 *Feith, H. & Castles, L. (eds.)*, Indonesian . . . ., p. 88.
63 Ibid., p. 395.
64 Ibid., p. 392.
65 *Legge, J.D.*, Sukarno . . ., pp. 346f.
66 *Anderson, B.R.O'G.*, The Language . . ., p. 92.
67 Ibid., p. 112.
68 Ibid., p. 93.
69 *Groenendael, V.M.C. van*, De Javaanse wayang in Indonesisch perspectief (unpubl. M.A. diss. Amsterdam 1974), pp. 40f.

BIBLIOGRAPHY

Anderson, B.R.O'G., Mythology and the Tolerance of the Javanese. Ithaca 1965.

Anderson, B.R.O'G., The Language of Indonesian Politics (in: Indonesia, 1, 1966, pp. 89-116).

Anderson, B.R.O'G., The Idea of Power in Javanese Culture (in: Culture and Politics in Indonesia, ed. by C. Holt, Ithaca & London 1972, pp. 1-69).

Babad Tanah Djawi, ed. by Meinsma,'s-Gravenhage 1941.

Bahan-Bahan Pokok Indoktrinasi, 3rd ed., N.Pl. 1965.

Benda, H.J., Democracy in Indonesia (in: Journal of Asian Studies, 23:3, 1964, pp. 449-56).

Benda, H.J., Decolonization in Indonesia: The Problem of Continuity and Change (in: American Historical Review, 70:4, 1965, pp. 1058-73).

Brandon, J.R., Theatre in Southeast Asia. Cambridge, Mass. 1967.

Brandon, J.R. (ed.), On Thrones of Gold. Three Javanese Shadow Plays. Cambridge, Mass. 1970.

Comaroff, J., Talking Politics: Oratory and Authority in a Tswana Chiefdom (in: Political Language and Oratory in Traditional Society, ed. by M. Bloch, London . . . 1975).

Dahm, B., Soekarno en de strijd om Indonesië's onafhankelijkheid. The Netherlands 1964.

Feith, H., History, Theory, and Indonesian Politics: A Reply to Harry J. Benda (in: Journal of Asian Studies, 24:2, 1965, pp. 305-12).

Feith, H. & Castles, L. (eds.), Indonesian Political Thinking 1945-65. Ithaca & London 1970.

Geertz, C., Ideology as a Cultural System (in: Ideology and Discontent, ed. by D.E. Apter, London 1964, pp. 47-76).

Geertz, C., Islam Observed. New Haven & London, 1968.

Groenendael, V.M.C. van, De Javaanse wayang in Indonesisch perspectief (Unpubl. M.A. diss. Amsterdam 1974.)

Heine-Geldern, R., Conceptions of State and Kingship in Southeast Asia. Ithaca 1956.

Kitab Primbon Betaldjemur Adammakna. Ngajogjakarta 1961.

Legge, J.D., Sukarno: A Political Bibliography. London 1972.

Moertono, S., State and Statecraft in Old Java: A Study of the Later Mataram Period 16th to 19th Century. Ithaca 1968.

Murwakala Lakon, (Leiden University Library: ms. LOr. 6431).

Pigeaud, Th., Java in the 14th Century. A Study in Cultural History, 5 vols. The Hague 1960-3.

Poerwadarminta, W.J.S., Kamus Umum Bahasa Indonesia. 3rd ed. Djakarta 1961.

Selosoemardjan, Social Changes in Jogjakarta. Ithaca 1962.

Bibliography

Soemosapoetro, S.R.M., Lampahan: Donorodjo. Serat Tutunan Tjaking Pakeliran Padalangan Ringgit Purwa (n.pl. 1963).

Tirtakoesoema, S.R., De viering van de garebeg Moeloed Dal 1863 in Jogjakarta (in: Djåwå, 12, 1932, pp. 41-9).

Tudjuh Bahan Pokok Indoktrinasi Republik Indonesia. 3rd ed. N.pl., n.y.

Uhlenbeck, E.M., A Critical Survey of the Languages of Java and Madoera.'s-Gravenhage 1964.

Weatherbee, D.E., Ideology in Indonesia: Sukarno's Indonesian Revolution. New Haven 1966.

Willner, A.R. & D., The Rise and Role of Charismatic Leaders (in: Annals of the American Academy of Political and Social Science, March 1965, pp. 77-88).

LANGUAGE POLICY AND LANGUAGE PLANNING IN INDONESIA AND MALAYSIA

Lars Vikør

INTRODUCTION

One of the most important problems confronting new states like Indonesia and Malaysia, is the development of a linguistic medium and a language policy which can promote the integration and progress of the people. In both countries, this has been seen as an important task for the government and other national institutions. This article will give a survey of these problems, viewed in an historical perspective, and the policy with which they have been and are being met. The chief accent will fall on Indonesia. It is introduced by some general remarks on language policy and language planning. Then, a short survey of the development of Malay is given. It is followed by a discussion of the Dutch language policy in colonial times, and the reactions to it from the side of the Indonesian nationalists. A somewhat more thorough discussion is given of the different aspects of modern Indonesian language planning, a similar, but shorter discussion of Malaysia follows, and the relations between the countries (especially the co-operation in the spelling question) are surveyed. Finally, the situation in Indonesia is tentatively summarized.

1. LANGUAGE POLICY AND PLANNING: DEFINITIONS AND GENERAL PROBLEMS

Language policy and language planning are relatively recent concepts, and it is often not easy to distinguish between them. I will define them in the following way:

Language policy includes all measures taken in order to influence or control the linguistic situation or language usage within a society or any sector of society. Usually governmental measures are meant, but language policy is also performed by non-governmental institutions like newspapers, broadcasting, publishing houses, schools and universities, commercial enterprises of all kinds, - in short, all institutions that function through mass communication. The fact that such communication in English-speaking countries is performed in standard English is the result of a certain language policy, even though nobody is conscious of it because there are (or seem to be) no alternatives. In most

Western countries there exists a standard language which claims to represent the whole nation, and which is acknowledged in this capacity by the whole nation, even those who speak other language varieties. Only in societies where competing standard languages exist, an overt choice presents itself to the language user, be it a person or an institution.

Language planning may be regarded as an element of language policy, or as a support for it. It may be given a wide definition, including all areas where decisions regarding language have to be taken, but it may also be restricted to the linguistic aspect in a narrow sense: the work with the language standard itself. The latter is more usual, and we shall stick to it here. Language planning then may be defined as the systematic and creative working with a specific language variety (including if necessary its creation or codification) in order to meet certain explicitly formulated longterm goals.

Einar Haugen[1] has formulated four elements in this process of language planning. They are: (1) The selection of a norm: Which language variety should be the basis of the standard language? (2) The codification of its form: What spelling, morphology and pronunciation should be used? (3) The elaboration of its functions: How should the vocabulary and the syntactic means of expression be extended and regulated? (4) Its acceptance by the society: How should it be propagated, and which social functions should it perform? (In our definition, of course, this is more a question of language policy than planning). It does not matter, of course, that one standard language should permeate the whole society and be compulsory in all formal situations. A division of function between e.g. a world language to be used in higher education, science and business, a national language to be used in internal politics and national culture, and regional languages and dialects to be used in primary education, is conceivable.

The most difficult question to answer in this context is, of course: Which aim should the language policy serve? Which criteria should be used in promoting certain linguistic varieties or variants rather than others? It is possible to use linguistic criteria, e.g. to maintain that irregularities and redundancies are a burden to the linguistic structure and should be eliminated. Valter Tauli[2] represents this line of thought, which leads him to reject strongly the notion that all natural languages are equally well suited to the needs of expression prevailing in their respective societies. In his view, a comparative evaluation of languages and language varieties on a structural basis is a necessary element in language planning.

Others have characterized this approach as too narrow. Social, psychological and political criteria are just as important elements in this sort of evaluation as the narrowly linguistic ones. If they are not taken into account, planning will not succeed. In such cases, of course, the question of conflicting interests arises. The use and promotion of a local language in primary education often give rise to such conflicts. It may be pedagogically sound and advantageous to the children, while at the same time being (or thought of as being) detrimental to society at large, if linguistic unity on a national scale is the aim of the official language policy, or if it is simply too expensive to produce teaching material in the local languages.[3]

2. THE DEVELOPMENT OF THE MALAY LANGUAGE

The history of the Malay language is commonly divided into three stages, viz. Old Malay, Classical Malay and Modern Malay. Old Malay is represented by several Southeast Sumatran epigraphs of the seventh century and some isolated inscriptions of the subsequent centuries. Classical Malay is the language of the Malay manuscript literature dating from the sixteenth to the nineteenth century, while Modern Malay is essentially a twentieth century phenomenon.

The criteria for this periodization are not linguistic, but cultural. The phonological and morphological structure of the most ancient language in which we have written specimens is fundamentally the same as that of the standard Malay written at present - especially if the most recent European influences are disregarded. But the different cultural orientations of the respective periods can be discerned in the script used in the prevailing texts, their lexicon and partly their syntax, and in the religious and cultural world they reflect. Old Malay is deeply influenced by the Indian cultural sphere in these respects. It uses the South Indian Pallava script, is full of Sanskrit loanwords, and functions entirely within a Hindu-Buddhist culture.

Classical Malay in the same way belongs to the Muslim world. It is written with the Arabic script, its most important sources of loanwords are Arabic and Persian, and even its syntax is often based upon Arabic patterns. Finally, modern Malay is in many ways a product of European influences, which is seen both in the fact that it uses the Latin script, its embracing of European loan-words and its orientation towards European syntactic models. We shall come back to this later on.

Traditionally, the written standard in the stage called Classical Malay has been regarded as rather fixed and uniform. A large part of the extant manuscripts were written at Riau, where a literary centre connected with the court of the Riau-Johore sultanate flourished in the eighteenth and nineteenth centuries. The spelling, morphology and idiom of this so-called Riau-Johore Malay has been traditionally accepted as the standard of good Malay, to the extent that even older texts written in other places have been judged by it, and their deviations from this 'norm' classified as mistakes or dialectal influences.[4] However, Teeuw[5] points out that such deviations are more likely to be attributed to older literary standards.

The most probable assumption is that at a certain time there existed several Malay writing standards concurrently connected with literary centres (usually identified with political centres) in different localities. These local standards must have been formed and moulded through different influences: from local speech, local spelling traditions, influences from other languages (Sanskrit, Tamil, Arabic, Persian) and from existing Malay writing traditions in other centres. It is reasonable to assume that the standard used at the politically most powerful centre of the region was prestigious also elsewhere and exerted more or less strong influences on other, local standards, which in their turn might take the lead later on as a result of historical developments. Such a leading centre must have been at Palembang around A.D. 700. Later centres were Pasai (North Sumatra) in the fourteenth and fifteenth centuries, Malacca in the late fifteenth century, Johore and especially Acheh from 1500 to 1700, Palembang in the eighteenth century, and Riau after 1700. The Riau norm was the most recent and therefore dominant one when the nationalist revival set in after 1900.

We have till now only discussed the written language. But there must have been large differences between this written language and its spoken counterparts throughout the period. From a sociolinguistic and functional point of view, we can divide the linguistic varieties that together constitute the Malay language into three groups, viz. the written language, the popular dialects and pidgin Malay. It is rather probable that each of these groups can be regarded as a separate entity, developing on its own through history, independently of the others (although not without mutual interference).

Both the Malay dialects and pidgin Malay have developed into many differing varieties. The dialects are spoken in East Sumatra and Malaya, the cradle of the Malay language, but also further eastwards, especially in Borneo. Pidgin Malay developed in the inter-ethnic trade of the archipelago, probably already as far back as the beginning of the Christian era. It has given rise to creolized varieties in many places, e.g. in Menado and Jakarta. The situation in Jakarta is especially interesting, because of the influential position of this city.

Here, there exist two clearly distinguished varieties of Malay: the official Bahasa Indonesia, used by the élite, and a creolized form of Malay used by the lower classes among the original inhabitants of the city (called *Betawi* or Jakartanese). Jarkartanese has been strongly influenced by Javanese, Sundanese and Balinese, and also by Portuguese, Chinese and Arabic. But the distinction between Bahasa Indonesia and Jakartanese is not discrete: There are many compromise forms, so-called colloquials, i.e. informal types of Bahasa Indonesia speech with heavy influences from Jakartanese. Such colloquials are used by anybody, so that there is no absolute division between popular and official speech. The division is partly functional: The respective varieties are used in different situations. Partly it is social: The social position of any individual is connected to his verbal repertoire.

In writing, colloquials are also used, but only in informal and humorous contexts, or in characterizations of common people. Here it is viewed and used as a distinct language variety.

The failure to distinguish properly between the different social/functional 'layers' of Malay has led to some vagueness concerning the roots of the present Indonesian and Malaysian language. It is, for instance, common to regard Bahasa Indonesia as a development of pidgin ('Bazaar') Malay, cf. Takdir: 'It can be said that gradually the Indonesian language has been satisfactorily transformed from a pidgin-like *lingua franca* into an official modern language.'[6]

I would regard it otherwise: modern Indonesian and Malaysian are further developments of the standardized Classical Malay written norm, while the 'pidgin-like *lingua franca*' has its modern successors in the creolized popular language of great cities like Jakarta, Menado and others. The core of the modern Malay standard (in both its national varieties) is inherited from the Riau norm. Of course, it has also been profoundly influenced by other languages and linguistic varieties, West European languages on the one hand, Javanese and Jakartanese on the other. But this influence is especially concerned with lexicon and syntax, not so much with phonology and morphology.

3. INDONESIA: LANGUAGE POLICY IN THE COLONIAL PERIOD

In the earliest phase of their colonial rule in Indonesia the Dutch took a passive attitude to the language problem by adjusting themselves to the prevailing situation. They kept their language to themselves and, in their contacts with the Indonesian population they used Malay, in the beginning also Portuguese, and later other of the more important regional languages. In the nineteenth century, however, a more conscious policy forced itself on them. Their administration of the colonies was to a large extent indirect. Members of the local nobilities were incorporated as lower civil servants, so that the colonial power could profit from their traditional authority among the local population. This was done on a fairly large scale, and it became necessary to give these persons an education that could make them fit for their functions. This led to an expansion of the formal schooling (on an elementary level) for Indonesians. It did not matter, of course, which language should be used in this.

There were three alternatives, viz. Dutch, Malay and the various regional languages. As it was common to use indigenous languages, particularly Malay, in the contacts with the population, these languages also got preference in education. So the most important regional languages, like Javanese and Sundanese, became the media of teaching in their own regions, while Malay was taught as a subject besides. Where no important regional language existed, Malay was used in teaching. Dutch was limited to the Dutch themselves and small groups of Christian Indonesians, especially in Ambon and Minahasa.[7]

This gave the impulse to a more intensive scientific research in the Indonesian languages and literatures. Pioneers were the missionaries, who described many hitherto unknown languages, codified spellings for them (in Latin characters) and published reading materials in them.[8] Most important was Van Ophuijsen's codification of an official Malay spelling, to which we shall return presently.

However, the Ethical policy (from 1900) brought a change in the language policy of the colonial regime. Now, it was seen as an aim in itself to 'cultivate' the Indonesians, i.e. to give them access to European culture. To reach this aim, a command of the Dutch language was seen as indispensable. Consequently, there took place a great expansion in the Dutch-language education for Indonesian children, particularly those of the upper classes.[9]

The result was the rise of a new Indonesian élite. Intellectuals oriented towards Western, i.e. Dutch, culture. The Dutch language and culture developed into the most important status symbol accessible for brown-skinned people. Conservative Dutch colonials often resented this, and even refused to let Indonesians address them in Dutch in order to keep the racial barrier intact. Instead they insisted on pidgin Malay, which was a great humiliation to an Indonesian aristocrat. The natural reaction from their side was to strive even harder to obtain a perfect command of Dutch, the only language that granted social promotion.

In other words, it was clear of course, which stand the Indonesian nationalists should take in the language question. The organization Boedi Oetomo, founded in 1908 in order to promote and renew the Javanese culture, resolved at its founding congress that the colonial government should extend the possibilities of learning Dutch to Indonesians on all levels. But the first nationalist mass organizations in Indonesia, the Sarekat Islam and its leftist offshoot, the PKI, chose Malay as their vehicle. The nationalist leaders who themselves largely belonged to the Dutch-educated élite and often were more fluent in Dutch than in Malay, understood fairly early that the Malay language was completely necessary if one was to get into contact with the masses of the people and mobilize them. It was the only language that could bridge the linguistic gap between the various ethnic groups as well as that between élite and masses. When this view was generally recognized and accepted, it was a small step to the theoretical and idealistic acceptance of Malay as the unifying language of all Indonesia. This acceptance got its classical form in the so-called Oath of the Youth *(Sumpah Pemuda)*, which was sworn at a nationalist youth congress in 1928. Their fidelity was promised towards the threefold ideal of one mother country, Indonesia, one Indonesian nation and one Indonesian language, *Bahasa Indonesia*.[10]

What was this Bahasa Indonesia? It was clear that the language meant was Malay, at any rate it was to be based upon Malay. But there were several varieties of Malay, of which the standardized school Malay was the most important. This variety was based on the Classical Malay (Riau) tradition as far as morphology and syntax was concerned, while its orthographical framework in the Latin alphabet had been laid down by Van Ophuijsen. But a strong Minangkabau influence made itself felt in those years, due to the fact that the Minangkabau ethnic group dominated the intellectual élite (especially the school teachers) at the time.

An important agent of this standard language was the official publishing house of the colonial government, Kantoor voor Volkslectuur or (in Malay) *Balai Pustaka*. Its most active period was the twenties and thirties of this century. It exerted a great influence upon the development of a modern Indonesian literature, by translating literary works from European languages as well as by giving Indonesian writers opportunity to publish and distribute their own works through schools, libraries and bookshops. The Balai Pustaka published books in all important regional languages, but particularly in Malay, and the figures of sale and lending indicate very clearly how strongly Malay was preferred by the reading public.[11] The linguistic usage in the Malay Balai Pustaka publications was corrected by Minangkabaus, particularly Nur Sutan Iskander, who worked as an editor in Balai Pustaka, and who used very rigid Sumatran standards in his work (i.e. traditional Malay with strong Minangkabau influences). Thus, this may be called the Sumatran period in the development of modern Indonesian - as opposed to the Javanese period after independence.[12]

But the victory of Malay as the Indonesian language was at this time not at all assured. The colonial government pursued a rather harsh policy towards the nationalist movement in the thirties, and its language policy was clearly aimed at spreading Dutch as soon and efficiently as possible among the population. The most famous advocate of this policy was the pedagogue G.J. Nieuwenhuis. His arguments were partly idealistic: He regarded Dutch as indispensable for the Indonesians if they wanted to get access to modern culture. But he also drew attention to the interests of the colonial power, stating that the 'spread of one's language and culture is the most direct road to economical expansion'.

It was regarded as important to create a cultural bond between Holland and the Indonesian élite. More and more people understood that the rigid racial segregation which had existed till then had to be abolished if a total and violent schism between colony and colonial master was to be avoided. Nieuwenhuis concentrated his attention particularly upon the middle stratum between the completely Westernized élite and the masses. He understood well that the social cleavage between élite and mass was a potential danger to the social order. He therefore proposed to give the lower ranges of the civil service (including primary school teachers and the like), who came in direct contact with the common people, intensive and comprehensive education in the Dutch language, so that they would be able to master it passively. Then they could function as a link between the masses of the people, who got no Dutch at all, and the élite, who learnt to master it also actively. In that way perhaps two million people would learn to read Dutch. This goal was never reached, but at the time of the Japanese invasion about half a million Indonesians had been taught Dutch.

The nationalists saw this policy as a potential danger to their ideal: Bahasa Indonesia as the unifying national language. They reacted similarly when regional languages were promoted. This happened in Acheh and Minangkabau (where local languages were taken up as medium of instruction in the governmental schools) and in Central Sulawesi (where the protestant mission used local languages in teaching). In Acheh, a local protest meeting was arranged in 1932 against the use of Achehnese in school, supporting Bahasa Indonesia.[13]

4. BAHASA INDONESIA - FROM IDEAL TO REALITY

Thus was the linguistic situation at the time of the Japanese invasion: Dutch was more actively propagated than ever before, Malay was commonly used as an auxiliary language among the Indonesians as well as between white and brown. Bahasa Indonesia as a national and unifying standard language was only the ideal of a limited group of Indonesian nationalists. The Japanese invasion was destined to make this ideal a reality, in an extremely simple, but effective way: through the instant and radical abolition of the Dutch language. Having done this, the Japanese were faced by the question of what language to use. But they had no real choice: almost nobody in Indonesia could understand Japanese. The new overlords did organize courses in their language everywhere, but the three years of occupation was too short a time for this endeavour to achieve any success. The most important immediate aim of the Japanese was to reach all Indonesians with their war propaganda, to mobilize and engage them in the war effort. The only suitable language for this aim was obviously Malay. The result was that more Indonesians than ever before were now brought into contact with the official, standardized variety of the language. More than ever before it was employed to serve all functions in public life.

In this way, the Japanese laid the foundations of the language policy in independent Indonesia. In the first (provisional) constitution of the Republic of Indonesia, later known as the Constitution of 1945, Bahasa Indonesia was proclaimed the official language of the state. In an explanation the following modification is given: 'In those regions where a separate language exists and is well taken care of by its own speakers (such as Javanese, Sundanese, Madurese), the languages in question shall be acknowledged and taken care of by the state too. Those languages are also parts of the living Indonesian culture.'

The most important instrument for the propagation of the language during the war of independence was, as could be expected, the army. It used Bahasa Indonesia not only as the most rational means in communicating with the population, like the Japanese, but also as an incarnation of the new national ideology: the unity and independence of Indonesia. After the transfer of sovereignty, Indonesian was introduced as the language of unity everywhere. The competitors from two sides were either eliminated or allotted a precisely defined and restricted place within the system. Thus, Dutch was abolished in 1950 as a language of instruction in high schools and universities, and the larger regional languages were given their place in primary education in their respective areas: the first three years Javanese, Sundanese and other children were taught in their own language, while given Indonesian as a subject, and afterwards the full transition to Indonesian took place.

The first fundamental language problem, the selection of a norm, was thereby solved without any conflict whatsoever. The position of Bahasa Indonesia as a language of unity has never been contested by anybody. But there remained enough problems to cope with. How should the appearance of this Bahasa Indonesia be, how should it develop? The most important themes of discussion were: 1. the spelling; 2. the extension of the vocabulary; 3. the opposition between traditional Malay standards and new developments in morphology and syntax.

5. *SPELLING*

In the nineteenth century, the Arabic script still dominated in the Malay language area. But already two centuries earlier, some European missionaries wrote the language with the Latin alphabet. However, there was no uniformity in spelling. The only guides the European students of Malay had were firstly their own ears, unconsciously adapted to English or Dutch phonology, secondly the English or Dutch spelling conventions and thirdly their possible knowledge of Malay written in the Arabic script. The use of the Roman script extended steadily in the nineteenth century, without any regularization or standardization taking place. Such a standardization was only felt to be necessary when the colonial powers began to develop a more extensive school system for the indigenous population. It is no accident, therefore, that a uniform and consistent spelling system for each of the two countries was first drafted by their respective school inspectors: Ch. A. van Ophuijsen for the Dutch East Indies and R.J. Wilkinson for British Malaya.

Ch. A. van Ophuijsen was an inspector of the (lower) education for the indigenous population of Sumatra and adjacent areas in the 1890s. In 1896, he was commissioned by the government to draft a consistent and scientifically based spelling system for use in teaching. He collected his data on a journey of the most important Malay-speaking areas (parts of the Straits Settlement, Riau, East Sumatra, Pontianak) and further drew strongly on the Riau spelling tradition in the Arabic alphabet as well as existing conventions of Malay spelling in the Roman alphabet. The result of his work appeared in 1901 as a word list preceded by a short exposition of the spelling rules, *Kitab Logat Melajoe*. This spelling was made official and compulsory in teaching and administration, and soon it was also adapted by the community at large. Even the Indonesian nationalists accepted it. This meant that the spelling question was settled for the time being.

The Van Ophuijsen spelling was phonemical and based on Dutch conventions. We may illustrate some of its features by comparing them with the English-based spelling of Malaya:

Malaya	ch	j	y	ny	sh	kh[1]	u	ě[2]	e[3]
Indonesia	tj	dj	j	nj	sj	ch	oe	e	é

(1) like *ch* in Scottish *loch*
(2) like *a* in *ago*
(3) like *e* in *bed*

One detail that did arouse some objection, was the digraph *oe* for the phoneme *u*. During the independence struggle, the Republican government issued a spelling reform where the transition from *oe* to *u* was made the central point. This spelling is known as the Republican spelling or the Suwandi spelling. (Suwandi was the minister of Education and Culture at the time of the reform - March 1947). The change from *oe* to *u* seemed to be inspired by nationalist and anti-Dutch sentiments, but it was soon accepted and adopted across political boundaries. Its scientific and practical advantages over the diagraph *oe* were quite obvious.

6. DEVELOPMENT OF VOCABULARY AND GRAMMAR

The Japanese appointed a language commission *(Komisi Bahasa Indonesia)*, which was to extend the vocabulary of the Indonesian language and provide it with a normative grammar. The secretary of the commission was Takdir Alisjahbana.[14] Its most concrete result was the coining of about 7000 new terms. Its other task, to compose a grammar, was not effected. During the independence struggle, the language experts on the Republican side continued this work as far as the circumstances allowed with support from the government. But only after full independence was attained was it possible to concentrate fully on language cultivation and language discussions, especially in connection with the rapid expansion of the general education. Several journals devoted to linguistic questions were published regularly throughout the fifties. A particularly large amount of energy was spent on the coining of new terms. The most important institution in this field was the Terminological Commission *(Komisi Istilah)*, which was formed in 1950. It was divided into sixteen sections, each dealing with a certain field and had about one hundred members. Lists of terms in the various fields were published regularly, from 1954 in book form. By 1972, fifteen such books had appeared, and in total 321,710 terms had been issued. Besides the Komisi Istilah, since 1975 there has existed an official bureau handling more general linguistic questions, called the Center of Language Cultivation and Development *(Pusat Pembinaan dan Pengembangan Bahasa)*.

Takdir Alisjahbana[15] gives an impression of the ideological problems involved in the terminological activities. The Japanese, whose propaganda was built on a 'pan-Asian' ideology, dictated a hierarchic structure for the possible source languages: New words should primarily be taken from the Malay language tradition itself. If this failed, other Indonesian languages should be tried. If this was unsuccessful, other Asian languages might be considered, and only in the last instance European sources could be involved. In practice, Takdir informs us, there were three factions in the commission, each with its own preference regarding the foreign sources. One faction preferred European (i.e.

ultimately Greek and Latin) terms, another preferred Sanskrit, the third Arabic. In certain fields, one source dominated. Chemical terms, for instance, were taken from the international nomenclature of Greek and Latin origin because of the internationally valid symbols. Also in other natural sciences and in medicine, there was no opposition to the use of the internationally acknowledged nomenclature.

Takdir has a strong preference for this policy also in a more general sense. His great aim is modernization, which he places in a framework where the opposition is between modern on the one hand, traditional, cultural and mental structures on the other. Modern man, according to Takdir, is characterized by an active attitude in relation to nature and his own fate. He can interfere with it and change it, while traditional man submits to it in fatalism. Modern man thinks rationally and in abstract terms, and he is egalitarian, while traditional societies (at any rate in Indonesia) are feudal, based on a very rigid hierarchy of ranks and classes. In addition, modern man is universal, living in a uniting world, while traditional man is bound within his own local community. Indonesia should take full part in this unification of the world. This view supports a technical and economical development of Indonesia along capitalistic lines and integration with the Western world.[16] It is no accident that Takdir in the fifties supported the PSI *(Partai Sosialis Indonesia)* which pledged for exactly such a policy. A far-reaching adjustment of the Indonesian language to the terminology of the modern Western languages is a natural consequence of this view.

Other motives were important for those who wanted to orient themselves towards Asian sources. Among the Indonesian regional languages Javanese naturally occupied the first place, as more and more users of Indonesian had this language as their mother tongue. Arabic too is important because of the strong religious and ideological value it carries for the orthodox Muslims, but the recent loans from this language are mostly limited to the religious and adjacent fields (Muslim jurisprudence and the like).

More striking is the role played by Sanskrit in modern Indonesia. This language was the exponent of a culture that formerly had an immense impact in West Indonesia, but which after five centuries exerts no direct influence any more. Nevertheless, Sanskrit is at present one of the most important sources of new terms in the Indonesian language, even including recently created terms. Sanskrit elements are used to construct new terms in the same way as Greek and Latin elements are used in Europe. How should this be explained? There is a possible linguistic explanation. The phonological system of Sanskrit does not differ radically from that of Indonesian, so that the phonetic and orthographical adjustment of Sanskrit words to the Indonesian system is relatively easy. But also here, the most important explanation is ideological.

It is an important fact in this connection that Java is the most dominating centre of Indonesia, economically, politically, demographically and culturally. This was so also in former, pre-colonial times, and important aspects of the modern nationalist ideology in Indonesia are inspired by the Old Javanese kingdoms flourishing from the eighth till the fifteenth centuries, and the great cultural and literary achievements of those kingdoms. The dominant cultural languages then were Sanskrit and the strongly Sanskrit-influenced Old Javanese, and that is the tradition on which one falls back in letting Sanskrit play a prominent role in the development of modern Indonesian. In this context, it is only natural that Sanskrit and Old Javanese words and elements are particularly prestigious in the political and military sphere, considering their nationalist appeal and the symbolic legitimation with which they can provide the army in its present political role.

In practice, a flow of loan words from European languages as well as from Sanskrit has entered Indonesian, and both sources are still exceedingly popular. Generally, it can be said that the European terms are adopted more or less spontaneously by the users of the language, while the Sanskrit terms are deliberately constructed. How penetrating this foreign influence on the vocabulary is, can be seen by the fact that new productive affixes have been adopted from various source languages, not least from Sanskrit. There is *swa-* for *self- (swadaya = self-relying)*, *swapraja = autonomous)*, *tuna-* for *lacking (tunakarya = unemployed, tunanetra = blind)*, *antar-* for *inter- (antarbenua = intercontinental, antarfakultas = interfaculty)* and *pra-* for *pre- (prakata = preface, prasejarah = prehistory)*. We must be aware, however, that such forms are usually only quasi-sanskritic. The elements *tuna* and *pra*, for instance, were never used like this in genuine Sanskrit. In fact, the largest part of these words are loan translations from European languages (primarily English, partly Dutch). Words like *prasaran = working paper*, and *praanggapan = prejudice* are obviously modelled on Dutch *preadvies* and *vooroordeel*.

Malay derivation morphemes have been used in the same way. The European influence has caused a marked increase in the use of nominalizations of verbs and adjectives, formed by the circumfixes *ke - an* and *pe - an*. Words like *keadilan = justice* from *adil = just*, *kemajuan = progress* from *maju = to go forward* and *pembangunan = construction, development* from *membangun = to build, construct* all indicate the increased abstractness of the language usage, as observed by Takdir.

Taken together, these examples indicate that the opposition between the two ways of word formation, viz. to import words from European languages or constructing them from Sanskritic or Malay elements, is in fact a superficial one. The models are in either case found in the West: Western concepts are transplanted into Indonesian through borrowing or loan translations. According to Haryati Soebadio[17] the Komisi Istilah has not played such an important role in this process as the number of terms it has produced suggests, due to the fact that it has no means available for the implementation of its proposals. Other institutions are more important, particularly the mass media, who create and use new terms more or less spontaneously.

A consequence of this situation is the excessive use of English words and expressions - completely unassimilated and, we may assume, unintelligible for many readers. Even more striking is the explosive growth of acronyms, often short-lived, in other cases remaining in the language as independent words. *Tapol* from *tahanan politik* (political prisoner), *mayjen* from *mayor jendral* (major-general) and *raker* from *rapat kerja* (working assembly) may serve as examples here. Such words multiply to such a degree that they probably make the newspaper language very puzzling at times to the average reader, also because there is no plan behind their formation, and no regular registration of them is made.

Of Western inspiration is also another, rather original, attempt at language reform. It concerns the personal pronoun of the second person. While the personal pronouns in European languages constitute a closed system of fixed elements, Indonesian has an open system where all kinds of words denoting a person's individuality or social status or position in relation to another person can function as pronouns of the first and particularly second person. This can apply to personal names, but also to titles of address and words denoting family relationships. The original ('real') pronouns are mostly felt to be rude when used with reference to people who are not intimate friends or relatives. A devaluation of these words is discernible: The original words for *I*, *aku*, normal a generation ago, are now seldom used, while the formal *saya* (originally a Sanskrit word meaning *slave*) is now common also in intimate relationships. As a consequence of this, some people feel that it is getting too informal and resort to *kami*, actually meaning *we* (exclusive) in formal situations.

It is clear that this whole system is adjusted to the needs of a feudal society where everybody's rank is defined within the framework of a strongly hierarchic system. The feudal structures have eroded in modern Indonesia, but have far from disappeared. This situation is bound to create great uncertainty in the usage of address forms. As a contribution to the defeudalization and democratization of Indonesia a new pronoun was introduced in 1957, *anda*. The intention was to provide an equivalent for the English *you*, which could stress the equality of all members of society. However, the experiment did not succeed, at any case not until the present time. The traditional, status-oriented way of thinking is still so deeply engraved in Indonesian social life that it *demands* an expression in the language structure. So, *anda* did not promote a simplification of the system; on the contrary, it provided another nuance in addition to those already in existence. Its particular area of usage is the formal and impersonal communication, such as commercial advertisements and letters to persons with whom one is not personally acquainted and does not stand in a well-defined social relationship. In addition, it is fairly frequent in literature. As to grammar (morphology) and syntax, there has been little deliberate planning, even though there has always been a strong desire among educated Indonesians to get an authorized normative grammar. However, there has been much disagreement as to the most desirable foundation for this norm. The basis of the present norm, as it is taught in schools and exposed in the existing grammars, is provided by traditional Malay. But there has been taking place fairly penetrating changes in the written norm through influence from above all European languages and Javanese. These influences manifest themselves through the transposition of foreign syntactical models into the existing Malay structure. Existing words and forms are used in new ways to provide new modes of expression.

7. *MALAYA/MALAYSIA*

The sociolinguistic scene of Malaysia differs completely from that of Indonesia. In the latter country, a large number of languages belonging to the same family and originating in the area itself are spoken, and the absence of strong ethnic tensions has made the choice of the *lingua franca* Malay as the national language of the country possible. In Malaysia, however, Malay is the only indigenous language whose impact is more than local, and it is tied to an ethnic group living in an uneasy social balance with another, immigrated group, the Chinese. In addition to that, the colonial language English was much more dominant than Dutch in Indonesia, being a world language and at the same time the only inter-ethnic elite language of the country.

The British followed the same policy here as elsewhere in their empire: They let local languages unfold themselves at the grassroot level while keeping the higher social domains for their own language. So, primary education in Malay was made available for the local population of this ethnic group, with the possibility of choosing English if the parents wanted to. And many did, as higher education was only available in English. English was the language of social prosperity and modernity, while Malay was still associated with the feudal culture of the still formally existing sultanates and the traditional village societies.

In the forties and fifties of this century, however, a Malay nationalism developed. One of its demands was that Malay should be made the national language. But this nationalism was just as strongly directed against the other ethnic groups of the country, particularly the Chinese, as against the colonial masters. The fear of being placed at a disadvantage by the economically so prosperous and powerful Chinese, caused the Malays to demand certain guarantees as to the maintenance of their political and social position after independence, and the formal supremacy of their language was one means to achieve this. This demand was heard, and as a part of the delicate political and social balance between the ethnic groups, Malay was proclaimed the 'national language' *(Bahasa Kebangsaan)* when the country became independent in 1957. However, a transition period of ten years was granted before English definitely was to be replaced by Malay in this position, in order to provide the language with the resources necessary to function (teachers, textbooks and other reading material, a technical vocabulary, etc.). The formal declaration of Malay as a national language for Malaya took place in 1967, four years after the proclamation of Malaysia. Sabah followed in 1973 and Sarawak in 1975.

The standardization of Malay in Malaya was initiated with the codification of a spelling in the Roman alphabet, following principles similar to those of Van Ophuijsen in the Dutch East Indies. In 1904, a system was agreed upon by a commission appointed by the government of the Federated Malay States (i.e. Perak, Negri Sembilan, Selangor and Pahang). Members of the commission were the British Residents of Perak and Selangor together with the Inspector of Malay schools, R.J. Wilkinson. It is probable that the substantial contributions to the system were made by Wilkinson, the only Malay scholar of the three. In any case, the spelling is known as the Wilkinson spelling. The Wilkinson system was used in the schools of Malaya and therefore also named the School Spelling. But there seems to have been more fluctuations and less certainty in the spelling here than in the Dutch East Indies. In 1923, the government set up a Translation Bureau for the writing, translation and editing of educational publications, novels and governmental publications. Through the work of the bureau, a certain uniformity of usage was achieved.

After the war, two trends manifested themselves in Malay language policy. One of them was conservative, tending to stick to the traditional Riau norm in a puristic way, while the other wanted to depart from this norm in order to develop Malay into a modern language, following the example set by Indonesia. The two trends were represented by two groups of language users, both active in Singapore and founded there in 1950. One, the Malay Language Institute *(Lembaga Bahasa Melayu* or LBM*)* consisted mainly of older people, especially teachers, employees in the radio, journalists, publishers and writers. It favoured the traditional approach. The other and more radical group called itself the 1950 Generation of Writers *(Angkatan Sasterawan 50* or *Asas 50).* It had a wider membership, but was led by a group of young writers. Both groups co-operated in sponsoring three language congresses in the 1950s, the last and most important of them being held in Singapore in 1956.[18]

That same year, a new language institute was formed, the *Dewan Bahasa dan Pustaka* in Kuala Lumpur. It was soon subordinated to the Ministry of Education, and is still the official language board of Malaysia. Its tasks are manifold: to develop and enrich the Malay language and literature, to publish books in the language, and to produce a standard dictionary. This dictionary, *Kamus Dewan*, was published in 1970. The Dewan Bahasa dan Pustaka has also been very active in coining new technical terms; up to 1973, more than 136,000 new terms had been issued.

The most dominant source of new terms in Malaysian is, obviously enough, English. However, the very different structure of the two languages has given rise to complicated problems of adaptation. The most frequently followed method was to adapt the spelling to the English (or an Anglicized) pronunciation: *haiderojan, ketelog, saikoloji, steshen, fakulti*. The most important alternatives to this policy have been the adoption of Arabic loanwords and the coining of new words from Malay elements (most often loan translations). Takdir[19] points to the preference of Arabic words like *diishtiharkan = being proclaimed, pentadbiran = administration, iktisad = economy* and *intikad = criticism*. The Indonesian words are respectively *diproklamasikan, tatausaha* or *administrasi, ekonomi* and *kritik*. The reason is the fact that Islamic religion and culture form a part of the ethnic identity of the Malaysian Malays. It must be noted, however, that in practice *ekonomi* and *kritik* even in Malaysia seem to be more frequent than *iktisad* and *intikad*. Hasan Ahmad[20] gives examples of Malay loan translations: *Faham komunis = communism, kediktatoran = dictatorship, kajihayat = biology, ilmu alam = geography, pengerusi = chairman*. Also here, the foreign terms in many cases seem to be more established in actual usage than the newly coined ones.

A rather special way of coining terms was the contraction of word compounds to single words, especially in the sixties applied on a fairly large scale. Hasan Ahmad [21] gives the following examples: *jabana (<jalan bawah tanah) = subway, maging (<makan daging) = carnivorous, gasar (<ganas + kasar) = barbaric, keretapi (<kereta api) = train, angkali (<angka kali) = coefficient*, and *gerakerja (<gerak kerja) = activity*.

8. LINGUISTIC CO-OPERATION BETWEEN THE TWO COUNTRIES: THE SPELLING QUESTION

The relations between Malaya/Malaysia and Indonesia have changed rather drastically several times, and this fact has been of direct consequence for the language planning. One of the first groups in any of the countries that actively advocated co-operation, was the Malayan Asas 50. They reflected a more general orientation towards Indonesia among young Malayan intellectuals, both because they were inspired by Indonesian nationalism and because they hoped for support from the large neighbour country in their struggle for the Malay language. From the middle of the 1950s, interest grew also on the Indonesian side. This development was stimulated by two important language congresses: that of Medan in Indonesia (1954) and that in Singapore (1956). At both congresses, the other country was represented, and both advocated further co-operation, particularly in the field of spelling.

The co-operation between the countries got a new dimension with the independence of Malaya in 1957. In April 1959, a cultural agreement was signed, and it was clear that it was to comprise co-operation in matters of language, including spelling. As a consequence of this, a delegation of Malayan language experts went to Jakarta the same year to engage in spelling negotiations. An indication of the importance attached to this question at the moment was the fact that the delegation was invited to meet President Sukarno himself at his palace.

An agreement was reached, and it has entered history under the name of *Melindo* (contraction of Malaya-Indonesia). It was marked by its strict adherence to the phonemic principle of one letter for one phoneme. Thus, the *ch/tj* was to be written *c*, the *j* and *y* were to have their English/Malayan values, and even more radically: the *ng* was to be written ŋ , and the *ny* ɲ or ɳ .

This proposal was not unforeseen. There had been a lively discussion about spelling problems within the literate communities of the two countries in the preceding years. In Indonesia, there was great discontent about the Suwandi spelling, particularly because it was not consistently phonemic. The distinction between ə and e (in Van Ophuijsen's spelling e and é) had been abolished through a regulation that *e* without any diacritical sign be written everywhere. Most comments on the spelling during the fifties criticized this regulation and pledged for the reintroduction of é in words like *memérah = to redden, pérang = a reddish or light brown colour, and pénanja = his* or *her pen,* to distinguish them from *memerah = to squeeze, perang = war* and *penanja = interrogator, questioner*. This demand was met in the Melindo spelling.

A special problem was the spelling of foreign words, and the admission of so-called loan phonemes like *f, x (ch* in Scottish *loch), sh* and *z*. These are frequent in Arabic and European loanwords, but in pronunciation they have often (but by no means regularly) been adapted to the indigenous phoneme system, e.g. *pikir* (<Ar. *fikr*) *= to think, kabar (<xabr) = news, sarat (<shart) = condition, jaman (<zaman) = time, period*. In Malaya, the tendency has been in favour of spelling these words with their Arabic sounds: *faham, khabar, sharat, zaman*. In Indonesia, however, already the Suwandi spelling prescribed that foreign words

should be adapted to Indonesian pronunciation as far as possible, and this trend dominated up till after 1960 and influenced also the modernists in Malaya. The Melindo spelling therefore excluded the *f, ch/kh, sj/sh, z* and other foreign sounds as regular elements in the system, even if it allowed for some of them as a possibility for those who wished to use them.

The Melindo spelling never became official, however. The following years, the plans for the creation of the new Federation of Malaysia proceeded, and the relations between the two countries accordingly deteriorated. In 1963, the Federation was proclaimed, and Sukarno started his confrontation policy. All official contacts between the two countries were broken, and also the Melindo spelling disappeared quietly in the governmental archives in Jakarta and Kuala Lumpur. Confrontation was not the only reason for this failure. The new letters of the Melindo spelling, which are not used in any normal orthography, would have required an enormous effort. In the words of Asmah Haji Omar,[22] it was 'linguistically speaking so good that it could not be prescribed at all to the public'.

After the installation of the Suharto regime in Indonesia in 1966, confrontation came to an end and the co-operation between the two countries was resumed. As far as spelling was concerned, the preparations for new negotiations started almost immediately, and in 1967, a Malaysian delegation once again arrived in Jakarta. A final draft was agreed upon and published. It showed that a major change in orientation had now taken place. While the scientific principle of phonemic representation had been predominant in the earlier reform attempts, the practical and economic aspects were now stressed. The principle of one letter for one sound thus had to yield to another principle: No new and alien letters should be introduced, not even diacritical signs. Another new development was that the resistance towards foreign elements (loan phonemes and certain consonant clusters) was given up.

The new spelling was generally welcomed in Malaysia, but met with resistance in Indonesia, to a large extent based on nationalist sentiment, but also on economic considerations (the fact that many books - particularly teaching materials - would have to be published in new and revised editions, people would have to change their established writing habits while the struggle against total or partial illiteracy was still an important task, and so on). The implementation of the new spelling therefore was delayed five years. Not until 1972 was the final decision taken, and the new spelling was formally given official status in both countries under the name of The Perfected Spelling *(Ejaan Yang Disempurnakan)*.

The basic features of this spelling can be summarized like this:

1. The consonants which had been spelt differently in the two countries now had this notation:

Malaysia	ch	j	y	ny	sh	kh
Indonesia	tj	dj	j	nj	sj	ch
Common spelling	c	j	y	ny	sy	kh

2. The distinction between ə and *e* was abolished, both being spelt *e*. This reform did not produce many problems because minimal pairs with ə and *e* are very rare.
3. The loan phonemes *f, v, z, kh, sy* were accepted as completely integrated parts of the system. This part of the reform was intended to make the language more receptive to European loanwords - an anti-purist measure, in other words. As for the co-operation in fields other than spelling, it has been less systematic and concrete. The factual influence of Indonesian upon Malayan Malay was considerable in the years preceding confrontation. Indonesia was then much ahead of Malaya in the production of books, regarding quality as well as quantity. So Indonesian books were read on a large scale in Malaya.

Confrontation stimulated the opposition towards 'indonesianisms' in the Malaysian language. The word for *television, talibisi,* was instantly changed to *talivishen*. But after the new rapprochement between the countries, a terminological co-operation was also initiated. Since 1972, there had been regular meetings between delegations from the two countries, alternately in Indonesia and Malaysia, to discuss terminological problems, among them the adaptation of foreign terms. If such terms are replaced by Malay (or, for instance, Sanskrit) elements, then this is done in such a way that the new term reflects the original as closely as possible, through systematic loan translations: *urbanization>pembandaran, misuse>menyalahgunakan, reprint> ulangcetak,* etc. When Western terms are admitted to Malay and adjusted to the structure of the language, then the basis of this adjustment is the internationally valid spelling, not the English pronunciation. Thus, we get forms like *geologi, prisma, nitrogen, katalog,* instead of the earlier Malaysian forms *jeoloji, prizam, naiterojan, ketelog* - in accordance with the system already prevailing in Indonesia.[23]

9. INDONESIA: RESULTS AND PERSPECTIVES

As this survey has shown, language policy and planning in Malaysia and Indonesia have to a large extent been regarded as relevant to the political authorities, and they have engaged actively in it. The most intense and systematic activities have concerned the spelling and the creation of a modern vocabulary. The results have been fairly satisfactory as far as the spelling is concerned. The reform of 1972 has been rather widely accepted, in any case the most important parts of it, which are mentioned above. Also the terminological activities have yielded impressive results as to the creation of terms. The implementation of them has been less impressive, as we have seen above. And the important areas of grammar and syntax have still not been regulated officially. There exists a number of school grammars, to a large extent based upon Classical Malay norms and European models for their description, but in spite of their influence, strong Westernizing and Javanizing tendencies make themselves felt in practice. One example: In possessive constructions, traditional Malay accepted only the construction *rumah bapak saya = the house of my father*. But today, one can use both *rumah dari bapak saya* and *rumahnya bapak saya*. The preposition *dari (= from)* is probably inspired by the English *of* or the Dutch *van*, while the construction *rumahnya bapak saya* is a calque from a Javanese and Sundanese model. In informal speech, the Jakartan construction *bapak saya punya rumah* is common, but it is not accepted and accordingly seldom used in writing.

It is not certain how successful the implementation of Bahasa Indonesia among the population has been. In the later years of his regime, President Sukarno launched a mass campaign for literacy. Short intensive courses were given to adults, who afterwards were sent back to their homes to teach their fellow villagers. While only about 15-20 per cent of all Indonesians above fifteen years of age could read and write in 1950, it has been estimated that more than 60 per cent of the whole population were literate (in Bahasa Indonesia); in 1964,65 per cent.[24]

This development stagnated after the change of regime in 1965-6, for a number of reasons. The new regime gave priority to the big economic problems, so there was no room for the large book production and distribution that would be necessary to extend literacy further or even maintain it. Another reason was that many village teachers of leftist persuasion were victimized by the large-scale massacres of late 1965, with accompanying mass arrests, dismissals and so on. In 1971, the literacy percentage was reduced to 40. The most important medium for the dissemination of Bahasa Indonesia today is probably the transistor radio, which is common all over the country.

The general sociolinguistic situation of Indonesia is marked by a deep cleavage - not between Malay/Bahasa Indonesia on the one side and the regional languages on the other, but between what I would call the 'public language' and the popular language (incl. popular Malay). The 'public language' is the more or less standardized Bahasa Indonesia - as used by the urban élite. It is abstract, rational and westernized, and thus adapted to the conceptual world of this élite. All formal usage in the 'modern' sector of society is pervaded by it.

While bilingualism is a very common feature in Indonesia, the demarcation line between the popular languages and the official or 'public' language is probably difficult to transcend. If a Javanese *becak*-driver from e.g. Surabaya moves to Jakarta, then he does not have to go to school in order to learn the Jakartanese spoken language. After a certain amount of time, he will learn it directly in the street. This is so because both these languages, like most other Indonesian languages, are adapted to the needs of common people and to the traditional cultural sphere in which they live. If he should want to learn the 'correct' formal Bahasa Indonesia, he would have to change his cultural and social environment completely, identify himself with a totally different status group, and undergo a long formal education. This sociolinguistic cleavage is strengthened by the role played by the English language in present-day Indonesia. This language has a dominant position in science and technology, in the economic life, in schools and universities, and to a certain extent in the media. It seems that English in Indonesia functions not only as the auxiliary language it was intended to be, but also as a real status language, a necessary condition for social advancement.

It is not easy to indicate how these problems should be solved - also because they are not purely linguistic, but belong in a much larger context: the social and political structure of the country. But it would seem advisable that they were taken into account in the further planning of the language. This would, in extremely general terms, mean that the planners should not one-sidedly strive to develop a standard language that is as 'developed' and 'modern' as possible, but that they should also consider making it a suited means of communication *with* (not only *to*) larger sections of the people. Such an approach might have consequences both for the grammatical structure of the official language and its general vocabulary, as well as for the notion of 'correctness' and the role it should play in the planning and particularly the teaching process.

NOTES

1 *Haugen, E.*, Language Conflict and Language Planning. The Case of Modern Norwegian (Cambridge, Mass. 1966), pp. 16-26.

2 *Tauli, V.*, The Theory of Language Planning (in: Advances in Language Planning, ed. by J. Fishman, Den Haag & Paris 1974).

3 *Rubin, J.*, Evaluation and Language Planning (in: Advances in the Sociology of Language, Vol. 2, ed. by J. Fishman, Den Haag & Paris 1972).

4 E.g. *Drewes, G.W.J.*, Een 16 eeuwse Maleise vertaling van de Burda van Al-Busiri (Den Haag 1955), pp. 78-9.

5 *Teeuw, A.*, The History of the Malay Language (in: Bijdragen tot de Taal-, Land- en Volkenkunde, 115, 1959).

6 *Takdir Alisjahbana, S.*, Language Planning for Modernization: The Case of Indonesian and Malaysian (Den Haag & Paris 1976), p. 106.

7 *Bodenstedt, A.A.*, Sprache und Politik in Indonesien (Heidelberg 1967), pp. 90-1.

8 *Swellengrebel, J.L.*, In Leijdeckers voetspoor. Anderhalve een bijbelvertaling en taalkunde in Indonesische talen, dl. 1:1820-1900, dl. 2: 1900-70 (Den Haag 1974-8).

9 *Takdir Alisjahbana, S.*, Language . . ., p. 37.

10 *Teeuw, A.*, Modern Indonesian Literature (Den Haag 1967), p. 22.

11 *Hooykaas, C.*, Modern Maleisch, zijne verspreiding, bruikbaarheid en toekomst (in: Koloniale Studiën, 1939), p. 423.

12 *Teeuw, A.*, Some Problems in the Study of Word Classes in Bahasa Indonesia (in: Lingua, 11, 1962).

13 Reported by Takdir Alisjahbana in an article from 1932, printed in *Takdir Alisjahbana, S.*, Dari perdjuangan dan pertumbuhan Bahasa Indonesia (Jakarta 1957), pp. 6-11.

14 *Takdir Alisjahbana, S.*, Language . . ., p. 69-72.

15 Ibid., pp. 72-7.

16 Ibid., pp. 58-60.

17 *Soebadio, H.*, New Sanskrit Loanformations in Bahasa Indonesia (in: Cultural Forum, 9:3/4, 1969, pp. 22-30).

18 The documents of this congress are collected in *Memoranda Angkatan Sasterawan 50* (Kuala Lumpur 1962). About the LBM and the Asas 50, see further *Li Chuan Siu*, Ikhtisar sejarah pergerakan dan kesusasteraan Melayu modern 1945-65 (Kuala Lumpur 1967), chapter 6.

19 *Takdir Alisjahbana, S.*, Language . . ., pp. 81 and 120.

20 *Hasan Ahmad*, Proses pemodenan Bahasa Melayu di Indonesia (in: Seminar Bahasa Indonesia 1968, Ende 1968), pp. 247-254.

21 Ibid., p. 252.

22 *Asmah Haji Omar*, Essays on Malaysian Linguistics (Kuala Lumpur 1975), p. 66.

23 See ibid., pp. 102-41.

24 *Bodenstedt, A.A.*, Sprache . . ., pp. 211-2.

BIBLIOGRAPHY

Asmah Haji Omar, Essays on Malaysian Linguistics. Kuala Lumpur 1975.

Bodenstedt, A.A., Sprache und Politik in Indonesien. Heidelberg 1967.

Drewes, G.W.J., Een 16de eeuwse Maleise vertaling van de Burda van Al-Būsirī. Den Haag 1955.

Hasan Ahmad, Proses pemodenan Bahasa Melayu di Indonesia (in: Seminar Bahasa Indonesia 1968, Ende 1968).

Haugen, E., Language Conflict and Language Planning. The Case of Modern Norwegian. Cambridge, Mass. 1966.

Hooykaas, C., Modern Maleisch, zijne verspreiding, bruikbaarheid en toekomst (in: Koloniale Studiën, 1939).

Li Chuan Siu, Ikhtisar sejarah pergerakan dan kesusasteraan Melayu modern 1945-65. Kuala Lumpur 1967.

Memoranda Angkatan Sasterawan 50. Kuala Lumpur 1962.

Rubin, J., Evaluation and Language Planning (in: Advances in the Sociology of Language, Vol. 2, ed. by J. Fishman, Den Haag & Paris 1972).

Soebadio, H., New Sanskrit Loanformations in Bahasa Indonesia (in: Cultural Forum, 9:3/4, 1969, pp. 22-30).

Swellengrebel, J.L., In Leijdeckers voetspoor. Anderhalve een bijbelvertaling en taalkunde in de Indonesische talen, dl. 1: 1820-1900, dl. 2: 1900-70. Den Haag 1974-8.

Takdir Alisjahbana, S., Dari perdjuangan dan pertumbuhan Bahasa Indonesia. Jakarta 1957.

Takdir Alisjahbana, S., Language Planning for Modernization: The Case of Indonesian and Malaysian. Den Haag & Paris 1976.

Tauli, V., The Theory of Language Planning (in: Advances in Language Planning, ed. by J. Fishman. Den Haag & Paris 1974).

Teeuw, A., The History of the Malay Language (in: Bijdragen tot de Taal-, Land- en Volkenkunde, 115, 1959).

Teeuw, A., Some Problems in the Study of Word Classes in Bahasa Indonesia (in: Lingua, 11, 1962).

Teeuw, A., Modern Indonesian Literature. Den Haag 1967.

PEASANTS AND POLITICS IN EARLY TWENTIETH-CENTURY WEST JAVA

Thommy Svensson

INTRODUCTION

The first political organizations among the indigenous population in Java were established just after 1900. They had been preceded by riots and smaller uprisings in the closing decades of the nineteenth century.[1] These had been peasant actions generated wholly within the rural society itself, and the reasons for discontent had been limited to the immediate, local environment: a particularly oppressive bureaucrat, the removal of some old rights belonging to the people or the imposition of new levies.

The actions were led by various religious leaders, the only alternative authority to the ruling bureaucracy at village level, and had a predominantly religious character. Oppositional ideas were clothed in legends and mysticism, stamped by age-old rural conceptions rooted in a social system crumbling away by colonial penetration. They were directed against encroachment and endeavoured a return to a lost, better way of life. They were of short duration, and had scarcely any effects beyond the local setting.[2]

Political organization did not originate in these rural areas but instead in emerging towns and trading centres growing out of the colonial economy at the turn of the century. Following Western models, Javanese social classes with modern and more powerful ideas, some organizational experience and newly-won education here created organisations to protect their interests: cultural societies, modest trading associations and small trade unions.

Initially, organizational work was limited to urban areas. Connections with rural society were established only in 1912-1913 when the first mass-organization, *Sarekat Islam*, was founded. The Sarekat Islam movement grew quickly, trying to attain political influence by enrolling a mass-following of such magnitude that its mere size would render the rulers open to reforms. Town-based leaders enlisted peasants in surrounding rural districts as members. It became a real mass-movement, at the end of the First World War claiming over two million members and still more sympathizers. The organization stood on a religious, Muslim foundation but bore secular traits as well, with demands for economic ameliorations and political rights.

However, the huge Sarekat Islam organization was heterogeneous. It constituted a conglomerate of local movements, and the large following of peasants was loosely organized, passive, and lacked continuity. Accordingly, the Sarekat Islam movement was weak. Following confrontations and alleged preparations for an armed uprising in one of the organization's strongest footholds, in Priangan in West Java, in 1919, regional leaders were arrested, and the government's counter-measures rapidly dissolved the mass-following all over Java. The organization fell to pieces during the first half of the 1920s.[3]

For a short time political activity became once again largely limited to urban areas. Soon, however, the fallen mantle of the Sarekat Islam was restored, this time in a communist form. The Indonesian Communist Party *(Partai Komunis Indonesia,* PKI*)* was established in 1920 and filling the vacuum left by Sarekat Islam, it quickly became the leading popular organization on the island. Since 1914 the party had in an earlier incarnation politicized within the Sarekat Islam movement, under the name of *Indische Sociaal-Democratische Vereeniging*. Now the PKI took control of the major part of the disintegrated local Sarekat Islam branches. By a resolution of the Party Congress in March 1923, these branches, denominated *Sarekat Rakyat,* became the party's base organization in particular among the peasants.

A dual structure of organization was formed. SR branches in rural areas were to be supervised by the nearest urban SR branch, in its turn subordinated to the nearest PKI branch. This PKI branch, being at the bottom of the party's hierarchical organization, was ultimately under command of the central PKI executive. Using this organizational structure, the Communist Party took over the mass-mobilizing role earlier performed by the Sarekat Islam.[4]

During its first years of existence, the party's agitation and activities had largely been limited to workers, lower middle-class groups living in urban areas and peasants settled in the immediate neighbourhood of larger towns. In 1923, however, directives were sent to regional branches to intensify Sarekat Rakyat's work in the countryside. A campaign was put into action all over the island to recruit members. Just as had happened to Sarekat Islam a few years earlier, the campaign was particularly successful in Priangan in West Java. The PKI section in the provincial capital Bandung soon became one of the most influential in the party, second only to that in the proletarian centre in industrial Semarang, where the party headquarters were situated.[5]

The peasant mobilization in Priangan in 1923 and 1924 took on a special character. The activities carried out challenged established groups in the local setting to the extent that local rulers took the drastic measure of constructing counter-organizations, called *Sarekat Hedyo* which mobilized other sectors of the rural population and, in violent confrontations with the communist followers, obliterated the Sarekat Rakyat organization in the area during the first half of 1925.

The *aim* of this study is to analyse the structure, development and social basis of the Sarekat Rakyat in Priangan and its function in local society thereby attempting to draw tentative conclusions regarding the conditions for the politicization of rural Java in the first decades of the twentieth century. The study focuses on the local Sarekat Rakyat branches in Priangan but also compares them to the Sarekat Islam movement in the area in the 1910s in an attempt to establish the more general pattern.

In trying to explain the course of events, the analysis concentrates on the role played by agrarian relations and agrarian economy. Mainly treated in a structural way, these independent variables do not directly and immediately explain what happened. Patterns of behaviour are not simple products of social and economic circumstances but the result of the interpretation people make of them, and base their actions upon, with the help of ideas and cultural resources they command at a given point in time. In this process ideological influences and individuals - and accidental occurrences - play a role. However, since earlier research on the anti-colonial movements in Java largely has concentrated on ideas, individuals and smaller groups of people, these are here being subordinated to the basic condition-setting framework within which politics took shape and could develop.

The *source-material* consists of the manuscript reports of the local administration in the area - mainly located in the Archives of the former Ministry of Colonies in The Hague - and some sequestrated documents of indigenous organizations. Another group of sources are Indonesian and Dutch newspapers published in Java during the period.[6] When studying social and economic conditions, these are supplemented by published and unpublished investigations made under the auspicies of the colonial government, and contained in Dutch and Indonesian archives.

1. SAREKAT RAKYAT AND SAREKAT HEDYO: THE COURSE OF EVENTS[7]

Sarekat Rakyat's mobilization campaign in Priangan in 1923 was initiated by itinerant propagandists from urban areas. They held meetings in the surrounding countryside. Agitation and organizational work was then carried further into the interior by people resident in the villages. These rural leaders could be activated due to their contacts with towns and trading centres. Schools built and run by the Sarekat Rakyat in many districts played an important infrastructural role. According to the sources the discontent that made people join was first and foremost the heavy burden of taxation, which recurs as the principal question around which the mobilization grew. In addition, demands for equalizing the uneven distribution of wealth and land were forwarded in a few districts.[8] The demands were expressed in concepts and representations fitting the local world of ideas, and accordingly received varying local disguises. Their basic content, nonetheless, was the same all over the province.[9]

The way in which the people were exploited by international capitalism was described. Often, examples from other parts of the world, both India and Latin America, were used. The capitalist system, which gathered wealth in the hands of a few foreign capitalists, who drained the riches of the country, was the cause of existing poverty. The people needed to wake up and demand their rights and share of the goods. Unity and struggle would in the end make possible the creation of a socialist society with an equitable distribution of wealth - often reference here was made to the Soviet Republic. The people in China were said to have shown that they no longer wanted to follow their rulers. It would not take long until the revolution would come also to Java. Time was short for getting organized. Often an impending great war between Japan and USA was hinted at.[10]

This was, briefly and crudely, the message of the itinerant propagandists. In a few places demands for redistribution of land seem to have been raised by village-leaders. But in most rural areas the general announcements of far-reaching structural changes in the social order were diluted and gradually disappeared. Here agitation was not directed against, for example, rural usurers or European plantations, but instead against native colonial officials, *pangreh praja*, and village officials. These were the capitalists' agents, in the pay of the Dutch extortionists. They survived and were nourished by the odious and

Land control systems in Java around 1900 (tentative distribution)

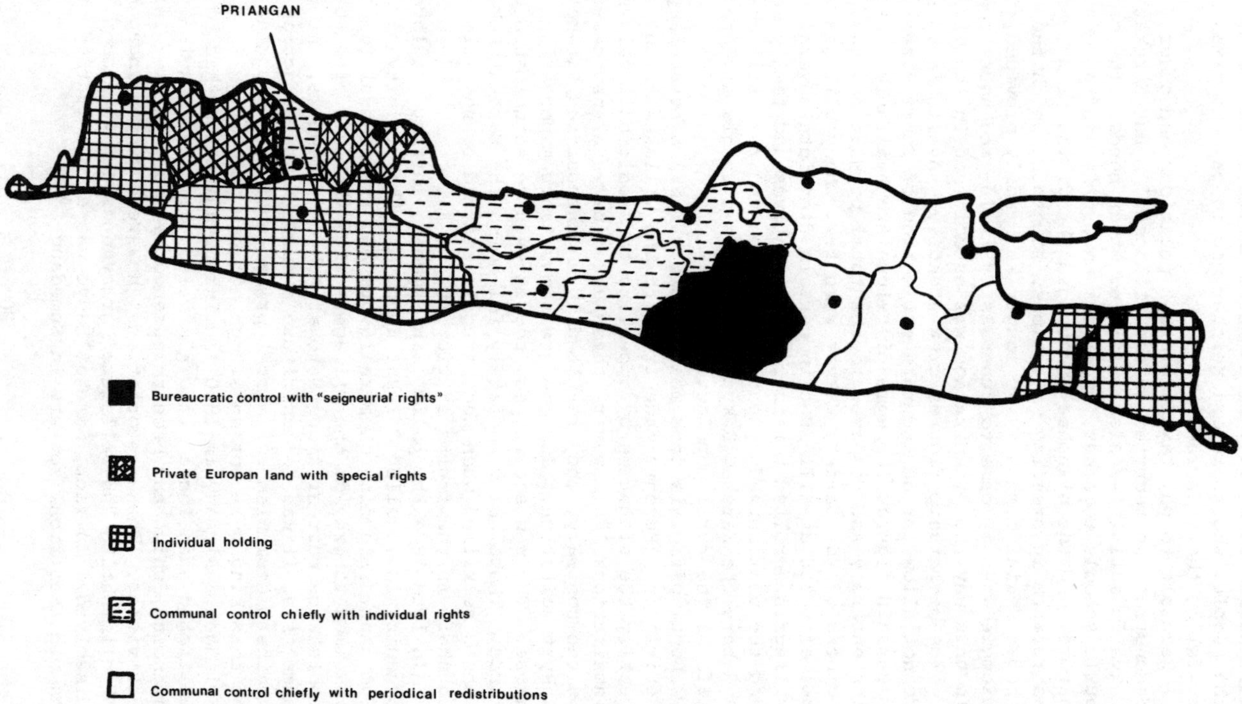

burdensome taxes. They no longer constituted the leaders of the people, who therefore neither had to pay the taxes nor to follow their decrees.

Refusals to pay taxes, protest petitions and other demonstrations recurred in the villages.[11] But Sarekat Rakyat's activities also fulfilled other needs. The members built schools together, undertook enterprises of an economic nature, and the branches encouraged the giving of mutual assistance in pressing situations, something which the eroded social community no longer so readily provided, for example when it came to funerals or field- and house-repairs. In this way the organization was established in the villages.[12]

The membership figures grew steadily. Available sources do not allow for an accurate estimation of their size. Only uncertain figures for some districts are available. Seen in its entirety and compared to the total population, the members of the Sarekat Rakyat were few. Many villages were not affected at all. But in certain districts several hundred villagers enrolled together with relatives and family members and the unorganized sympathizers accounted for still more. And here the Sarekat Rakyat activities strongly affected the life of the rural population.[13]

Local officials took measures to curtail Sarekat Rakyat's activities. Regents made trips to the villages trying to rectify the situation by appealing to traditional values and institutions.[14] However, these attempts were unsuccessful. On the contrary, they resulted in an intensified Sarekat Rakyat agitation. In some areas messianic expectations arose. The new society now should even be established by force. Those not immediately following the Sarekat Rakyat should be killed when the struggle started or not allowed to share in the fruits of victory.[15]

In late 1924 the *patih*[16] in Sumedang initiated a local organization, called *Sarekat Hedyo,* in the vicinity of Sumedang. Standing on a religious and traditional foundation, it aimed to provide the villagers with the sort of mutual assistance current among Sarekat Rakyat's members. At the same time, it was to constitute a bulwark and an action group against 'communism'.[17] Local priayi-activated associations of this kind were not an altogether new phenomenon in Priangan. Already in 1920 similar organizations had been initiated when local officials tried to fortify their standing, which had been threatened by local Sarekat Islam activities. These associations, however, proved incapable of eliminating the villagers' grievances and were soon dissolved. In fact, Sarekat Hedyo was a reactivation of an old theatrical society in Sumedang.[18]

The situation in Priangan became more and more tense. Groups of police and local officials supervised well-attended Sarekat Rakyat meetings. Provocations increased and finally open clashes between police and Sarekat Rakyat members took place, in Bandung on the 17th, 24th and 29th January 1925, in Sumedang on the 30th January, and in Ciamis on the 1st February. Arrests followed. Houses were searched. *Jimats* and various kinds of weapon were confiscated.[19] At the disturbances in Sumedang many Sarekat Hedyo members participated on the side of the police. At once conflicts broke out. Violent confrontations spread over the countryside.

From Sumedang the idea of anti-communist counter-organizations was spread by local officials to the other regencies. The new associations created got different names, all with traditional connotations. They stood on a religious foundation. Religious officials, both at village and district level, together with secular village officials, carried out the membership enlistment. Established influence and direct contacts with higher priayi enabled them to mobilize quickly thousands of followers. Both within the government and the national Indonesian organizations it became common to designate the associations with the name of their predecessor, *Sarekat Hedyo*. In one important respect, however, the original Sumedang organization differed from its successors. The latter did not possess any programme of mutual assistance. And they did not attempt to eliminate the sources of discontent, which constituted the basis of Sarekat Rakyat's appeal to the people. They were plain anti-organizations, created with the purpose of destroying 'communism'. Moreover, the later these Sarekat Hedyo were established, the smaller their organizational ambitions became. In some districts they were just groups of hired bandits, paid by local officials, passing through the villages searching for 'communists'.[20]

Sarekat Hedyo actions spread like wildfire in the province. They were particularly active in the Bandung regency, but also in Tasikmalaya and Ciamis. Sarekat Rakyat members - primarily the local leaders - were mauled and driven out of their villages, economic and social boycotts against them were initiated, and houses and fields destroyed. The Sarekat Rakyat schools were closed and the buildings demolished. The actions were passively supported by local officials and the police. Reports against assailants were ignored. Demands for an investigation of the occurrences, raised by national Indonesian leaders as well as the Dutch press and the representative assembly, *Volksraad*, were rejected.[21]

In most areas the members immediately withdrew from the Sarekat Rakyat. The Dutch Resident in Bandung wrote, for instance, on the 18th of February, in his report on the political situation:

> In the once so troublesome Sarekat Rakyat districts Sumedang, Banjaran, Soreang, Ujungberung, Ciwedey and Cililin in the department of Bandung no single member is left and all the schools of the organisation have been dissolved or closed. Also from Tasikmalaya and Ciamis information is coming in stating that, for instance, in Ciamis, which is a very violently communist area, at present 800 members have left the organization and the notorious school there has closed . . .[22]

Certainly, these reports were exaggerated. For instance, local Sarekat Rakyat branches established self-defence groups in Bandung in March, called *Anti Ribut Bond*, in an attempt to suppress actions of the anti-communist groups.[23] And incidents were reported in the Indonesian press as late as in June.[24] But nonetheless, the Sarekat Hedyo actions had the desired effect. Sarekat Rakyat's resistance was restricted to urban areas and the lion's share of adherents withdrew from the organization. The movement's political activities ceased from the second half of 1925 onwards.[25]

Looking at Java as a whole, the rural campaign of the Communist Party/Sarekat Rakyat in 1923-1925 had its greatest appeal in Priangan - despite the fact that the activities were so quickly and effectively curtailed by the Sarekat Hedyo. It is also clear that the mobilization in some respects constituted a continuation of, and a new phase in, the widespread activities of the local Sarekat Islam branches in the area during the period 1917-19.

In fact, in relation to both of the large mass-organizations during colonial times - the Sarekat Islam and the Communist Party - Priangan holds a special position. The province was the area in Java where rural campaigns became particularly strong, and more than in other areas challenged the rulers. On both occasions the activities culminated in violent confrontations with local potentates. Firstly, in 1919 the so-called Afdeeling B affair, resulted in the imprisonment of hundreds of local Sarekat Islam leaders in Priangan, as well as members of the top echelons in the national organization, contributing to the disintegration of the mass-base and decomposition of the whole movement.[26] Secondly, in 1925 the confrontations between Sarekat Rakyat and Sarekat Hedyo led to arrests, suppression of the right to political activity and other measures against the Communist Party nationally to such an extent that the party henceforth was largely driven underground.[27] Thus, the political activity carried out in Priangan was of strategic importance to the development of both of the two mass movements in Java during the colonial period. It may be asked if discontent with existing agrarian conditions was more widespread among large population groups in Priangan than elsewhere in Java, and subject to being canalized into forceful rural action. Was this the case and, if so, why?

In order to answer these questions we must analyse the general features of Priangan rural society. Thereafter, we can turn back to the events just described and try to interpret them on the basis of this information.

2. *JAVA'S AGRO-ECONOMIC SYSTEMS*

When the basic question of who controlled the land and its use is considered, it appears that in the first decades of the twentieth century a number of different agrarian systems existed in Java. A preliminary attempt to establish the geographical distribution of the major types of land control around 1900 is shown in map 2.[28]

In colonial times Dutch scholars concluded that there existed three distinct areas, *adatrechtkringen,* in Java each one characterized by its own system of indigenous customary law *(adat)* - West Java, Yogyakarta-Surakarta (Vorstenlanden), and Central and East Java.[29] If European agriculture is omitted and we concentrate our attention on that operated by Indonesians, the variations in adat law are largely concomitant with the three major types of land control.

Furthermore, studies establish that the difference with regard to land-control corresponds also to variations in the organization of production, in village-organization, and in different mechanisms used by non-cultivating classes to acquire a surplus product.

Thus, if European holdings are not taken into consideration, it may tentatively be argued that around the turn of the century, when agrarian commercialization had taken a firm hold on the island, at least three basic types of *agro-economic systems* existed in Java. These systems reacted in different fashions to the penetrating forces and conditioned the rise of different patterns of land distribution and social structures.[30]

PRIANGAN AROUND 1925

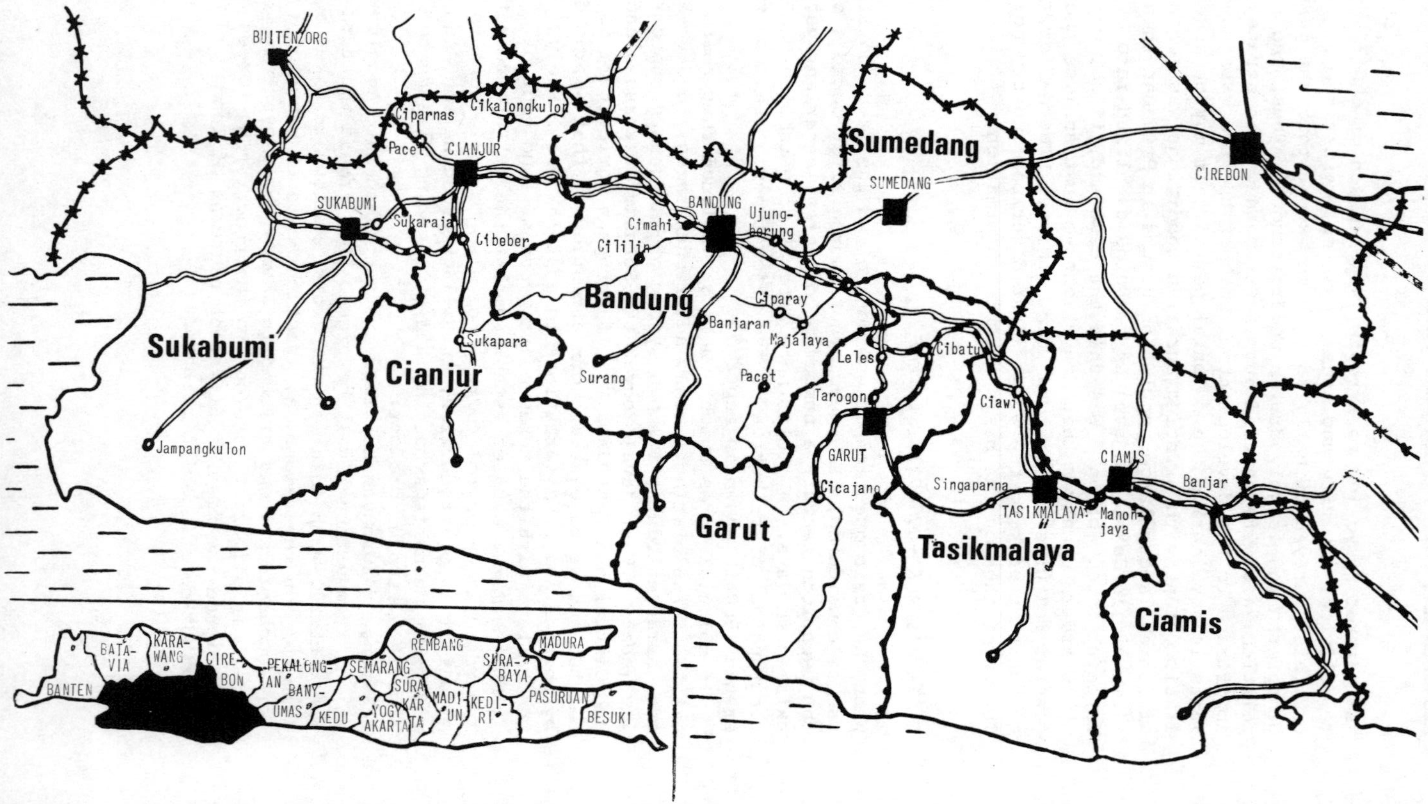

In some areas in south Central Java what may be called a *bureaucratic* system prevailed.[31] All land ultimately belonged to the princely rulers of Yogyakarta and Surakarta, who over the centuries had granted smaller and larger lease areas, *apanage,* to officials and favourites. Hereby, holdings existed with extensive 'seigneurial rights' attached to them. The peasants lacked permanent rights and cultivated the fields for the lord in various types of share-cropping arrangements, and supervisors and harvest collectors were employed directly by the lord. No administratively autonomous village communities existed. When in the late nineteenth century European companies started to lease land more frequently, and rights attached to it, from the apanage holders, the system became extraordinarily exploitative. During the 1910s and 1920s the colonial authorities carried out a land reform aimed at abolishing the system. The new arrangements tried to mix individual rights with communal control within newly-created village communities. Nevertheless, remnants of the old system survived for several decades.

In other areas of Central and East Java various forms of *communal* control of land existed, exercised by the village communities independently of higher administrative levels. The peasants either had permanent shares in the village land, or recurring redistributions were made. In both cases the peasant had fixed, individual *rights of cultivation,* which could seldom be taken away from him and often derived from his descent from the original founders of the village. But the community ultimately disposed the land and exercised an overall control of production, which made it difficult to sell a piece of land without the village's permission and decision as to the new holder. This communal control was very strong in inland areas, and not so fully developed in the coastal, *pasirir,* areas.

Burdensome taxes, the market forces, activities of money-lenders, the swelling of the population and the steady growth of a landless group - to which no shares in village land were available - were all forces that contributed to growing poverty among most peasants in Java. But at this point in time the collective control of land prevented a minor group of strategically placed people from taking advantage of the situation and accumulating larger holdings.[32] Although the differences between coastal and inland areas with regard to land-rights conditioned a more developed market economy in the *pasirir,* and increased the social differences between the areas as time passed by, the general picture was that the population growth and the increased external exploitation of the villages' resources led to a *fragmentation of land holding*. Complicated patterns of tenancies and sub-tenancies arose, by which economic resources were redistributed, and the villagers together fell into deeper and comparatively equally shared poverty.

In contrast, *individual*, hereditary *right of disposal* of land prevailed in West Java where Priangan constituted the largest area. In the decades around 1900, when the market economy had penetrated rural areas and taxes and levies were monetarized, here - by Javanese standards - a strong *concentration of land* in a few hands took place, accompanied by the rise of a large group of regular agricultural wage-earners, absentee landlords and a more accentuated social stratification. The precondition for this differentiation process was the individual holding of land in combination with weak collective structures at village level making possible indebtedness and sales of land without communal restrictions preventing the transactions.[33]

Possessing different types of social structures and varying intensity in class conflicts, these agrarian systems formed different preconditions for the Communist Party/ Sarekat Rakyat's and Sarekat Islam's political mobilization campaigns. To what extent were the particularly accentuated class divisions in Priangan expressed in Sarekat Rakyat's activities? Does the individualistic agrarian system explain Priangan's outstanding position as a battleground for peasant struggle during the period?

To answer these questions, we first have to study the agrarian system in Priangan, attempting on crucial points to compare it with the dominant collectivistic systems in East and Central Java.

3. THE AGRARIAN SYSTEM IN PRIANGAN[34]

3.1 The agrarian-bureaucratic state (to 1870)

Our knowledge of the agrarian conditions in Priangan in older times is very scant. In contrast to the core-areas of the island where wet-rice cultivation in *sawah*-fields was established much earlier, the Priangan highlands were sparsely populated. For a long time slash-and-burn cultivation prevailed and made people mobile and difficult to control, preventing the establishment of larger social and political units. During the sixteenth century the first evidence of a more permanent, but still rudimentary state-bureaucratic superstructure occurs. Probably this development was connected with the gradual spread of wet-rice agriculture - a process which was expedited in the beginning of the seventeenth century when the area was annexed as a border region to the realm of Mataram centred in south Central Java. Mataram's influence seems to have stabilized the floating relationships between various chiefs and local rulers in Priangan. Gradually the foundation for an administration covering and integrating the whole area was established. In pace with the accelerated spread of the more productive sawah-fields, the population became domiciled, creating conditions for the rise of a more stable ruling class - an *agrarian bureaucracy* living on that part of the peasantry upon which it was able to impose taxes. Rents were levied in kind and combined with various types of corvee-labour and subjects could also be conscripted as soldiers.

More detailed knowledge is scarce as to landholding, types of land, duties and rights attached to it and how the extraction of surplus product was organized.[35] It must be noted, however, that the opportunities for potentates to demand taxes and labour by no means were a matter of course, but varied geographically and over time. Furthermore, incessant changes in the balance of power often made rival rulers claim the right to tax the same settlements or parts thereof.[36]

In the late seventeenth and early eighteenth centuries Priangan was placed under *Dutch suzerainty*. Treaties concluded with Mataram transferred rights to rents and services owed to the princely ruler in Surakarta by the tributary vassals in Priangan to the Dutch East India Company. Hereby, the company could begin to utilize existing systems of taxation for commodity deliveries to its overseas trade. Initially, the peasants' deliveries to the company were crops long since grown in the area, for instance cotton, spices and indigo. Then, commencing in 1720, tax-cultivation of coffee was introduced and expanded steadily during the following century. Landholding households were imposed to hold a number of coffee-plants for the company. Indigenous potentates - led by the five *bupati* in Bandung, Cianjur, Sumedang, Limbangan (Garut) and Sukapura (Tasikmalaya) - were made responsible for collection and transport of the goods to the harbour. For this they were remunerated with a sum of money to be divided with their subordinates and proportional to the amount of commodities delivered. In 1850 coffee was cultivated in 55 of Priangan's 66 districts, in total over 40 million plants.[37]

This so-called Priangan System *(Preanger stelsel)* was gradually extended to other crops as well, principally tea and tobacco, especially when the Dutch Crown took over the company's undertakings in 1800. It was in force until 1871, and then gradually liquidated. The Priangan System was the model for the so-called Cultivation System *(Cultuur stelsel)* introduced in Central and East Java in 1830. Here the peasants were compelled to grow sugar, which the Dutch sold on the world market.

The two systems filled the same purpose and were, as tax-cultivation, on the surface very similar. However, they differed on two crucial points, and here can be traced one of the reasons why agrarian developments went in different directions in Priangan and in Central and East Java, within the joint colonial framework.[38]

Firstly, sugar-cane required other ecological conditions than coffee, tea and tobacco. Since careful irrigation was needed, the best habitat was found to be the peasants own *rice-fields*. Accordingly, a system of rotation of sugar and rice in the same fields was introduced. This differed from the cultivation in Priangan where export crops were grown on mountain slopes only to a limited extent utilized by the peasants themselves, *independently of the rice-fields*.

In order to manage the food supply under constant sugar-production, a rotation was necessary, demanding joint control of most of the village land and irrigation systems. Accordingly, *the village* here became the unit of taxation and an extensive, communal control and administration came into existence. The Cultivation System strengthened the village's productive unity and established a communal organization of the means of production and control of the peasants' economic and social activities.[39] In Priangan, on the other hand, the *individual households* were production and taxation units, and administrative roles for the villages did not develop. The Priangan System did not stimulate, in fact it even contradicted the development of a communal village organization.

Secondly, the more comprehensive regulations of the Cultivation System made direct Dutch influence in local circles stronger in Central and East Java than in Priangan. Sugar factories and supervisors arrived and the colonial administration was extended into rural areas and downwards in the ruling hierarchy. The power and independence of indigenous officials diminished accordingly.[40] Priangan experienced a contrary development. Here the agrarian bureaucracy was strengthened and grew on the back of the colonial system.

Colonial supremacy in Priangan rested on a consistently realized *indirect rule*. Apart from commodity deliveries, higher appointments and commercial and judicial regulations, the indigenous bureaucrats were left free to tax and rule over the population as they thought best. The number of Europeans settled in the area remained slight. In 1860 there were still just above a hundred. Both private Europeans and Chinese were prohibited from living in the area, and the influx was meticulously regulated.[41]

It was, therefore, not until the 1860s, when influential political groupings in The Hague started to demand an opening of the colony to private capital, that more detailed investigations were carried out concerning agrarian and administrative relations in the province. These investigations give the first more comprehensive picture of Priangan society.[42]

They revealed a voluminous and powerful agrarian bureaucracy of several thousand office-holders on a number of levels radiating from the five bupati. The Dutch tried to conceive of it as a hierarchically arranged system, but a lot of overlapping and unclear boundaries prevailed. Secular power was strongly mixed with religious. Religious officials maintained most of the daily contacts with the peasantry. Within the framework of rice-cults and fertility rites, which played a central role in a cultural system interwoven with popular Sundanese folk beliefs and the Islamic faith, they exercised a fundamental role in society's reproduction: *they supervised and regulated the irrigation systems of the rice fields*. In other parts of Java this task was fulfilled by the village communities and sugar factories. The religious bureaucracy in Priangan thus had a stronger position than elsewhere. It constituted an integrated part of material life, at the same time as it ideologically sanctioned the state and the social order.

In practice, official positions were hereditary and a rank order founded on privileges accentuated, as in other areas.[43] The officials' families were large; kinship and lineage of fundamental importance. This hereditary nobility, which the Dutch, using an ethnocentrical analogy, called aristocracy, and which here will be referred to by the indigenous term, *priayi*, was maintained by the peasants. It received royalty on the coffee deliveries, tithes on the rice crop *(padi cuku)*, *njambungan*-deliveries for ceremonials and festivities, corvee-labour *(herendienst)* and various special levies. Lower officials were reimbursed by bupati, but also had certain rights of their own to levy taxes.[44]

The burdens these imposts laid on the peasants were certainly exaggerated in Dutch reports of the time. Nevertheless, independent sources give concordant evidence of an increased exploitation and impoverishment of the population during the nineteenth century, despite the increased productivity of the land during the same period.[45] Most often on the initiative of bupati and depending upon organizational work by lower officials, irrigation was extended and sawah-fields constructed. It was either done using corvee-labour or by creating incentives among the peasants through temporary tax-exemptions or -reductions. More extensive reclamation seems to have started some decades into the nineteenth century, with an especially intensive phase during the 1860s when about 57,000 ha of sawah were constructed in 1863-7 alone.[46] Hereby, the still shifting slash-and-burn peasants finally became settled.

The improvements were of necessity collective efforts, in other parts of Java often conducted by the village communities themselves. In Priangan, however, they were instigated and organized by the ruling bureaucracy in attempts to increase revenue.

With regard to the expropriation of surplus product, the fields fell into two broad categories: *tax land* and *bureaucratic land*. Sawah raised under temporary tax-reductions, together with earlier reclaimed tax land, belonged to the peasant by way of the work carried out when constructing the fields. But irrespective of the peasant's private-like right of disposal, which made alienation of the holdings possible, he was subordinated to priayi's demand of taxes, services and deliveries. Fields raised by using corvee-labour became bureaucratic land. It was at the disposal of priayi - the right in theory being tied to the office - and was tilled under serf-like conditions by so-called *rahayat*-peasants belonging to different priayi-houses.

Thus, reclamation and intensification of production did not directly originate from the peasants themselves. One of the reasons was the lack of politically-administrative village communities in Priangan. In Java's core areas such communities had developed and gained strength under the Cultivation System and the villages, *desa*, constituted autonomous unities, led by a village head, *lurah* or *bekel*, and a cadre of functionaries. These village officials maintained the contacts with superior officials, as well as the villages' internal affairs, such as distribution of land and water, religious practices, police functions, some jurisdiction and the upkeep of joint establishments such as buildings, roads and bridges. In Priangan autonomous village communities of this type never seem to have existed. Instead, landholding households fell directly under some office-holder, while the collective tasks were regulated by local priayi and religious officials.

This administrative pattern does not conflict with the *social* communities prevailing within smaller settlements, *kaluruhan,* delimited by the irrigation networks. Social solidarity was in line with the subsistence economy and is evidenced by sources from after 1870.

To sum up, around 1870 politically-administrative village communities were non-existent in Priangan, as well as communal undertakings resting on the peasants' own initiative. The ruling bureaucracy reached all the way down to village-level, being just an extension of the ruler's private sphere of influence. This situation contrasts sharply with the communalistic structures, which had developed in East and Central Java (with the exception of the Yogyakarta-Surakarta area). Within the framework of wet-rice agriculture and a strong alliance between secular and religious power, the regulation of the Priangan-peasants' joint affairs was instead exercised by bupati's direct representatives on the spot, where religious officials played a crucial part. The villagers' administrative influence, political independence and possibilities for joint action was reduced to the same extent.

The peasants were divided into three principal classes: *taxed freeholders,* having hereditary right of disposition of land and being taxed by the office-holders, *tenants and sharecroppers* on these tax lands, and *rahayat-cultivators,* tilling the bureaucracy's fields under serf-like conditions in return for a share in the crop. The *nobility* lived on these classes and the state it upheld was autonomous within the colonial framework. Exploitation was extensive and the pressure on the population increased during the nineteenth century despite the coeval spread of wet-rice agriculture.

3.2 The colonial state (after 1870)

In the 1870s agrarian relations changed. Private European capital started to exploit the colony's resources of men and land, and the old agrarian-bureaucratic state broke up.

The new agrarian legislation in 1870-1 started the process of liquidating the Priangan System, giving Europeans and other non-natives opportunity to rent land from the peasants and uncultivated land from the state to grow export crops. Favourable conditions and a climate suited to Europeans up in the mountains, soon gave Priangan the heaviest density of export-plantations in Java. In 50 years - up to 1920 - more than 1,400 larger and smaller plantations were established. In 1890 45,000 ha were cultivated on behalf of non-natives. By 1926 the figure had risen to 220,000 ha. The number of Europeans settled in the area rose from a few hundreds in the 1860s to over 27,000 in 1930.[47]

This development transformed agrarian relations in the area.

3.2.1 The transformation of the agrarian bureaucracy

The agrarian bureaucracy lost its independent position. Bureaucratic landholding was abolished and the land distributed to the peasants. Rights of taxation were abrogated and the use of corvee-labour heavily reduced, and was to cease altogether in due course. Instead, the indigenous rulers became directly employed by the Dutch state.

Following the same pattern as elsewhere in Java, the number of officials was fixed and a hierarchical administrative structure created. Hereby, the old lords were transformed into a professional administrative corps, *pangreh praja,* with fixed salaries and patterns of promotion.

The reforms required time to be accomplished. The independence of indigenous officials diminished at the same pace as Europeans arrived and took place at lower levels of administration. The period between 1870 and 1900 constitutes a transitional stage and from the turn of the century onwards the contours of the modern colonial state were established.[48]

Public administration was financed by a government taxation system, which replaced the old unregulated revenues. It had three major parts. The first was the land tax *(land rente),* originally a tithe but after a few years extended to delivery of 3/20 of the harvest. Soon it was monetarized and calculated from the size and quality of the production unit. Secondly, the different types of corvee-labour were replaced by one single system of *herendiensten,* by which landholding households were obliged to work a certain number of days for the state, mainly in transport and road works. Later on these services were transformed into a head-tax, so-called *hoofd-geld.* Thirdly, the state began to put charges on activities deriving from the new economy, such as trade and commerce fees, charges on animals and vehicles, stamp duties, etc.[49]

A stricter levying according to the rules, and a reduced income level of indigenous officials, undoubtedly alleviated the population's burdens in the 1870s. But the rapid expansion of state activities, and the swell of bureaucracy, soon again increased the pressure of taxation.

The most important change was the *monetarization* of the taxes, a conversion starting before the turn of the century and almost completed at the outbreak of the First World War. The transformation had revolutionary effects. It was caused by, and at the same time reinforced, the spread of the market economy, thereby being one of the major propelling forces of change. Forced to pay taxes in money, the rural population had to hire out their fields to European firms, earn money-wages by seeking temporary or seasonal employment at the plantations, or by selling parts of the crops.

Incomes from land lease, plantation work and cash cultivation extended indigenous commodity trade. *Local markets* developed. But it was a geographically uneven development, intimately connected with the expansion of the transport system. The construction of the railway in this respect meant another veritable revolution. For the first time Priangan was physically linked to other parts of Java. And old centres - Sukabumi, Cianjur, Bandung, Tasikmalaya and Ciamis - were connected with each other. New centres grew up where the tracks were laid down, supported by an extended and improved network of roads. These developments created new conditions for economic and social communication.

Accordingly, Priangan's population began to travel at the turn of the century. Although the railway was intended primarily to serve European export agriculture, the Sundanese - on their third-class tickets - soon constituted the major part of the traffic. Hereby new markets for indigenous goods were opened. *Small-scale trade* expanded and was encouraged by special freight rates. The lion's share of commerce became a part-time activity, mostly carried out by women in order to raise necessary cash.

Subsequently a small class of *full-time traders* emerged, settling in new, urban-like population centres and no longer directly earning their living by agriculture. In most other areas in Java this niche in the economic system became commandeered by the Chinese minority; but *not* - at this point - in Priangan. The reason was, apart from a more intensive indigenous capital formation - which will be discussed later - that the Dutch had earlier prohibited Chinese settlement in the area.[50]

The structure of the *religious bureaucracy* was also formalized. Muslim officials had to be acknowledged by the state. Legislation codified by the bupati as religious heads and penghulu- and jaksa-offices were more strictly defined. Unclear, intermediary levels were restructured or abolished.

The most important change, however, was that the religious élite lost its direct influence in agricultural production. By a decision of the Governor-General in September 1870, 'the muslim priests (should) withhold from exhortions regarding the irrigation of the fields and all endeavours connected with rice cultivation . . . [The bupati] are injuncted to look after that the muslim priests in no way interfere with the material interests of the people.'[51]

Losing one of its major bases of power, the local religious élite was allowed to retain rights to collect fees and duties, especially the so-called *zakat* and *pitrah*, 'in accordance with the Koran and prevailing local custom'. According to local, colonial reports, the fees were, in theory, voluntary contributions, but in actual fact were forcibly extracted from the villagers, who regarded them as remuneration for tasks performed, as a kind of tax.[52] When the religious officials, however, lost their active role in the rice-cycle, the fees became more difficult to collect. In order to mitigate the effects, the government exempted religious officials from paying taxes.[53] It is nevertheless questionable how voluntary the contributions became. The native officials of the state, *pangreh praja*, in an old-established symbiosis with religious power, used their traditional influence to raise zakat and pitrah to the mosques and their servants. Already in the decision of September 1870, which was cited above, it was made clear that bupati - in accordance with the office instruction[54] - 'is compelled to make sure that the indemnifications to the clergy remain within the limits prescribed by religion and that the collection is carried out without any help from or interference by native chiefs.'

Nonetheless, abuses prevailed in the following period, and the use of means of compulsion augmented as the religious élite and its ceremonialism were separated from production. The religious fees became considered by parts of the population as iniquitous.[55] Colonial authority could not do much about it. Still in 1915 reports were being sent to Batavia about 'the religious parasitism', said to be particularly common in Priangan, where several mosque-functionaries, but also higher officials, accumulated wealth through collections sanctioned by pangreh praja.[56]

By control of religious practices and the removal of its position in the production cycle, a religious bureaucracy thus ranged into the colonial state, depending on more unwilling villagers for its incomes.[57]

The role played by local officials in village affairs was taken over by *newly-constructed, administrative village communities (desa)*, designed from the model of East and Central Java. As has been discussed earlier, the cultivation of non-irrigated land and a small population had created a high mobility among Priangan's peasants. The population growth, concomitant with the extension of sawah-fields, decreased vagabondage, and larger permanent settlements with a socially related village system of *kaluruhan* arose. These kaluruhan were now arranged into desa-units, which were given administrative autonomy, enabling them to rule their own, internal affairs. Each desa was led by a village head, *lurah*, and a cadre of functionaries subordinated to him. The lurah had the right to levy village taxes and services, and together with the other officials he upheld contacts with higher levels of administration and executed the state's more and more frequent directives downwards.[58] Formally, the lurah-office was elected by the adult, male inhabitants of the village, but ultimate control rested with the right of veto of the state. The lurah appointed the other functionaries himself, such as deputy-heads, supervisors of irrigation, police, village-clerk and others.[59]

Judged in general terms, the position of village officials in Priangan became weak compared with that in East and Central Java where the ultimate control of the communally disposed village-land gave their counterparts a key to strong influence. In Priangan the lurah and his functionaries were from the start regarded as representatives of higher office and executors of tasks given from above.

Even more important, however, is that as far as class-position is concerned, the Priangan lurah was separated from his fellow villagers - a feature quite peculiar to this area. Together with the more important functionaries, the lurah-group came to constitute an *exploitative rural class*.

At this time Java's lurah had five types of income attached to office:

- *ambtsvelden,* i.e. land kept within the village for the office-holder indigenously termed *bengkok*.
- royalty on the collected *land tax*
- *pancen*-money, originally being services performed by the village's landholders, later on transformed into a levy in cash
- remuneration for *work on behalf of the state,* foremost the running of government rural credit
- irregular *special levies* when needed.

In those parts of Java where various forms of communally regulated rights to land prevailed, ambtsvelden provided the major part of the lurah's income, making him a part of the working community. With the exception of the regency Ciamis - which until the beginning of the 1920s belonged to the Cirebon province - and a few pieces of land that had become ambtsvelden after the land reform in the last decades of the nineteenth century, no collectively disposed land existed in Priangan and, accordingly, no office-land. Instead, Priangan's lurah relied solely on direct taxation of the villagers.

This is shown by data from an investigation into the village system conducted in the middle of the 1920s.[60] In Table 1 the composition of the lurah's income in Priangan is compared with that in the provinces of Cirebon and Madiun. In Madiun land was chiefly disposed communally and a strong village community prevailed, as elsewhere in Java's core-areas. In Cirebon - a pasirir province adjacent to Priangan - the money economy was more widespread than in Madiun, the village communities weaker and the disposition of land mixed in collective and individual parts. The three areas, therefore, can be said to represent strategic points on a scale of more and less collectively styled agrarian systems on the island.[61]

It can be concluded that in Madiun and Cirebon half of the lurah's income derived from office land. In Priangan with the exception of Ciamis, this part was instead taken directly from the villagers by a proportionally higher levy of pancen-money. The figures also suggest a higher standard of living for the lurah in Priangan, where the average yearly income was estimated at 1,165 Guilders, compared with 894 in Cirebon and 637 in Madiun.

Although the lurah office was upheld by election, it tended to become hereditary. In fact, in 1926 about 40 per cent of Priangan's lurah had inherited their offices within the family.[62] Consequently, the special interests

Table 1. Composition of lurah-incomes in Priangan, Cirebon and Madiun in 1926. Percentage-distribution on various income-categories.

PROVINCE	Office land (1)	Royalty on collection of land-tax	Pancen-money	Government remuner-ation (2)	Irregular levies	Total per cent	Average yearly income (3)	Number of lurah
PRIANGAN	6	27	53	7	7	100	1165	1240
Bandung	1	31	55	8	5	100	1300	276
Ciamis	48	20	22	5	4	99	706	117
Garut	1	30	63	3	2	99	1280	148
Sukabumi	0	23	68	5	3	99	1614	147
Cianjur	0	35	43	8	14	100	1253	133
Tasikmalaya	3	25	50	8	13	99	986	281
Sumedang	2	25	61	6	5	99	964	138
CIREBON	47	23	22	3	5	100	894	1001
Cirebon	51	24	20	3	2	100	1226	305
Kuningan	63	15	7	3	12	100	756	240
Indramayu	22	31	37	5	5	100	716	189
Majalenka	44	22	29	2	3	100	763	267
MADIUN	54	18	18	3	6	99	637	1151
Madiun	58	22	12	5	4	101	775	233
Ngawi	53	20	20	5	2	100	753	215
Magetan	58	13	20	3	7	101	671	236
Ponorongo	58	17	13	3	8	99	628	303
Pacitan	37	23	32	1	6	99	257	164

Commentary: (1) estimated net-income; (2) running of credit bank; (3) Guilders.

Source: *Eindverslag over het desa-autonomie-onderzoek op Java en Madoera*, ingesteld krachtens Gouvernementsbesluit dd. 8/5 1926, no. 3x (Weltevreden 1929), staat 2.

deriving from the lurah office's place in the social system became permanent and were reinforced as time passed by.

It can be concluded, that the village heads in Priangan constituted a non-producing class with material interests in certain important respects contradictory to those of other villagers. The village office-holders did not belong to the peasantry, but tended instead, with regard to class position, to mix with priayi.[63]

3.2.2 Agrarian classes and the rise of big landlords

We have discussed earlier how land in Priangan was disposed individually. The right was in theory tied to the work carried out when constructing the fields. We have further noticed the two major forms of holding with regard to rent: tax-disposal of private type and bureaucratic landholding.

After 1870 bureaucratic landholding was liquidated and the land distributed among the peasants. It was either given to the original reclaimer of the fields or to the actual cultivator. In addition, a small part was set aside as ambtsvelden for a few lurah. The lack of systematic figures makes it impossible to establish the proportion of the turnover.[64]

Immediately following this levelling, however, a process of land concentration started, which created a new class situation in the countryside. Sales of land certainly took place in the 1850s, probably also earlier,[65] but the holdings had barely any market value before 1870. The reason was the heavy levies and services attached to them. The reforms of 1870-1 lightened the pressure of taxation and made land a profitable object of investment. Prices soared and those disposing capital quickly could expand their holdings.[66]

The source-material for a study of the development of landholding can be divided into two major categories. Initially, colonial investigations were made of more or less representative samples of villages, mainly by interviews carried out by state-employed personnel. It has to be taken into consideration that those interviewed gave information which they anticipated would favour low taxes. Thus the figures are unreliable. Nonetheless, it is possible to conclude that the concentration process started immediately following the reforms of 1870-1.[67]

Only when a land-register was established, do we get a better factual foundation. After the introduction of the land-tax system, surveys and registration of holdings were made during the 1890s and 1900s, and the information was gathered in a cadastral register.[68] Albeit no longer preserved, these registers at various times provided the basis for government investigations, as well as for current reports of colonial officials in different parts of the province. These give us a rough picture of the developments.

It is, however, clear that the cadastral information *underestimated* the volume of large landholding.[69] Firstly, because many landlords held land in more than one village. Since the desa constituted a registration unit, it was impossible to establish the total amount of land held by a person.[70] Secondly, concealed holdings were common, as fields were withheld from registration or held in another person's name.[71] Thirdly, rural indebtedness quickly developed.[72] It is, therefore, impossible to determine the number of bigger landlords in Priangan at any certain time. It can only be concluded, that large landholding increased over a period of time and was much more widespread in Priangan than elsewhere in Java. This is illustrated in Table 2, based on figures from two special investigations made in 1905 and 1925. The picture given is confirmed by data from sources of other provenance distributed over the time period.[73]

Considering what has been said about the bias in the material, it is obvious that the concentration of land in Priangan was greater than the figures indicate. But apart from Batavia, Banten and Cirebon in West Java - where, as in Priangan, individually controlled land existed - the figures more accurately reflect the actual situation, since communal control largely prevented the transfer of land to people outside the village and concealed holdings. Thus, the proportional differences between the areas in West Java and other parts of the island were larger than the figures indicate.

The concentration process speeded up when taxes were monetarized, and the recession during the First World War was another accelerating factor. The process was strongest in areas adjacent to towns, trading centres and along the transport routes where contacts with the market were more intense. Especially in the vicinity of the provincial capital, Bandung, the development was faster and stronger than elsewhere.[74] This is shown when the figures in Table 2 are broken down for the regencies in the province (Table 3).[75]

The necessary condition for the rise of big landlords was the existing individual rights to the land, combined

Table 2. Number of persons holding more than 30 bouw of land in Java's provinces in 1905 and 1925 according to official figures

PROVINCE	NUMBER OF HOLDERS WITH MORE THAN 30 BOUW 1905	1925
Priangan	559 x)	1226
Pekalongan	212	106
Surabaya	104	79
Semarang	95	250
Madiun	45	78
Pasuruan	38	137
Banyumas	28	207
Kediri	25	107
Rembang	23	43
Kedu	20	80
Besuki	18	223
Cirebon	15 x)	268
Madura	15	50
Batavia	7	376
Banten	5	157

x) Ciamis (Galoe) in 1905 belonged to Cirebon, in 1925 to Priangan. The figures have been recalculated and Ciamis assigned to Priangan on both occasions.

Sources: Onderzoek naar de mindere welvaart der inlandsche bevolking op Java en Madoera, dl. IXc (Batavia 1911), bijl. 10, p. 134. *Onderzoek naar den belastingsdruk op de inlandsche bevolking*, door J.W. Meijer-Ranneft & W. Huender (Weltervreden 1926), bijl. 8, staat B.

Commentary: 1 bouw = 0.7 ha. The figures refer both to individual disposal of land and such under collective control.

Table 3. Landholders in the Priangan Regencies distributed according to the size of holdings in 1905.

REGENCY	SIZE OF HOLDING (bouw)						TOTAL
	<1	1 - 3	4 - 8	9 - 14	15 - 29	>30	
Bandung	26 562	18 732	8 984	2 758	1 060	196	52 292
Garut	17 942	14 413	10 587	2 842	719	115	46 609
Tasikmalaya	24 891	21 257	14 224	3 036	757	114	64 279
Sukabumi	15 265	13 649	7 013	1 230	306	62	37 525
Cianjur	19 043	13 248	4 360	829	231	47	37 758
Sumedang	10 688	9 796	4 816	1 136	250	22	26 708
Ciamis x)	15 554	13 975	3 556	305	48	3	33 448

Source: see Table 2

Commentary: see Table 2

with weakly developed village communities. An additional factor was the customary, Sundanese law of inheritance, which, as a rule, prevented the fragmentation of holdings.[76] The direct cause was the increased economic pressure on households living with low margins of maintenance due to cash cultivation dependent on the fluctuations of the market and the increased pressure of taxation. In addition, the herendienst were independent of the size of holdings, to the disadvantage of the smallholders.[77]

These pressures frequently put smaller peasants in the hands of money-lenders. Already at the turn of the century rural usurers were notorious in Priangan.[78] Just after 1900 an investigation was carried out regarding private money-lending in the area. It revealed that the two largest creditors that were found had a yearly turnover of between 200,000 and 250,000 guilders - figures to be compared with, for example, the average estimated lurah-income of 1,165 guilders in 1926. For 56 money-lenders the turnover was over 5,000 guilders each and together they commanded a circulating capital of over 2,350,000 guilders. In addition, there was found a large number of smaller creditors.[79]

Loans were not seldom given with security in land. Consequently many small peasants lost their fields. The above investigation - only disclosing a part of the activities - shows, for example, how 23 people in this way obtained over 2,150 ha.

The concentration of land created an increasing number of *landless* peasants. Many sought temporary employment as wage-earners at the plantations or moved in to the growing urban areas. Accordingly, Bandung - in the vicinity of which the land concentration surpassed all other areas - experienced the largest growth of Java's towns, from ca. 47,000 inhabitants in 1905, 102,000 in 1921 to 157,000 in 1930; an average yearly increase of about 10 per cent.[80]

The migrants formed new social classes hitherto unknown to Priangan society: a proletariat, predominantly in service and transport sectors, small-scale traders and a few white-collar workers. The old, established order was broken up and society got a more diversified structure. No reliable figures on these new classes' proportional share of the population are available before 1930. From the census material of this year, in Table 4, we can see not only how the dominance of agriculture had decreased, but also that the intensity of change varied regionally. At this point especially the Bandung-plateau had developed a differentiated structure, whereas Sumedang, which the railway

Table 4. Percentage of Priangan's population with agriculture as main occupation in the census of 1930

Regency	Peasants
Bandung	39.9
Ciamis	57.3
Garut	57.3
Sukabumi	57.7
Cianjur	66.0
Tasikmalaya	67.7
Sumedang	72.9

Source: *Volkstelling 1930*, dl. 1 (Batavia 1933), p. 86.
Commentary: peasants = households predominantly working in indigenous agriculture.

never reached, Tasikmalaya and Cianjur were still heavily stamped by agricultural activities.

The landless remaining in native agriculture worked as sharecroppers, tenants or wage-earners on other peoples' land. The size of this group is difficult to estimate. It is also a question of definition, since smallholders added to their income with own tenancies, and by performing temporary wage-labour outside indigenous agriculture and various subsidiary activities - just as the landless. Nevertheless, it is evident, that a large class of landless peasants existed in Priangan and that this group was proportionally bigger than in other parts of Java. Data from 1905 illustrates the situation. The summary of the so-called Lesser Welfare Reports gives figures of the number of landholding households and households which earned their living in agriculture without land of their own. These figures have been compiled in Table 5 where Priangan is compared with the five provinces showing the largest number of big landlords the same year according to Table 2.

For many years the landless worked as sharecroppers and tenants in a multitude of arrangements that varied geographically and over time. Generally, conditions became less favourable as the pressure on the land increased.[81]

Table 5. Landholding and landless households in Priangan, Pekalongan, Surabaya, Semarang and Madiun in 1905.

Province	Landholding households	Landless households	Per centage total	Total number
Priangan	39	61	100	664,744
Pekalongan	48	52	100	406,043
Surabaya	61	39	100	465,107
Semarang	65	35	100	578,785
Madiun	51	49	100	302,379

Source: Algemeen overzicht van de uitkomsten van het Welvaarts-onderzoek, gehouden op Java en Madoera in 1904-5, door C.J. Hasselman ('s-Gravenhage 1914), bijl. E.

Commentary: The Regency Ciamis is not included in Priangan's figures; in 1905 it belonged to Cirebon. *Landholders* includes both those with individual disposal and those having shares in communally controlled land. *Landless* contains those working in agriculture without land of their own (sharecroppers, tenants, day-labourers, plantation-workers).

But as capital formation among the bigger landlords augmented production was more commercialized. In some areas - especially in the Bandung plateau - this process during the 1910s and 1920s led to increased productivity owing to changes in the *organization of work*. Regular wage-labour was introduced within indigenous agriculture. Instead of leasing out the land seasonally or for longer periods of time, in which case the cultivator himself conducted the whole production-cycle and the landlord just collected his rent after harvest, it became more common to cultivate the fields by using day-labourers hired for shorter periods. Larger areas of land could thereby be integrated and better capital resources utilized. Hired labourers now performed only lesser specific tasks, directed by a supervisor employed by the landlord.[82] Some areas of Priangan became rice-surplus areas and the growing of commercial crops increased. From the 1910s onwards native production started directly for the world market of tea, but also coffee, tobacco and rubber.[83]

Preconditions for a more developed capitalist economy arose. Commodities, means of production and labour were increasingly sold on the market.

To sum up, a market- and money-economy arose in Priangan and extended into rural areas to a higher degree than elsewhere in Java, permeating most aspects of the rural population's material life. Although the export cultivation initiated in the area during the eighteenth century by the Dutch East India Company had put money in circulation for a long time,[84] the real breakthrough came with the entry of private, European plantations after 1870. Land was hired out to European firms, regular wage-labour came into existence, taxes were monetarized and indigenous cash-cultivation spread quickly. Labour, land and goods were increasingly sold on the market.

The entry of the market-economy and the rise of European capitalist production affected directly and indirectly the whole of rural Java. But the effects of this development on agrarian relations varied depending on the preconditions prevailing in local contexts, especially with regard to control over land.

In Central and East Java - with the exception of Yogyakarta and Surakarta - various forms of *communal* control of land prevailed. It was regulated by the village communities, who, within certain frameworks, decided about the distribution of land.

The establishment of more differentiated economic systems, in conjunction with the introduction of overwhelming market forces, the activities of money lenders, burdensome taxes and the rapid population growth, were all factors which contributed to increased poverty among the majority of Java's peasants. But at this stage the communal control of land prevented a minor group of strategically placed people from taking advantage of the developments and to accummulate larger properties, since mostly the fields could not be sold without the village's permission and decision about the successor.[85]

Accordingly, the population growth, together with an increased external exploitation of the villages' resources led to a *fregmentation of landholding* and a complicated system of tenancies, sub-tenancies, redistribution of economic resources and the spread of the burden of taxation, which prevented the rise of more permeating commercial production and, actually, seem to have strengthened village bonds.

This communal control did not exist in Priangan. Here the right of disposition of land rested fully and unequivocably with the *individual landholder*. Accordingly, the money and market forces had different effects. Private sales and accumulation of land were possible and the penetration resulted in a *concentration of land* in a few hands. Thus, with regard to the basic, material conditions - founded on the prevailing pattern of land distribution - fully-developed class conflicts with regard to land came into existence. In this respect Priangan differed from other parts of Java.

In the vicinity of urban areas, along the railway and major roads, a class of big, *wealthy landlords* arose, which in the 1910s and 1920s began to develop more purely capitalistic interests. *Smaller landholders* were increasingly threatened with the loss of their fields and *sharecroppers and tenants* faced the danger of being reduced to low-paid *day-labourers*. Many landless moved into towns or sought temporary employment at the European plantations for wages barely at subsistence level. Social bonds in the villages broke up and poverty spread among lower layers of the population.

The changes were most strongly felt in areas adjacent to towns and trading centres. Further away into the interior rural areas the dissolving processes had started but change had not gone so far. Life remained to a greater extent within the old, established patterns.

To what extent were these accelerating and complementary processes of commercialization, land concentration, capitalization and proletarization reflected in the activities of the local Sarekat Rakyat organization in Priangan in 1923-5?

4. THE DIRECT REASONS FOR DISCONTENT

Proletarization and pauperization, first of all, lay behind Sarekat Rakyat's efforts with regard to joint, member-based enterprises trying to better material living. Another reflection were the attempts to stimulate mutual aid and membership solidarity. In these respects the organization replaced the social bonds broken by the capitalized economy.[86] The aid provided was of direct importance to the poor and is one of the explanations for their willingness to enrol. It also elucidates the character of mutual-aid society, revealed by the early Sarekat Hedyo organization.

The opposite interests with regard to land and labour were to a minor degree expressed in Sarekat Rakyat's agitation in a few districts adjacent to Bandung and a few other big towns. Here vague demands for redistribution of land were on some occasions put forward in an attempt to attract small landholders, tenants and day-labourers. But the sources do not indicate that any concrete actions aimed at changing the prevailing agrarian conditions ever took place. The question is of no importance when trying to explain the mass-following.

Instead, *taxation* stands out in the sources as the main reason for Sarekat Rakyat's success. Campaigns against high taxes were the central theme in rural areas. Questions of land redistribution were put into the background. Demands for tax-reductions were raised, writs of protest written and actions brought for refusal to pay.[87]

Accordingly, Sarekat Rakyat's activities in rural areas did not follow the cleavage between landlords and landless. Seen as a whole, the organization's mobilization was not directed against landlords or European plantations, but instead against local officials, the Muslim establishment and village officials. These were the tax-collectors, lacking dominant interests in land and living upon the burdensome levies. Sarekat Rakyat's agitation and actions against land-tax, hoofd-geld, pancen-money and religious fees directly affected these groups' age-old rights, undermined their social standing and the traditional ideological system. Therefore, it was through these groups, at the bottom of the colony's administrative hierarchy, that the Sarekat Hedyo organizations were initiated and brought forward as a weapon against the challenge. The lurah and local, religious officials played the central role, supported by superior pangreh praja - and not directly by the Dutch officials as so many Indonesian observers, placed at central levels within nationalist organizations, argued at the time. In fact, a couple of reports from Dutch officials in the area after some time began to reveal hesitation of the methods used by their colleagues. But they had to grin and bear it. In the end they faced a situation they could not control and tried to stem the worst excesses.[88]

Thus, the Sarekat Rakyat activities concerned taxes and the position of the local bureaucratic élite, and not the cleavage between landlords and landless. Nonetheless, the distinction between landholder and landless was of crucial importance, because, with some exceptions, *only landholders were liable to taxation*.

Apart from the tax-like religious fees, two types of taxes prevailed: the state taxes, which defrayed the expenses of the state administration and its employees, and village taxes collected to cover the villages' own expenses, including pay to the lurah. At this time both of these had been transformed from deliveries in kind and corvee-labour to charges in money.[89]

The most important *state tax* was that on land. Land tax was paid by all landholders in proportion to the estimated value of the harvest. The charge depended on the size and quality of the fields, after deduction of the cost of production. In most of Priangan the tax-scales were modified during the years just before 1923, whereby charges in many cases were raised by over 100 per cent. This created discontent of such a magnitude, that the question even achieved national importance. Amongst other things it was recognized at the central administrative conference in Batavia in 1925. The land tax was collected by the lurah, who kept for himself 8 per cent of the revenue. This made him the direct target of local Sarekat Rakyat agitation.

Also, most other state taxes directly affected bigger, commercially producing landlords and only indirectly the landless, through less favourable tenancy arrangements and lower wages.

As we have discussed above, *village taxes* were comparatively high in Priangan. In most other parts of Java village land was set aside from which the village head got the largest part of his income. Such office-land, with a few trifling exceptions, did not exist in Priangan and resulted in a higher charge in pancen-money.

Just as was the case with the land tax, in most cases only landholders were liable to village taxation, although a direct transfer of a part of the burden to non-landholding groups seem to have taken place in the 1910s and 1920s. The most important village-tax was the *pancen-money*. initially it was services to the lurah but now almost everywhere paid in cash. Originally the sum of money was unrelated to the size of holdings, whereby smaller holders felt the strongest burden due to the concentration of land. Therefore, at the time under discussion here, pancen was changed into a proportional levy calculated on the land tax unit, which was disadvantageous to larger landholders.

Also unpaid compulsory labour existed, for example to maintain buildings, roads, bridges and irrigation systems and for watch at night. These services applied directly to the landholders and only indirectly to the landless.

The concentration process created absentee landlords, which withdrew parts of the land from the village's taxable area and increased the pressure on landholders settled in the village. The size of revenue increased successively in concordance with the enlarged range of village administration.

On these grounds discontent among landholders was widespread and provided fertile soil for Sarekat Rakyat's agitation. At the same time, the local Sarekat Rakyat branches *represented the interests of the landholders,* partly at the expense of the landless. Considering the developed class-situation in Priangan this is, perhaps, a surprising fact. However, it can be explained on the grounds that the organization was forced to make use of the local leadership that was available.

5. *SAREKAT RAKYAT'S LOCAL LEADERSHIP AND MEMBERSHIP STRUCTURE*

In urban areas Sarekat Rakyat had regional, consciously communist and relatively well-educated leaders. They were mainly intellectuals and teachers, often professional propagandists. Travelling around holding meetings in the countryside adjoining the towns, where social and economic cleavages were mostly developed, they induced people to enrol and looked for individuals within the local setting that could carry on the work. The available rural leadership was provided by wealthier villagers who had good contacts with the towns, elementary education and some organizational experience. These the organization was forced to use, if larger and more permanent activities were to be carried out. They were to some extent local, secular teachers, but mainly richer peasants and traders rooted in the new economy. They were bearing the tax-burden and were highly discontented. After a propaganda meeting or social party they enlisted in Sarekat Rakyat and started to form local circles in their home villages by attracting fellow villagers, who came to constitute the membership base. In this process, however, the programme and strategy of the central and regional leaders were distorted.[90]

The national Communist Party had decided upon a programme against 'colonialism and capitalism', by which it tried to assemble all discontented social groups. It looked towards a national revolution as a first step towards the socialist one further ahead. At propaganda meetings in urban areas leaders agitated against foreign capitalism and the oppressive, colonial state, which impoverished the population and took the fruits of men's labour over the ocean to Europe. They also spoke against the indigenous officials *as a class,* which ran the errands of the Dutch capitalists and thereby maintained the existing, degrading order.

Out in rural areas, however, where agitation and organizational work was taken over by the local, village-settled leaders, this general message was adapted to locally prevailing images of the social order and to the palpable wrongs and injustices on the spot. The inner, philosophical connections and long-term goals were lost. Here agitation became directed against the close, evident scape goats - often mentioned by name, either it was bupati himself, a local official or lurah - and not against the structure as such.

Political agitation and action often took a religiously inspired form within the framework of the local tradition. Messianic expectations became common, such as the belief in the arrival of the righteous Sundanese prince, *Ratu Sunda*, or an approaching holy war, *perang sabil*, against the unbelievers. This deprived the movement of much of the modern, secular appearance it showed in urban settings.

In addition, Sarekat Rakyat's local activities assumed a character reflecting the local leaders' own immediate interests and the directives and intentions of the national communist leaders were transformed. Often these rich peasants or traders held a strong position in the village and the role as leader of a big, nation-wide organization enhanced their social standing, for instance in relation to the village officials. Sarekat Rakyat's activities turned out to be not primarily a national struggle, but instead a part of a combat between different indigenous social groups.

The central organization nonetheless needed these local leaders. They were the key to membership enrolment. When local leaders enlisted, they almost automatically brought with them into the organization friends and relatives, and poorer and landless peasants tied to them by bonds of patronage. Joint activities and mutual aid-arrangements then induced others to join as well. Therefore, membership was not so much dictated by the level and content of agitation but rather by people's contacts with the local leader.[91]

Accordingly, Sarekat Rakyat in rural Priangan was a loosely structured organization composed of locally-oriented branches without any convinced marxist leader-or membership. It was impossible for the leaders at central level to uphold discipline, since most members had joined only because of their ties with local leaders. When the latter were forced out of the organization by the Sarekat Hedyo activities, their followers immediately handed over their membership cards. Thus, the membership structure and the way in which the mobilization was built up explains the rapid mass-withdrawal and collapse of the Sarekat Rakyat during the first half of 1925.

6. *THE ACTIVITIES OF SAREKAT RAKYAT IN PRIANGAN AND NATIONAL POLITICS*

The events that have been described give a picture of a Communist Party unable to put its ideas into practice. The base organization's activities could not be controlled and thereby jeopardized the very existence of the party, since actions carried out by local Sarekat Rakyat branches occasioned severe government repression against PKI.

The national communist leaders were certainly aware of the problems. But differences of opinion as to the role and structure of the Sarekat Rakyat and a lack of knowledge of local conditions resulted in a vacillating policy without strength and continuity. As the mobilization campaign accelerated in 1923-4, problems of discipline became serious. Militant local actions took place, which were not sanctioned by the party headquarters. But the arrests that followed, and government restrictions on the right to political activity, affected the national Communist Party organization, whose cadre of leaders shrank.

The Party Congress, held in 1924, concluded that discipline, the formation of conscious cadres and teaching of the foundations of marxism and the party's aims and strategy must take precedence over agitation and mass-mobilization. It was decided to allow local Sarekat Rakyat branches only where there existed local PKI-cadres with real potential to control their activities. The school-building programme should be intensified and a cleaning up of the heterogenous party press was to be carried out only allowing newspapers which followed the party line. Newspapers and periodicals - it must be remembered - were the main line of contact between national leaders and local branches, as other lines of communication were poorly developed.[92]

However, it was impossible to put the decisions into practice. The mobilization campaign continued locally. Membership figures rose and local militancy grew apace. Deviations from the party line manifested themselves more and more. PKI leaders began to travel around in Priangan urging the Sarekat Rakyat branches to moderate agitation and put forward more realistic demands.[93] The central executive decided on restrictions on the holding of public meetings. But the local leaders could not be controlled, resulting in factional strifes within the party as to how to solve the problems.

In desperation an extraordinary Party Convention was summoned in Yogyakarta and Surabaya in December 1924. The Central Executive suggested that the Sarekat Rakyat should be liquidated. The party instead ought to turn to a purely proletarian line. Organizational work should be limited to urban areas and plantations where firm, reliable and homogeneous cells could be built. Opposition hereto was put forward by other groups. The Executive was unable to procure a majority for its proposal. A compromise was arrived at. The Sarekat Rakyat organization should gradually be liquidated. By education it would be possible to bring the proper Sarekat Rakyat leaders into the Communist Party's cadres, while the others, lacking central support, as time went on would fall out by themselves and Sarekat Rakyat accordingly slowly die.[94] But this decision did not solve the Communist Party's problems.

Sarekat Rakyat's activities in Priangan - carried out in discord with party directives and despite exhortations from the headquarters to moderation and discipline[95] - incurred the government's wrath. Following the violent confrontations in the area in early 1925, arrests were made and other measures taken of such a severe nature that the Communist Party was in practice driven underground. Its mass following was rapidly dissolved and opportunities to work openly both in rural and urban areas vanished.

This development contributed to further struggles within the party, dissolving it into a number of factions. Regional branches could only with great difficulty maintain contacts. In the end an ill-planned and badly co-ordinated armed uprising was carried out in late 1926, which was immediately crushed by the government. Thousands of party members were imprisoned and the Communist Party disappeared from the political arena for the rest of the colonial period.[96]

7. *THE GENERAL PATTERN: A COMPARISON WITH SAREKAT ISLAM IN PRIANGAN IN THE 1910s*

It has been concluded that wealthy landholding or trading villagers constituted the core of local leaders behind the Communist Party/Sarekat Rakyat's rural mobilization in 1923-5. What may be called the problem of local leadership arose. The people used as rural agents were the only ones available to the Communist Party. If they were not utilized, no activities at all could be carried out. But they were never really committed to the party and certainly were not communists. As activities grew they deviated more and more from the Communist Party's programme and intentions. Instead, the local leaders used the Sarekat Rakyat branches in a struggle against their adversaries within the local context. Politics turned out to be a combat between different native groups, which obstructed the whole party's chances of success.

The problem of local leadership seems to have been a general feature of anti-colonial mass-movements in rural Priangan in the early twentieth century. A pattern of development similar to that of Sarekat Rakyat is shown by *Sarekat Islam* in the area in the preceding years, in the 1910s.

The *Muslim religion* was the ideological vehicle of Sarekat Islam's mass-mobilization. Although practised in many different forms, more or less mixed up with older animist and Hindu-Buddhist beliefs, Islam provided a basis of identification for most Indonesians against the foreign power.

Apart from trying to ameliorate material life by various projects and struggles against high taxes, Sarekat Islam showed many traits of a'free-church movement'. This was especially the case in Priangan where its local activities were directed against the government's attempts to regulate religious life, against the bupati's position as religious head, against laws enforcing religious teachers to obtain government recognition, against the iniquitous fees of the Muslim establishment and other forms of what was called 'religious parasitism.' In the heydays of 1917-9 these were the questions around which the local Sarekat Islam built much of its mobilization. But religious struggle was also a central element in, for instance, the activities of the Sukabumi branch in rural areas as early as 1914-5; just as in Cianjur in 1924-5, when the only remaining Sarekat Islam branch in Priangan was affected by Sarekat Hedyo activities in the same way as the Sarekat Rakyat movement in the other regencies.[97]

In the closing years of the agrarian-bureaucratic state - in the middle of the nineteenth century - the Muslim religion, which had arrived in the area some centuries earlier, had aged and become an integrated, even dominant part of Sundanese culture. Its religious élite was very influential and maintained daily contacts with the peasants both in religious practices and production. In its

Sundanese form Islam had become institutionalized; a religion of and for the state.

Dutch administrative reports show that just after 1870 Islam, in various secret brotherhoods, was a source of priayi's resistance to the Dutch take-over of regional administration.[98] But the struggle was short. Soon the religious officials became tied to the colonial state as well, lacking an independent source of power in landed estates. Divorced from material production when they lost control of the irrigation systems, religious officials were also separated from the villagers at a time when rural world views gradually became incapable of explaining the accelerating social and economic changes. Hereby many peasants became susceptible to new beliefs. A vacuum emerged which was filled, amongst other things, by a Muslim revitalization movement opposing pangreh praja and established religious officials, their usurpation, iniquitous imposts, distortion of Muslim law and co-operation with the impious Dutch. This Muslim rejuvenation movement became particularly strong in Priangan. It is a well-known fact that from then on - up to the present - the province became Java's most orthodox and militant Islamic area.

The revitalization undoubtedly originated in broadened contacts with the faith's home in the Middle East during the closing decades of the nineteenth century when the number of pilgrims to Mecca, *hadj,* swelled sharply. One of the reasons was the opening of the Suez Canal in 1869. Hereby the Holy Lands became much easier to reach on board the ships to and from Europe, earlier going around the Cape. For most Javanese hadj, the visit to the Middle East lasted only for a few months, but for more ambitious students considerably longer. Mecca gave vital impressions. It was often the first town the pilgrims had visited where they were not subordinated to colonial authority.[99] At the same time they enhanced their knowledge of a world view independent of - even in opposition to - that of the West, as well as the traditional Islam practised at home.

When back, most hadj returned to their previous occupations in agriculture or trade with an intensified faith. They were not regarded as real religious teachers, *kiayi,* but could now assist in educating the village's youngsters. They could perform some rituals and participate from a more prominent position in the Muslim brotherhoods, *tarekat.*

Some returning hadj, however, after further studies chose to dedicate themselves more wholeheartedly to religious leadership as kiayi in the villages or in Muslim schools, *pesantren.* The number of pesantren increased sharply during the late nineteenth and early twentieth centuries. In 1912 there were fully 1,900 registered in Priangan, with 48,650 students.[100]

Among these groups new religious doctrines emerged. They wanted to rejuvenate Islam, restore the basic doctrines, purify the faith and increase the zeal of its adherents by removing the mystical, pre-Islamic practices, in opposition to the established religious learning.

During the 1850s and 1860s an average of about 1,500 pilgrims from the whole of Indonesia were registered. During the following three decades the figures were multiplied. Table 6 gives a picture of those from Java 1876-88, showing that the number of hadj from West Java was very high, and that Priangan exceeded by far all other areas.[101]

The reasons for Priangan's special position are to be found in the individualistic social structures. When the colonial state was established in the area from the 1870s onwards, there came into existence the accumulation of economic resources in the hands of traders and a rising landholding class, which gave some sections of the population an unusual wealth compared with other parts of Java.

The *Koran* exhorts all Muslims to make the pilgrimage during their lifetime, *provided* they possess sufficient economic means, so that their absence does not affect the material life of family members remaining at home.[102] This means, that only comparatively rich people could make the hadj, and since the accumulation of indigenous capital in Priangan exceeded that in other parts of Java, a proportionately larger share of hadj came from the area. Thus, the capitalization process in the Sundanese economy - based on the individual landholding - was one of the major conditions for the strength of the revitalization movement.

At the same time, it was precisely those more commercially related groups that were touched by Muslim regeneration. For instance, the investigation cited above regarding rural money-lending found that hadj totally dominated rural credit in Priangan as early as 1901.[103]

The hadj were mainly capital owners, rich peasants and traders. They differed from other members of the population by their economic activities and an accompanying way of life, which achieved a system of standards more strictly and consistently based on Islam. Accumulation of capital, commercial activity and a corresponding ethos of frugality and thrift stood outside the traditional, Javanese-oriented, collectivistic cultural pattern. Being an individually based religion, in contrast to the old Javanese syncretic apprehensions, Islam therefore became the prime system of

Table 6. Number of registered hadj departed from Java's provinces 1876-88.

Regency	Number of hadj		Percentage	
Priangan	8,833		22.1	
Banten	3,867		9.6	
Batavia	2,721		6.8	
Cirebon	2,535		6.3	
Karawang	157		0.4	
WEST JAVA		18,113		45.2
Semarang	3,266		8.2	
Bagelen	1,966		4.9	
Pekalongan	1,311		3.3	
Kedu	1,267		3.2	
Tegal	903		2.2	
Banyumas	534		1.3	
CENTRAL JAVA		9,247		23.1
Surakarta	550		1.4	
Yogyakarta	352		0.9	
VORSTENLANDEN		902		2.3
Surabaya	5,322		13.2	
Madura	1,368		3.4	
Pasuruan	1,284		3.2	
Madiun	782		2.0	
Rembang	700		1.8	
Japara	684		1.7	
Kediri	641		1.6	
Besuki	602		1.5	
Probolinggo	403		1.0	
EAST JAVA		11,786		29.4
JAVA AS A WHOLE	40,048	40,048	100.0	100.0

Source: Opgave van vertrokken en terguggekeerde hadjis. Java en Madoera 1876-88 (KITLV: Collectie Gobée, no. H1085/4).

values for many within these new progressive groups. And in its turn the hadj's prestige in local society reinforced their activities. More and more they applied themselves to activities that were considered to agree with their enhanced status, such as commercial production, trade and religious practices.[104]

The rise of these new social classes and the concomitant new cultural values of revitalized Islam constitutes one of the explanations of the forceful politicization of Priangan's countryside by local Sarekat Islam branches in the 1910s. Most of the local leaders of these branches were hadj. This is recounted in many reports from the local colonial administration in the area and also quantitative evidence can be provided. In Table 7 is shown the proportion of hadj among the board-members of local Sarekat Islam branches in Java's provinces at the time when each of them applied for legal status. Priangan has the highest figure, following Banten, the sparsely populated area further to the West.

With a few exceptions Sarekat Islam's activities in Priangan between 1913 and 1916 were limited to urban areas, trading centres and their immediate neighbourhoods. A larger mass-following, the spread of organization further out in rural areas and increased militancy in relations with local bureaucracy started in 1917 and reached a peak during the first half of 1919.[105]

Just as was the case in the Sarekat Rakyat branches in the 1920s, bigger, commercially expanding landholders and traders played a central role as local leaders. In this case they were also hadj. Since religious issues had a dominant role in the organization, the local branches also enlisted several religious teachers, kiayi, as mobilizers, who almost automatically brought their pupils and followers with them into the organization.

The factor which made a lot of hadj engage in the Sarekat Islam during 1917, 1918 and 1919 seem to have been the government's *rice policy*. Those years were years of famine, with bad harvests in the shadow of the First World War. Rice-supplies became insufficient and prices soared. Starvation spread in many parts of Java. The situation also deteriorated in Priangan where a proportionately larger number of households were dependent on buying rice at the markets. The government introduced a maximum price for rice and started forcibly to buy up fixed amounts of the crop to lower prices from the bigger peasants, for distribution in deficiency areas. A lot of prosperous peasants regarded the compulsory sale to the government as a flagrant encroachment of their rights.[106] Those cultivating for market

Table 7. Percentage of hadj among board members of established Sarekat Islam branches in Java's provinces 1913-16.

Regency	Number of board members	Percentage hadj
Banten	26	77
Priangan	88	*69*
Batavia	45	47
Cirebon	53	43
WEST JAVA	212	59
Pekalongan	58	60
Banyumas	74	47
Semarang	141	30
Kadu	102	26
CENTRAL JAVA	375	37
Yogyakarta	10	50
Surakarta	25	8
VORSTENLANDEN	35	20
Surabaya	86	26
Madura	67	24
Rembang	95	23
Pasuruan	79	23
Kediri	99	18
Besuki	93	17
Madiun	37	8
EAST JAVA	556	21
JAVA AS A WHOLE	1,178	33

Source: Uittreksel uit het register der besluiten van den Gouverneur-Generaal van Nederlandsch-Indië (KA:Vb 31-3-19-10, 28-7-17-28, 8-3-16-50, 15-3-15-8, 13-5-14-10, 7-11-14-10).

saw profits disappear, and so did the rice traders. Hadj, together with allied kiayi, flocked into Sarekat Islam.

Just as happened in the case of Sarekat Rakyat, the resistance was rooted in local traditions. In this case Muslim brotherhoods, *tarekat*, played a central role, with secret oaths, signs and plans that were directed against the immediate scapegoats and rice-collectors: the indigenous officials.

The national Sarekat Islam organization also opposed the policy of forced rice-sales and advocated other measures. In particular it demanded that land should be withdrawn from European export agriculture and be planted with rice.[107] But pressure was put on the government by using parliamentary means, whereas on the local plane militancy increased. Sarekat Islam's national strategy was transformed and its local branches in Priangan could not be controlled. It culminated in June 1919 in the so-called *Garut affair*, when a rich peasant and hadj refused to sell his rice and offered resistance to the local authorities. It developed into an encounter with the military and the peasant and a number of family members were killed.[108]

Local officials used the opportunity to crush their adversaries. All over Priangan local Sarekat Islam leaders were quickly arrested and put into custody. Local branches were broken up.[109] The officials claimed that Muslim brotherhoods had constituted a secret, subversive section within the Sarekat Islam organization aiming to overthrow the government. In their argumentation a number of suspicious meetings held between local Priangan leaders and prominent representatives of the national Sarekat Islam played an important role. Finally, legal proceedings were also brought against the top echelons of the national Sarekat Islam, which - together with other government measures - conditioned the decline and fall of the whole movement.[110]

The counter-measures against Sarekat Islam in Priangan were - just as the Sarekat Hedyo associations later on - initiated by local, indigenous officials and not directly by the Dutch administration, which neither this time exercised full control over those maintaining the direct contact with the people.[111]

8. CONCLUSIONS

The individualistic agro-economic system in Priangan - based on individual holding of land and poorly developed village communities - when it was penetrated by colonial capitalism after 1870, generated - by Javanese standards - a strong concentration of land. In its turn, this process produced a strongly developed market-economy already before the turn of the century. Wealth was accumulated by groups *within* the indigenous rural society. Big, commercially oriented landholders and native traders emerged. Because of the circumscriptions placed on their initiatives by the colonial economy, these groups developed radical ambitions. They became the nucleus of the local branches of both Sarekat Islam and Sarekat Rakyat in the area and used the organizations to forward their interests against the indigenous representatives of the colonial state within the local context.

At the same time the process of land concentration impoverished sections of the rural population. Wage-incomes came to constitute an increasing part of most families' budgets and the old, largely subsistence-based economy - with its corresponding cultural patterns and world views - could no longer make their existence secure.

These transformations created particularly propitious conditions for the rise of indigenous political activities and Priangan was politicized more thoroughly than other areas of comparative size in Java during the first decades of the twentieth century. It took the form of a struggle between new, emerging classes and bureaucratic officials upholding the colonial state at local level. There were oppositional local leaders available, who were engaged in new economic activities and pauperized, partly proletarized, groups susceptible to agitation, who could be mobilized chiefly through existing patron-client relations.

The situation in Priangan contrasts with that in most other areas of Java which displayed collectivistic agro-economic systems. Here no larger capital formation took place within native agriculture, mainly because of the communal restrictions on land and well-developed village communities. The market- and money-economy certainly penetrated these areas too, but the surplus released was *taken out* of the villages and the inhabitants sank into deeper and relatively equally distributed poverty. Therefore, in these parts of Java new, progressive classes were formed only in growing urban areas, culturally and ideologically separated from the villages. Accordingly, indigenous political activity of longer duration became here limited to the towns. It was difficult to establish more continuous and forceful political activity in the countryside.[112] Leadership was not at hand, and discontent over poverty was instead largely endogenously channelled into traditional paths lacking political potential and explosive force.

NOTES

1 The article has been written within the framework of the research-project *'Peasants and Politics in Twentieth Century Java'* at the Department of History, University of Gothenburg. The archival studies were financed by grants from The Swedish Agency for Research and Co-operation with Developing Countries (SAREC), Stockholm,and the Scandinavian Institute of Asian Studies, Copenhagen.

2 See *Sartono Kartodirdjo,* Protest Movements in Rural Java. Singapore 1973.

3 Ibid. *Niel, R. Van,* The Emergence of the Modern Indonesian Elite. The Hague 1960. *Sutherland, H.,* Pangreh Pradja (unpubl. PhD-thesis, Yale University 1973).

4 *McVey, R.T.,* The Rise of Indonesian Communism. Ithaca 1965.

5 Ibid., pp. 181-2.

6 With a few exceptions the Indonesian newspapers have been consulted through the Dutch periodical compilation *Overzicht van de Indlandsche en Maleisch-Chineesche Pers* (cit. IPO); the Dutch mainly in the knipselarchief of the Stokvis collectie, Internationaal Instituut voor Sociale Geschiedenis, Amsterdam.

7 The basic source for this description is *Nota over de volksbewegingen in de Preanger* (cit. Nota . . .) written by Patih Toemenggreng and dated 15/5 1925 (Koninklijk Instituut voor Taal-, Land- en Volkenkunde (KITLV), Leiden Collectie Gobée, no. H 1085/4.) This account undoubtedly presents the most reliable information. The author was attached to the Advisory Bureau of Native Affairs (Adviseur van Inlandsche Zaken). He travelled to Priangan to collect information when all calls, made both by Dutchmen and Indonesians, for a thorough investigation of the role played by the local administration in the events were repudiated by the Priangan officials. In the reports to Batavia the local bureaucracy depicted its actions as utterly innocent, describing the acts of violence against the Sarekat Rakyat members as spontaneous actions by the villagers. However, in the archival sources there are reports which ascribe to the local native officials much more active part in the occurrences, thus corroborating the information given in *Nota* . . . The trustworthiness of this source is further confirmed on crucial points by accounts given in the independent Indonesian Press. Consequently,

the description given below is based on *Nota . . .* supplemented with material referred to consecutively in the text.

8 See e.g. *Politiek rapport. Regentschap Tasikmalaja,* 15/8 1924 (Archives of the former Ministry of Colonies (KA), The Hague, mr. 722x/24 Vb 5-1-25-F).

9 See e.g. *Missive of Resident Priangan,* 18/2 1925 with enclosures; *Report of Patih Bandung,* 5/2 1925 (KA: mr 196x/25, 178x/25 Vb 23-12-25-K18).

10 See e.g. *Algemeene Recherche: Extracten uit redevoeringen gehouden in leden en cursusvergaderingen (6/10-14/11 1924)* (KA: mr 1031x/24 Vb 31-10-25-R15).

11 See e.g. *Politiek rapport. Tjiamis,* 20/8 1924 (KA:mr 794x/24 Vb 5-1-25-F). *Missive of Resident Priangan,* 6/2 1925 (mr 171x/25 Vb 23-12-25-K18). *Missive of Adviseur van Inlandsche Zaken,* 24/10 1924, 15/6 1925 with enclosures (mr 903x/24; mr 580x/25 Vb 29-5-28-H9). *Indische Courant,* 9/2 1925.

12 See e.g. *Nota Procureur-Generaal,* 31/1 1925; *Missive of Resident Priangan,* 18/2 1925 with enclosures (KA: mr 127x/25, 200x/25 Vb 23-12-25-K18).

13 At 1930 about 4.5 million people lived in Priangan. *Volkstelling 1930,* dl. 1. Batavia 1933.

14 *Missive of Bupati Ciamis,* 20/8 1924 (KA: mr 794x/24 Vb 5-1-25-F). *Missive of Resident Priangan,* 18/2 1925 with enclosures (mr 196x/25 Vb 23-12-25-K18).

15 *Missive of Resident Priangan,* 6/2 1925 with enclosures (KA: mr 178x/25 Vb 23-12-25-K18). *Nota Procureur-Generaal,* 27/2 1925 (mr 224x/25 Vb 31-10-25-R15).

16 High official.

17 Compare also *Missive of Resident Priangan,* 18/2 1925 (KA: 200x/25 Vb 23-12-25-K18).

18 *Memorie van overgave, Priangan, Res. L. de Steuers, 1921,* pp. 138 et seq. (KA: mr 182/22).

19 See e.g. *Missive of Resident Priangan,* 31/1, 6/2 1925 with enclosures (KA: mr 148x/25, 171x/25 Vb 23-12-25-K18). *Api,* 28, 30/1, 2-7/2 1925.

20 See, apart from *Nota . . .*, *Api,* 7/3, 14-18/4 1925. *Hindia Baroe,* 10/3 1925; *Soerapati* 9/2, 11-24/4 1925 (in: IPO).

21 See e.g. *Missive of Bupati Bandung,* 16/2 1925; *Missive of Assistant Resident Tasikmalaya,* 9/3 1925; *Letter from Gouvernement Secretaris to Voorzitter Volksraad,* 5/6, 21/9 1925 with enclosures (KA: mr 216x/25, 268x/25, 890x/25 Vb 23-12-25-K18). *Api* 17, 23/2, 2-7/3 1925; *Hindia Baroe* 5-6, 10/3, 6-16/5 1925; *Sedio Tomo,* 6-10, 30/4 1925 (in: IPO). *Algemeen Indisch Dagblaad,* 31/1 1925.

22 *Missive of Resident Priangan*, 18/2 1925 (KA: mr 199x/25 Vb 23-12-25-K18).

23 Ibid., 19/5 1925 (KA: mr 534x/25 Vb 23-12-25-K18). *Api*, 25/5 1925. See also *Dingley, S. [*psued. for Semaun?*]*, The Peasants' Movement in Indonesia (Berlin 1926?), pp. 44-5.

24 E.g. *Api* 3-9/6 1925; *Sedio Tomo*, 8-12/6 1925 (in: IPO).

25 In the regency Cianjur a remaining local Sarekat Islam branch - and not Sarekat Rakyat - was the leading political organization in the countryside. The conflict between Sarekat Islam members and local officials here arose mainly over religious issues, but also over taxes. When the Sarekat Hedyo actions against Sarekat Rakyat started in the other regencies, local officials in Cianjur used the same measures against Sarekat Islam. Acts of violence were also extensive here and continued for a longer period than elsewhere. It seems that the Sarekat Islam members managed to resist the attacks better and for a longer time than those of the Sarekat Rakyat. See, in addition to *Nota . . . ., De vereeniging Sarikat-Islam in het regentschap Tjiandjur; geheim rapport van den Regent*, 5/5 1925; *Missive of Advizeur van Inlandsche Zaken*, 9/6, 21/9 1925 (KA: mr 851x/25, 594x/25, 910x/25 Vb 23-12-25-K18).

26 See e.g. *McVey, R.T.*, The Rise . . .; *Oates, W.A.*, The Afdeeling B: An Indonesian Case Study (in: Journal of Southeast Asian History, 1968, pp. 107-16).

27 See e.g. *Geheim rapport over PKI, eind juni 1925*, met bijlagen (KA: Vb 29-4-26-Q7, the enclosures in mr 761x/25 Vb 31-10-25-R15). *Rapport over neutraliseering en bestrijding van revolutionaire propaganda onder de inheemsche bevolking*, 1927 (KA: mr 457/x/28 Vb 1-5-29-C9).

28 Based mainly upon *Onderzoek naar de mindere welvaart der inlandsche bevolking op Java en Madoera* (cit. Rapportmindere welvaart), dl. IXa (Batavia 1911), pp. 108 et seq.

29 *Vollenhoven, C. van*, Het adatrecht van Nederlandsch-Indië. Leiden 1931. Research into customary law in the colonial period is reviewed in *Koentjaraningrat*, Anthropology in Indonesia ('s-Gravenhage 1975), pp. 86-113.

30 The three systems discussed are generalized, isolated types. In their concrete forms the structures of the systems were sometimes locally mixed with each other, but with some types dominating at an aggregated level, setting the pattern of the regional system as a whole.

31 The following brief outline of the three systems is elaborated in *Svensson, Th.*, Javanesisk verzuiling (in: Indonesia 1980: politikk, økonomi, kultur, red. av J.-P. Myklebust, Bergen 1980, pp. 32-50).

32 In some areas the village officials undoubtedly got hold of a proportionately large share of land, but this does not affect the general argument.

33 In addition, individual disposal of land existed in the eastern parts of Java. Also here a concentration of land took place, although not to the same extent as in Priangan. (See Robert Elson's very interesting and deep-going study: *Elson, R.*, Sugar and Peasants: the Social Impact of the Western Sugar Industry on the Peasantry of the Pasuruan Area, East Java. Unpubl. thesis, Monash University, 1979.)

The reasons for the different development in Eastern Java compared to Priangan seem to a high degree to be found in the widespread sugar cultivation carried out by European companies in the Eastern regions. Here sugar was cultivated on leaseholds in rotation with the peasants' own rice crops. This system of cultivation gave rise to a powerful communal village structure, which never developed in Priangan. See also *Verslag van de Suiker-enquête-commissie*. Surabaya 1921.

34 The agrarian system in Priangan is discussed in the author's article 'Bönder och politik i Parahyangan 1870-1925. Del 1: Den strukturella bakgrunden' (Publ. of The South-East Asian History Project, Dept. of History Univ. of Gothenburg, January 1979), pp. 23-70, where further references can be found. Here the central sources will be noted consecutively in the text.

35 *Hoadley, M.C.*, Man, land, and ruler, Cirebon-Priangan administration of ca. 1700 (Paper for the Scandinavian Conference on Indonesian and Malaysian Studies 1977).

36 *Hoadley, M.C.*, Javanese Procedural Law. A History of the Cirebon-Priangan Jaksa-College, 1708-32 (PhD-thesis, Cornell University, 1975).

37 *Verslag van de uitkomsten van het onderzoek betreffende het koffie-cultuur, ingesteld 21/2 1865, Preanger-Regentschappen (1867)*. (Arsip Nasional Republik Indonesia (ANRI): Archieven Cultures, no. 294).

38 On the earlier history of Priangan, see foremost *Haan, F. de* Priangan. De Preanger-Regentschappen onder het Nederlandsch bestuur tot 1811, dl. 1-4, Batavia 1910-12; and *Klein, J.W.*, Het Preanger-stelsel (1677-1871) en zijn nawerking, Leiden 1931.

39 See *Fasseur, C.*, Organisatie en sociaal-economische betekenis van de gouvernementssuikercultuur in enkele residenties op Java omstreeks 1850 (in: Bijdragen tot de Taal-, Land- en Volkenkunde, 1977, pp. 261-93); and *Geertz, C.*, Agricultural Involution, Berkeley 1963.

40 See *Sutherland, H.*, Pangreh Pradja . . .

41 *Regeeringsalmanak voor Nederlandsch-Indië. Nota inzake toelating van Chineezen, Arabieren en dergelijke Oosterlingen, Preanger-Regentschappen, 1857.* (ANRI: Archieven Financien, no. 1158).

42 *Rapport van het lid van den Raad van Nederlandsch-Indië O. van Rees, 30/10 1867.* (partly published in Verhandelingen van het Bataviaasch Genootschap van Kunsten en Wetenschappen, dl. 39 (Batavia 1880); the complete report is preserved at the Algemeen Rijksarchief (AR), Schaarsbergen; cit. Rapport-Rees); *Kinder de Camarecq, A.W.*, Bijdrage tot de kennis der volksinstellingen in de oostelijke Soenda-landen (in: Tijdschrift voor de Taal-, Land- en Volkenkunde van Nederlandsch-Indië, 1861, pp. 259-90); *Eindresumé van het onderzoek naar de rechten van den inlander op den grond van Java en Madoera,* dl. 1-3 (Batavia 1876-80); cit. Rapport-grondrecht).

43 *Sutherland, H.*, Pangreh Pradja . . .

44 A huge number of various services and unpaid labour existed, see *Klein, J.W.*, Het Preanger-stelsel . . ., pp. 100 et seq.

45 See e.g. *Vitalis, L.*, De invoering, werking en gebreken van het stelsel van cultures op Java (Zaltbommel 1851), esp. pp. 21-2; *Eindresumé van het onderzoek naar de verplicte diensten der inlandsche bevolking op Java en Madoera (Gouvernementslanden), door F. Fokkens,* dl. 1:1 (Batavia 1901), pp. 37-46, dl. 1:2 (Batavia 1902), pp. 45 et seq, 89 et seq; *Kinder de Camarecq, A.W.*, Bijdrage . . .; *Rapport-Rees*. Compare *Scheltema, A.M.P.A.*, De ontwikkeling van de agrarische toestanden in Priangan (in: Landbouw, 1927/8, pp. 271-305, 317-68).

46 *Koloniaal Verslag*, 1870; *Rapport-grondrecht*.

47 *Memorie van overgave, Priangan, Res. de Steuers, 1921,* p. 56 (KA: mr 182/22). *Schelema, A.M.P.A.*, De ontwikkeling . . ., p. 298. *Volkstelling 1930*, dl. 1. Batavia 1933.

48 *Klein, J.W.*, Het Preanger-stelsel . . .; *Scheltema, A.M.P.A.*, De ontwikkeling . . .

49 *Fokkens, F.*, De Preanger landrente-regeling, N.y. 1904. *Teng Sioe Tjhan*, De Landrente-belasting. Rotterdam 1933. *Memories van overgave, Priangan, Res. Oudemans*

1913, Res. de Steuers 1921; Midden-Priangan, Res. Gessler Verschuir, 1929 (KA: mr 799/13, 182/22, 648x/30). *Rapport betreffende den afkoop van herendiensten, 1907, 1909-10* (KA: mr 363/09, 614/09, 1025/11 Vb 24-5-12-41).

50 *Rapport-mindere welvaart,* Samentrekking van de afdeelingsverslagen, handel (Batavia 1907), Priangan. *Gonggrijp, G.,* Schets eener economische geschiedenis van Nederlands-Indië (Haarlem 1949), p. 214.

51 Cit. in *Rapport-mindere welvaart,* dl. Va, p. 16.

52 See *Circulaire aan Hoofden van het Gewestelijk Bestuur, no. 1926,* 4/8 1893 (Osterse Instituut (OI), Leiden, Archief Snouk Hurgronje, "stukken door Snouk Hurgronje in 1907/8 ontwangen uit het archief van dr. Hazeu").

53 *Besluit, Res. Priangan,* 30/10 1905, no. 1703a/16 (KITLV: Collectie Kern, no. 37).

54 *Indische Staatsblad,* 1867 no. 114.

55 See *Verslag van een onderzoek naar de wenschen der bevolking ten aanzien van grondbezit en belastingen, Preanger-Regentschappen, ca. 1890.* (ANRI: Archieven Cultures, no. 148). *Letter from L. Junmetman(?), Sukabumi, to C. Snouk Hurgronje,* 14/8 1897 (OI: Archief Snouk Hurgronje, "Div. part brieven, stukken enz. van europ. en inl. ambtenaren"). *Snouk Hurgronje, C.,* Ambtelijke adviesen ('s-Gravenhage 1957-65), dl. 1-3, pp. 1243-84.

56 *Missive of Adviseur van Inlandsche Zaken,* 22/3 1915 (KA: mr 937/15 Vb 8-3-16-50).

57 The exact size of this group is not possible to establish. In 1926 religious functionaries at village level numbered just over 1,800; a proportionately higher figure than in other parts of Java. See *Eindverslag over het desa-autonomie-onderzoek op Java en Madoera* (cit. Rapport-desa-autonomie) (Weltevreden 1929), staat 1, pp. 92-3.

58 *Scheltema, A.M.P.A.,* De ontwikkeling . . .; *Klein, J.W.,* Het Preanger-stelsel . . .

59 See *Berg, L.W.C. van den,* De inlandsche gemeentewezen op Java en Madoera (in: Bijdragen tot de Taal-, Land- en Volkenkunde, 1901, p. 55).

60 *Rapport-desa-autonomie;* and *Regentschapsverslagen op het desa-autonomie-onderzoek op Java en Madura* (cit. Rapport-desa-autonomie, regentschapsverslagen) (Weltevreden 1929), pp. 39-124.

61 This reasoning does not consider the conditions in the Yogyakarta-Surakarta area, which had a wholly different character at this time.

62 *Rapport-desa-autonomie,* staat III.
63 In 1926 they were 1,240 lurah and some 12,000 functionaries, see ibid., staat I, pp. 92-3.
64 See esp. *Scheltema, A.M.P.A.,* De ontwikkeling . . ., pp. 294-5, relying on landrente-monografien compiled from surveys made in 1890-1910 and no longer preserved, with the exception of data published in *Adatrechtbundel no. 8* (1914), pp. 2-46.
65 *Nota van den Resident Overstrand,* 5/2 1849. (ANRI: Archieven Cultures, no. 294). *Rapport-grondrecht,* dl. 1, p. 45, bijl. C.
66 *Scheltema, A.M.P.A.,* De ontwikkeling . . ., p. 291; *Gogol,* Losse gedachten van de heeren- en desadienstplichtige, III (in: Tijdschrift Binnenlandsche Bestuur, 1898), pp. 97-8.
67 *Rapport-grondrecht,* dl. 2, pp. 362 ff.
68 See *Besluit 24-3-1898, no. 21* (ANRI: Algemeene Secretarie).
69 *Stukken van het aantal personen dat landrente betaald heeft over de jaren 1898-1907* (KITLV: Collectie Kern, no. 34).
70 *Scheltema, A.M.P.A.,* De ontwikkeling . . ., p. 321, based on landrente-monografien compiled in 1893-4, mentions data from a village in Cicalenka where 57% of the land was disposed by holders not living in the village, and from two villages in Majalaya where the figures were 41%. Corresponding data is given in 1926 by *Rapport-desa-autonomie, regentschapsverslagen,* pp. 84-124.
71 *Vollenhoven, C. van,* Belastingspractijk en -practijken in Nederlandsch-Indië (in: Indische Mercuur, 1/2 1924).
72 See below p. 102.
73 *Kern, R.A.,* Prijangsche toestanden: 't Grootgrondbezit (in: Indische Gids, 1904, pp. 1816-24. *Memories van overgave,* cited in note 49. *Agrarische toestanden in het regentschap Sumedang, Assistent Resident Ruys, 1930* (Koninklijk Instituut voor de Tropen (KIT), Amsterdam, handschrift Aad. 2/R). *Rapport betreffende het landbouwcredietonderzoek in de Preanger-Regentschappen,* door W. van Westerrode. Batavia 1904. (cit. Rapport-credietonderzoek). *Overzicht van den economischen toestand der inheemsche bevolking op Java en Madoera,* door W. Huender. 's-Gravenhage 1921. (cit. Rapport-economische toestand 1921).
74 District-statistics contained in *Stukken van het aantal personen dat landrente betaald heeft . . .*
75 See also *Rapport-grondrecht,* dl. 2, pp. 362-3.

76 See *Vollenhoven, C. van,* Het adatrecht . . ., dl. 1, p. 1731.

77 *Scheltema, A.M.P.A.,* De ontwikkeling . . ., pp. 300-1. *Velders, A.F.,* Eenige aantekeningen omtrent het grondbezit in de Preanger (in: Tijdschrift Binnenlandsche bestuur, 1909), pp. 87-115.

78 *Algemeen overzicht van de uitkomsten van het Welvaarts-onderzoek, gehouden op Java en Madoera 1904-5,* door C.J. Hasselman, 's-Gravenhage 1914, (cit. Overzicht-mindere welvaart). *Rapport-economische toestand 1921.*

79 *Rapport-credietonderzoek.*

80 *Gemeente Bandoeng. Dienst van het grondbedrijf. Prospectus voor de uitgifte van gronden* (Bandung 1931), p. 4. *Volkstelling 1930,* dl. 1-3 (Batavia 1933).

81 *Scheltema, A.M.P.A.,* Deelbouw in Nederlandsch-Indië (Wageningen 1931), pp. 122-30, 153-61, 281-9, 343-52.

82 *Memorie van overgave, Midden-Priangan, Res. Gessler Verschuir, 1929* (KA: mr 648x/30). *Missive of Adviseur van Inlandsche Zaken,* 24/10 1924 with enclosures (KA: mr 903x/24). *Missive of Res. Priangan,* 18/3 1920 (KA: 309x/20 Vb 7-7-21-21). *Rapport-desa-autonomie, regentschapsverslagen,* pp. 39-124.

83 See e.g. *Indonesia's Export Crops 1816-1940,* ed. by P. Creutzberg (The Hague 1975), pp. 37 et seq, 77 et seq, 85 et seq, 99 et seq, 113 et seq, graph III, p. 142.

84 *Kultuur-verslag, Preanger-Regentschappen, 1852-76* (ANRI: Archieven Cultures, no. 1621). In fact, it seems as if the intensity in coffee-cultivation and the coffee-reimbursements to the population concomitants with the strength of the land concentration process after 1870. (See esp. *Kultuur-verslag 1856, 1861,* compared to the figures in *Stukken van het aantal personen dat landrente betaald heeft . . .)* However, the author has not yet had time and opportunity to investigate deeper into this connection.

85 Some concentration of land certainly took place, mainly in the hands of lurah and village functionaries, but only to a comparatively small extent and in a way qualitatively different from that in Priangan. See *Elson, R.E.,* The Cultivation System and "Agricultural Involution" (Working Papers of the Centre of Southeast Asian Studies. Monash University, Melbourne 1978.)

86 *Nota Procureur-Generaal,* 31/1 1925; *Missive of Dir. Binnenlandsche Bestuur,* 5/3 1925 (KA: mr 127x/25, mr. 263x/25 Vb 23-12-25-K18).

87 *Missive of Assistant Resident Garut*, 29/2/1924; *Missive of Res. Priangan*, 28/8 1924 with enclosures; 8/9 1924 with enclosures; *Missive of Adviseur van Inlandsche Zaken*, 24/10 1924 with enclosure; *Missive of Ass. Res. Tasikmalaya*, 5/2 1925 (KA: mr 231x/24 Vb 5-11-24-87; mr 722x/24 Vb 5-1-25-F;mr 47x/25 Vb 14-4-27-38; mr 903x/24; mr 171x/25 Vb 23-12-25-K18). *Nota . . .*

88 Ibid.

89 The following section on the taxes is founded on: *Brink, M. van den*, Aantekeningen omtrent pantjen-inkomsten van het desabestur op Java en Madoera (in: Koloniaal Tijdschrift, 1941, pp. 88–101). *Afkoop van alle desadiensten ter afdeelingshoofdplaats Tjiandjoer*, dated December 1908 (KA: mr 241/09 Vb 24-5-12-41). *Onderzoek naar den belastingsdruk op de inlandsche bevolking*, door J.W. Meijer-Ranneft & W. Huender, Weltevreden 1926. *Rapport-desa-autonomie, regentschapsverslagen*, pp. 39-124. *Derde verslag van de Commissie tot herziening van het belastingsstelsel in Nederlandsch-Indië, 1925*, esp. enclosures 3-4; *Nota op de belastingsdruk op de inlandsche bevolking op Java en Madoera voor de Java-residentien conferentie, 1925*, enclosures (KA: mr 269x/25 Vb 6-5-25-26; mr 47x/25 Vb 14-4-27-28). See also note 87.

90 *Missive of Res. Priangan*, 6/2 1925 with enclosures, 18/2 1925 with enclosures, 21/2 1925 (KA: mr 171x/25, 178x/25, 196x/25, 199x/25, 200x/25 Vb 23-12-25-K18; mr 235x/25 Vb 29-5-28-H9).

91 See *Nota Procureur-Generaal*, 22/9 1924, 27/2 1925 with enclosures; *Missive Res. Priangan*, 6/2 1925 with enclosure, 18/2 1925 with enclosures (KA: mr 794x/24 Vb 5-1-25-F; mr 224x/25 Vb 31-10-25-R15; mr 178x/25, 196x/25 Vb 23-12-25-K18).

92 *Verslag van het 9de PKI-congres te Batavia, 7-10 juni 1924* (KITLV: Collectie Kern, H797/311); *McVey, R.T.*, The Rise . . ., pp. 190 et seq.

93 E.g. *Missive of Ass. Res. Tasikmalaya*, 15/8 1924 (KA: mr 722x/24 Vb 5-1-25-F).

94 *Missive of Adviseur van Inlandsche Zaken*, 3/1 1925; *Rondschrijven Procureur-Generaal*, 19/2 1925 (KA: mr 32x/25, 214x/25 Vb 29-5-28-H9). *Letter from Semaun to Hoofdbestuur PKI*, 25/12 1924 (KA: 761x/25 Vb 31-10-25-R15). *McVey, R.T.*, The Rise . . ., pp. 263 et seq.

95 *Geheime instructies van het Hoofdbestuur PKI aan secties en onderbouw, nr. 1-6B* (first half of 1925) (KA: mr 761x/25 Vb 31-10-25-R15).

96 *McVey, R.T.*, The Rise . . ., pp. 257-346. *Pluvier, J.M.*, Overzicht van de ontwikkeling der nationalistische beweging in Indonesië in de jaren 1930 tot 1942. 's-Gravenhage 1953.

97 *Missive of Adviseur van Indlandsche Zaken*, 22/3 1915 with enclosure (KA: mr 937/15 Vb 8-3-16-50); and note 25, p. 82.

98 See e.g. *Missive of Res. Priangan*, 20/1 1871 with enclosures (AR: Vb 30-1-73-33); *Godsdienstige bewegingen in de Preanger Regentschappen* (1885-6) (AR: mr 642a/85, 647c/85, 807b/85, 262/86). *Politiezaken met betrekking tot de inlandsche bevolkning, Preanger-Regentschappen, 1881*. (ANRI: Residentie Archieven, no. 73).

99 *Snouk Hurgronje, C.*, De hadji-politiek der Indische regeering (in: Verspreide geschriften (Bonn 1924), dl. 4:2, p. 184).

100 *Memorie van overgave, Priangan, Res. Oudemans, 1913*. The Muslim education was particularly widespread in Priangan, which partly constitutes the explanation for the province's high rate of literacy at the time - double that of any other province in Java, see *Volkstelling 1930*, dl. 1 (Batavia 1933), pp. 66-73.

101 *Vredenbregt, J.*, The Haddj: Some of Its Features and Functions in Indonesia (in: Bijdragen tot de Taal-, Land- en Volkenkunde, 1962), esp. pp. 139-48

102 Ibid.

103 *Rapport-credietonderzoek*.

104 Compare *Vredenbregt, J.*, The Haddj . . ., pp. 114-5.

105 *Memorie van overgave, Priangan, Res. de Steuers, 1921*, pp. 130 et seq.

106 See *Missive of Res. Priangan*, 18/3 1920, 7/4 1920, 16/7 1920 (KA: mr 309x/20, 826x/20 Vb 7-7-21-21; mr 416x/20 Vb 19-1-21-67).

107 *McVey, R.T.*, The Rise . . ., p. 38. *Verslag Sarekat Islam Congres, 20-27/10 1917* (Batavia 1918), pp. 50-7.

108 A very extensive archival material exists on the Garut-affair and its sequel. It also illuminates the development of Sarekat Islam in Priangan in general. The most important parts are contained in KA: Vb 4-42-19-2, 10-12-19-S9, 28-12-21-C14, 28-3-22-E3, 2-5-23-D6. In addition, complementary documents and most of the newspaper reports are found in KITLV: Collectie Hazeu, H1083/36.

109 See esp. *Missive of Regeeringscommissaris voor Inlandsche en Algemeene Zaken*, 25/9 1919 (KA: mr 673x/19 Vb 28-12-21-C14). Compare *Letter from pres. Sarekat Islam, Wignjadisastra to G.A.J. Hazeu*, 18/8 1919

(KITLV: Collectie Hazeu, H1083/36).

110 The developments are described in *Oates, W.A.*, The afdeeling B . . .

111 See esp. *Betr. Memories van verdediging van den Ass. Res. en den Regent van Garoet* (KA: mr 1147x/20 Vb 28-3-22-E3, mr 43x/21, 193x/21 Vb 2-5-23-D6).

112 See e.g. the description of the political activities in Pasuruan, East Java in *Elson, R.*, Sugar and Peasants . . .

BIBLIOGRAPHY

I. MANUSCRIPT SOURCES

1. Algemeen Rijksarchief, Schaarsbergen (AR)

Ministerie van Koloniën

Rapport van het lid van den Raad van Nederlandsch-Indië. O van Rees, 30/10/1867.

Verbaal (Vb)
1873: 30-1-73-33

Mailrapporten (mr)
1885: 642a, 647c, 807b
1886: 262

2. Arsip Nasional Republik Indonesia, Jakarta (ANRI)

Algemeene Secretarie
Besluit 1898: 24-3-98-21

Archieven Cultures
no. 148: Verslag van een onderzoek naar de wenschen der bevolking ten aanzien van grondbezit en belastingen, ca. 1890.
no. 294: Verslag van de uitkomsten van het onderzoek betreffende het koffiecultuur, ingesteld 21/2 1865, Preanger Regentschappen, (1867).
no. 1621: Kultuurverslagen Priangan 1852-76.

Archieven Financien
no. 1158: Nota inzake toelating van Chineezen, Arabieren en dergelijke Oosterlingen, Preanger Regentschappen, (1856-7).

Residentie Archieven (Pasar Ikan)
no. 73: Politiezaken met betrekking tot de inlandsche bevolking, Preanger Regentschappen, 1881.

3. Internationaal Instituut voor Sociale Geschiedenis, Amsterdam (ISG)

Stokvis Collectie: knipselarchief Indonesia, no. 35-54.

4. Ministerie van Binnenlandse Zaken: Archieven van de Overzeese Rijksdelen, The Hague

Archief van het voormalige Ministerie van Koloniën (KA)
Verbaal
1912: 24-5-12-41

1914: 13-5-14-10, 7-11-14-10
1915: 15-3-15-8
1916: 8-3-16-50
1917: 28-7-17-28
1919: 31-3-19-10, 4-12-19-2, 10-12-19-S9
1921: 19-1-21-67, 7-7-21-21, 28-12-21-C14
1922: 28-3-22-E3
1923: 2-5-23-D6
1924: 5-11-24-87
1925: 6-5-25-26, 5-1-25-F, 31-10-25-R15, 23-12-25-K18
1926: 29-4-26-Q7
1927: 14-4-27-38
1928: 29-5-28-H9
1929: 1-5-29-C9

Mailrapporten
1924: 903x

Memorie van overgave
Priangan, Res. Oudemans, 1913
Priangan, Res. de Steuers, 1921
Midden-Priangan, Res. Gessler Verschuir, 1929

5. *Koninklijk Instituut voor de Tropen, Amsterdam (KIT)*

Handschriften
Agrarische toestanden in het Regentschap Sumedang, 1930 (Aad. 2/R)

6. *Koninklijk Instituut voor Taal-, Land- en Volkenkunde, Leiden (KITLV)*

Collectie Gobée, H 1085
no. 4: Hadji-statistiek 1848-88
no. 8: Nota over de volksbewegingen in de Preanger, 1925

Collectie Hazeu, H 1083
no. 36: Over "Garoet-zaak", knipsels en afschriften

Collectie Kern, H 797
no. 34: Stukken van het aantaal personen dat landrente betaald heeft over de jaren 1898-1907
no. 37: Besluiten over vrijstelling van herendiensten in de Preanger-regentschappen, 1905
no. 311: Verslag van het 9de PKI-congres te Batavia, 7-10 juni 1924

7. *Osterse Instituut, Leiden (OI)*

Archief Snouk Hurgronje
Stukken door Snouk Hurgronje in 1907/8 ontwangen uit het archief van dr. Hazeu

Div. part. brieven, stukken enz. van europ. en inl. ambtenaren

II. *PRINTED SOURCES*

Adatrechtbundel, no. 8 (1914).

Algemeen overzicht van de uitkomsten van het Welvaarts-onderzoek, gehouden op Java en Madoera in 1904-5, door C.J. Hasselman. 's-Gravenhage 1914.

Api, (Semarang), 28/1-25/5 1925.

Brink, M. van den, Aantekeningen omtrent pantjen-inkomsten van het desabestuur op Java en Madoera (in: Koloniaal Tijdschrift, 1941, pp. 88-101).

Dingley, S., [psued. for Semaun?], The Peasant's Movement in Indonesia. Berlin 1926(?)

Eindresumé van het onderzoek naar de rechten van den inlander op den grond van Java en Madoera, dl. 1-3, Batavia 1876-80. (Cit. Rapport-grondrecht).

Eindresumé van het onderzoek naar de verplichte diensten der inlandsche bevolking op Java en Madoera (Gouvernementslanden), door F. Fokkens, dl. 1:1-2, Batavia 1901-2.

Eindverslag over het desa-autonomie-onderzoek op Java en Madoera, Weltevreden 1929. (Cit. Rapport-desa-autonomie).

Fokkens, F., De Preanger Landrente-regeling. N.pl. 1904.

Gemeente Bandoeng. Dienst van het grondbedrijf. Prospectus voor de uitgifte van gronden, Bandung 1931.

Gogol, Losse gedachten van de heeren- en desadienstplichtige, III (in: Tijdschrift voor de Binnenlandsche Bestuur 1898).

Indische Courant, 9/2 1925.

Indische Staatsblad, 1867, no. 114.

Indonesia's Export Crops 1816-1940, ed. by P. Creutzberg The Hague 1975.

Kern, R.A., Prijangsche toestanden: 't Grootgrondbezit (in: Indische Gids, 1904, pp. 1816-24).

Kinder de Camarecq, A.W., Bijdrage tot de kennis der volks-instellingen in de oostelijke Soenda-landen (in: Tijdschrift voor de Taal- Land- en Volkenkunde van Nederlandsch-Indië, 1861, pp. 259-90).

Koloniaal Verslag, 1870.

Onderzoek naar de mindere welvaart der inlandsche bevolking op Java en Madoera, dl. Va, IXa, afdeelingsverslag, handel, Priangan, Batavia 1906-11. (Cit. Rapport-mindere welvaart.)
Onderzoek naar den belastingsdruk op de inlandsche bevolking, door J.W. Meijer-Ranneft & W. Huender, Weltevreden 1926.
Overzicht van de Inlandsche en Maleische-Chineesche Pers, 1919, 1924-5. (Cit. IPO.)
Overzicht van den economischen toestand der inheemsche bevolking op Java en Madoera, door W. Huender. 's-Gravenhage 1921. (Cit. Rapport-economische toestand 1921.)
Rapport betreffende het landbouwcredietonderzoek in de Preanger-Regentschappen, door W. van Westerrode. Batavia 1904. (Cit. Rapport-credietonderzoek.)
Rees, O. van, Overzicht van de geschiedenis der Preanger-Regentschappen (Verhandelingen van het Bataviaasch Genootschap van Kunsten en Wetenschappen, dl. 39, Batavia 1880).
Regeeringsalmanak voor Nederlandsch-Indië, 1860.
Regentschapsverslagen op het desa-autonomie-onderzoek op Java en Madoera, Weltevreden 1929. (Cit. Rapport-desa-autonomie, regentschapsverslagen.)
Snouk Hurgronje, C., Ambtelijke adviesen, dl. 1-3, 's-Gravenhage 1957-65.
Snouk Hurgronje, C., De hadji-politiek der Indische regeering (in: Verspreide geschriften, dl. 4:2, Bonn 1924).
Velders, A.F., Eenige aantekeningen omtrent het grondbezit in de Preanger (in: Tijdschrift Binnenlandsche bestuur, 1909, pp. 87-115).
Verslag Sarekat-Islam Congres, 20-27/10 1917, Batavia 1918.
Verslag van de Suiker-enquête-commissie. Surabaya 1921.
Vitalis, L., De invoering, werking en gebreken van het stelsel van cultures op Java. Zaltbommel 1851.
Volkstelling 1930, dl. 1-3. Batavia 1933.
Vollenhoven, C. van, Belastingspractijk en -practijken in Nederlandsch-Indië (in: Indische Mercuur, 1/2 1924).

III. LITERATURE

Berg, L.W.C. van den, De inlandsche gemeentewezen op Java en Madoera (in: Bijdragen tot de Taal-, Land- en Volkenkunde, 1901).
Elson, R.E., The Cultivation System and "Agricultural Involution" (Working Papers of the Centre of Southeast Asian Studies, Monash University, Melbourne 1978).

Bibliography

Elson, R., Sugar and Peasants: the Social Impact of the Western Sugar Industry on the Peasantry of the Pasuruan Area, East Java, from the Cultivation System to the Great Depression. Unpubl. thesis, Monash University, 1979.

Fasseur, C., Organizatie en sociaal-economische betekenis van de gouvernementssuikercultuur in enkele residenties op Java omstreeks 1850 (in: Bijdragen tot de Taal-, Land-, en Volkenkunde, 1977).

Geertz, C., Agricultural Involution. The Processes of Ecological Change in Indonesia. Berkeley 1963.

Gonggrijp, G., Schets eener economische geschiedenis van Nederlands-Indië. Haarlem 1949.

Haan, F. de, Priangan. De Preanger-Regentschappen onder het Nederlandsch bestuur tot 1811, dl. 1-4, Batavia 1910-12.

Hoadley, M.C., Javanese Procedural Law. A History of the Cirebon-Priangan Jaksa-College, 1708-32. (PhD-thesis, Cornell University, 1975).

Hoadley, M.C., Man, Land, and ruler. Cirebon-Priangan administration of ca. 1700. (Paper for the Scandinavian Conference on Indonesian and Malaysian Studies, 1977).

Klein, J.W., Het Preanger-stelsel (1677-1871) en zijn nawerking. Leiden 1931.

Koentjaraningrat, Anthropology in Indonesia. 's-Gravenhage 1975.

McVey, R.T., The Rise of Indonesian Communism, Ithaca 1965.

Niel, R. Van, The Emergence of the Modern Indonesian Elite, The Hague 1960.

Oates, W.A., The Afdeeling B: An Indonesian Case Study (in: Journal of Southeast Asian History, 1968).

Pluvier, J.M., Overzicht van de ontwikkeling der nationalistische beweging in Indonesië in de jaren 1930 tot 1942, 's-Gravenhage 1953.

Sartono Kartodirdjo, Protest Movements in Rural Java. A Study of Agrarian Unrest in the Nineteenth and Early Twentieth Centuries, Singapore 1973.

Scheltema, A.M.P.A., De ontwikkeling van de agrarische toestanden in Priangan (in: Landbouw, 1927/8).

Scheltema, A.M.P.A., Deelbouw in Nederlandsch-Indië. Wageningen 1931.

Sutherland, H., Pangreh Pradja. Java's Indigenous Administrative Corps and Its Role in the Last Decades of Dutch Colonial Rule (PhD-thesis, Yale University, 1973).

Bibliography

Svensson, Th., Javanesisk verzuiling (in: Indonesia 1980: politikk, økonomi, kultur, red. av J.-P. Myklebust, Bergen 1980).

Teng Sioe Tjhan, De Landrente-belasting. Rotterdam 1933.

Vollenhoven, C. van, Het adatrecht van Nederlandsch-Indië Leiden 1931.

Vredenbregt, J., The Haddj: Some of Its Features and Functions in Indonesia (in: Bijdragen tot de Taal-, Land- en Volkenkunde, 1962).

RURAL CHANGE IN SUHARTO'S INDONESIA: COMMUNAL RIGHTS AND HARVESTING METHODS IN A JAVANESE VILLAGE

Lien Pekih Aass and Svein Aass

INTRODUCTION

This essay[1] is based on material from fieldwork in a village in East Java, in the period December 1973 to June 1974.

The village chosen for the study, 'Bangsal',[2] lies about 7 km from the town with the fictitious name of 'Mojokuto', that gained notice after a group of graduate students from Harvard carried out research in the area in the mid-1950s under the auspices of the Massachusetts Institute of Technology (M I T).[3] The village is about 4 km from the main road leading to Jombang and Surabaya to the north, and to Mojokuto, Malang and Kediri to the south. Transportation is mainly by foot, bicycle or the 'dokar' (horse-drawn carriage) in the village as it is mainly a dirt road. Once on the main road, however, a steady stream of 'colts' (Japanese Mitsubishi minibuses)and buses assures transportation to the cities.

The village of Bangsal is divided into eight sub-villages or hamlets and it is in one of these sub-villages that we lived during the main part of our research. Empirical material used in the study is for the most part taken from this village.

1 THE VILLAGE OF BANGSAL

1.1 The Setting

Bangsal is a village complex of approximately 8,000 inhabitants, spread over an area of 760 hectares. This amounts to a population density of about 1,000 inhabitants per square km. (The average population density for the whole of Java is 565 per square km).[4]

The area lies on a flat plain in the Brantas River Basin, one of the richest agricultural areas of Java. Volcanic ashes from Gunung Kelud periodically fertilize the region. Bangsal is also favoured as regards irrigation, this being due to natural springs, outlets of the Brantas River, as well as a complex of canal systems built by the Handelsvereniging Amsterdam sugar company during the colonial period.

The village administration is composed of a village head *(Lurah)* and secretary *(Carik)* responsible to the *Camat* or Sub-District head at Mojokuto. They are aided by a religious official *(Modin)*, a security official *(Jogoboyo)*, and an irrigation official *(Jogotirto)*. On the level of the *pedukuhan* or sub-village there is also a village chief *(Kamituwo)* responsible to the lurah, and his assistant the *Kebayan*.

Village *warungs* (small shops) and hawkers supply day-to-day household items such as food, soap and the like. For clothes, tools and more important articles the villagers will go to Mojokuto. Most peasants will prefer to do their shopping in Mojokuto as not only will they have a wider choice but they will also avoid yet another middleman.

One also goes to Mojokuto for entertainment. There is one movie theatre in Mojokuto showing an assortment of films from the home-made variety to Chinese, Indian and Western films. Besides this, an open-air theatre presents the Javanese classics as well as the *ludruk* (transvestite theatre) and the *gambus* (Arab-inspired musical). Lack of transportation and money will however compel the majority to remain in Bangsal and await such entertainment as might offer a wedding, circumcision, or the *slametans* given on various occasions. Slametans are religious thanksgiving meals typical of traditional Java. These may be given singularly by a family on the occasion of a birth, death, marriage, circumcision, (the two latter often accompanied by gayer forms of entertainment as plays, music and traditional dances) or other events requiring the blessing of God, the spirits and the community. The giving away of food is said to bring health and well-being to the family. Collectively, slametans may be given by the village as a whole on the day of the clearing of the village, national holidays or other occasions of importance to the whole village.

There are three primary schools and two religious schools *(madrasah)* in Bangsal. The educational system in Indonesia, not counting the university, consists of three stages comprising altogether 12 years of study - the 'sekolah dasar' or primary school (6 years), the *'sekolah menengah pertama'* or junior high school (3 years), the *'sekolah menengah atas'* or senior high school (3 years). Most of those who do go to school in the village do not go further than the sixth grade; those who do go to Mojokuto or the other cities.

As in other parts of Java, the dominant religion in Bangsal is Islam. Of the whole population only about 40 are non-Muslims. Besides the religious schools mentioned above, there are four mosques in the village and at least one *langgar* (prayer house) in each sub-village.[5]

1.2 Land Use

Over 65 per cent of the total land area of the village is *sawah* (irrigated wet-rice land). The rest is divided into *tegalan* (non-irrigated land), *pekarangan* (household compound), and *perumahan* (housing). Because of the abundant water supply rice is the main crop and is grown the year round. (This is in fact rather atypical of the region most known for its onions and where the rice crop is most often rotated with corn and soya.) Since the introduction of the green revolution, Bangsal farmers have been able to grow up to three harvests a year although the most usual is five harvests in two years. The green revolution in Indonesia means the introduction of the High Yielding Variety seeds (e.g. the PB5 variety developed at the International Rice Research Institute in the Philippines and the Pelita 1-1 variety developed locally at the Institut Pertanian at Bogor) under the BIMAS programme sponsored by the government. In Bangsal this was introduced in the late sixties. The BIMAS programme extends to the farmer, at the beginning of each harvest season, a 'package' including in addition to the seeds initially distributed, fertilizers, insecticides and cash. This loan has to be repaid after the harvest.

Tegalan or dry land, found only in two of the sub-villages, comprises in all just about ten hectares. It is mostly used for growing secondary cash crops as a sideline and is not important in comparison to the paddy. The household compound on the other hand is often an important source of income. A well-stocked compound can provide the household with such items as spices, fruits and vegetables so that extra expenses could be spared.[6] Besides growing these plants, the space could also be used to keep such livestock as chickens, ducks, as well as animals like goats and water buffaloes. The total area of household compound is approximately 180 hectares so that it is second in importance. Still, Bangsal is above all a rice village.

2 LAND AND LABOUR IN BANGSAL

2.1 The Cultivation of Rice

Most characteristic of wet-rice cultivation is that it is labour intensive. According to our field notes, approximately 330 man-days are necessary for the cultivation of one hectare of land (1 day - 6 hours).[7] The number 330 man-days includes ploughing, harrowing, hoeing, planting, weeding - in short all labour excluding the harvest. The labour is distributed among the various tasks in the agricultural cycle as shown in Table 1.

Table 1. Average labour use per hectare in rice cultivation according to task in the village of Bangsal.

A.	sowing	1 day
B.	1. time ploughing	35 days
C.	2. time harrowing	17 "
D.	2. time ploughing	30 "
E.	2. time harrowing	15 "
F.	hoeing	7 "
G.	pulling of seedlings	2 "
H.	planting	84 "
I.	1st weeding	105 "
J.	2nd weeding	35 "
	Total pre-harvest labour use:	331 days

The labour-absorptive nature of rice agriculture in Java in general is very pronounced even if compared to other countries where rice cultivation forms the foundation of agriculture. This can be seen from Table 2.

The first phase is the preparation of the land - ploughing, harrowing, hoeing, and fixing of the dykes and the terrace walls. Most farmers will prefer to plough the land twice (with several days' interval) as this gives better results. Cows or buffaloes (the asiatic water buffalo or carabao) are used for ploughing and harrowing, the rest are done manually. Manipulations with a hoe (or

Table 2. Average labour use in rice cultivation per hectare in different countries.[8]

Country	*Cultivation method*	*Man-days per ha*
South Vietnam	one seedbed	70
	two seedbeds	75
Japan	manual labour	231
Philippines		ca 55
USA	direct sowing and complete mechanization	5

pacul) are used for cultivating the corners of the fields which are out of reach of the ploughs. Besides this, the dykes and the terraces are also renewed with the help of the pacul. Sometimes, scarcity of draught animals and the nature of the soil can compel the use of hand labour for the whole preparation of the land.

Seeds are sown at about the same time that one begins with the preparation of the land. The best stalks from earlier harvests are selected for the seeds. These are strewn in a small bed reserved for this purpose. When the seeds are ready for planting, usually after 25 to 35 days, they are removed from the seedbeds and planted in the fields prepared earlier. The transplanting of the seedlings demands a lot of labour. This consists of pulling up the seedlings, binding them into sheaves and transporting them to the fields where they are placed in clusters over the areas to be planted. Planters will then take each seedling one by one and plant them in regular rows over the field.

In the period of about three months when the plant is allowed to grow, the work-pace slows down. What is left now is the checking of water (to ensure that there is enough or not too much), weeding (although time consuming, this can be done inside a longer period), and the application of insecticides and fertilizer at the appropriate moments.

2.2 Labour Relations: the traditional labour organization

According to informants, the *dukuh* of Sarangmanuk (the sub-village of our residence) was originally cleared by five men in the 1870s. By clearing the land and cultivating it, these men became the owners of the land. In this enterprise they were usually aided by young men who were their followers or *bolo*. A man with a larger following will thus be able to acquire more land than those more modest. In exchange for their labour, these men were given board and lodging as well as moral leadership. *Nyantri*[9] is the Javanese term for the system. Mornings were spent in the fields whereas evenings were consecrated to studies with the head of the household who was considered not simply as an employer but a spiritual leader as well.

From of old, the peasants have always tried to satisfy their labour needs as far as possible by making use of the labour of their families (or in the case of Sarangmanuk by the labour of their households). However, self-reliance in labour also depends on the size and composition of the household, the extent of ground to be tilled, as well as the time within which a given piece of work must be finished. Where the household proved insufficient for the realization of a given piece of work, neighbouring households were called in for assistance. This mutual help system is called *sambatan*. Requests for help were always granted, stimulated by the understanding that each in turn would need such help from his neighbours. At the time, all villagers were more or less at the same social level, all owned land, and the prosperity of the different families did not vary greatly. In this way the cash requirements of the villagers were reduced as the sambatan system excluded the need for payments in cash. Inversely, the system itself is a clear indication of the feeble role that money earlier played in the peasant economy.

It was only during the harvest season, when a lot of work had to be done inside a limited time and when each household was busy reaping its own harvests, that extra labour had to be brought in.

With the years the situation changed. Landholdings became smaller as each plot went to the next generation and the system of nyantri died out. Earlier 'disciples' formed their own families and moved out of the landlords' households. Further the total population increased as a result of immigration. The economy continued nevertheless to be tied to the land. The more lucky may have been able to acquire a small plot of land, the rest turned to agricultural labour.

As a result there has been a steady differentiation through the simultaneous and complementary processes of accumulation and proletarization. The fragmentation and parcelling of the soil also made possible the concentration of wealth in the hands of few through the increasing monetization of the peasant economy. Although a very gradual and drawn-out process, the role of money has for a long time been important in the village economy. First of all, money was needed to buy clothing. The domestic industry in Java started to lose ground in the competition with foreign manufactured textiles even before 1850. Moreover, in the later period of Dutch rule, the taxes in money increased. In addition, more and more essentials were procured through the market, articles like salt, petroleum, frying oil and salt fish.

2.3 Land Tenure and Occupations in Bangsal

Today, of the 81 households[10] in Sarangmanuk, there are 25 landowners to the 56 landless. In spite of this, only a very small percentage are independent of agriculture for their livelihood. Tables 3 and 4 will give the reader a better idea of landholdings and the economic activities of the villagers.

Besides the sub-village of Sarangmanuk we have also included the percentage of landholdings in two of the other sub-villages of Bangsal. In Sarangmanuk and Banyurejo the proportion of landowners is clearly under 50 per cent, and of these over 50 per cent own under 0.5 hectare of land. Gerbong is an exception but shows nevertheless the tendency for fewer but larger landholdings. At the time that Indonesia was still a Dutch colony, the area (that is now Gerbong) 'belonged' to the Handelsvereniging Amsterdam who used the land for their sugar plantation. The factory was destroyed during the war and upon independence the land became a property of the State. A motion by the *Barisan Tani Indonesia* (Indonesian Peasant Organization, a peasant organization affiliated with the Communist Party of Indonesia) gave the 'right of use' or *hak pakai*[11] of the land to its inhabitants. Each family was given a plot of land according to need, the average allotment being 0.5 *bau* or 0.350 hectare. Not 30 years later, the uniformity is wearing out. Although the percentage of landownership is over 50 per cent, 25 per cent own over 0.5 hectare of land whereas 30 per cent are landless. The case of Gerbong thus offers an excellent illustration of the history of Bangsal, how an egalitarian community turned into one based on the opposition between landholders and the landless.

Occupation in Table 4 denotes the occupation of the head of the household. This is important as most households are supported by several of its members. Wives and almost all children over 13 years help in the family economy.[12] Only the aged and disabled are unproductive. As with the male

Table 3. Landholdings in the subvillages of Bangsal

Size distribution (in ha.)	Percentage of households Sarangmanuk no.	Sarangmanuk per cent	Banyurejo per cent	Gerbong per cent
over 15	0	0	1	0
10-15	1	1	2	0
5-10	1	1	1	0
2-5	2	3	1	4
1-2	4	5	2	10
0.5-1	4	5	10	10
under 0.5	13	17	28	45
Total:		32	45	70

Table 4. Occupations in Sarangmanuk

Occupation	*Percentage of households*
farmer	10
farmer + other labour	10
farmer + agricultural labour	10
agricultural labour	40
agricultural labour + other labour	20
other labour	10

population, the majority of women are also agricultural labourers, and almost without exception participate in harvests.[13]

(1) Farmers and farmers with a secondary occupation form the 'upper class'. 'Other labour' here are such prestigious sidelines as the post of village official, school teacher, or entrepreneur trader. The extra labour is not a necessity. This group represents 20 per cent of the total population; the remaining 80 per cent of the villagers are either partly or completely dependent on wage labour in one way or another, generally agricultural work.

(2) Farmers also engaged in agricultural labour are those with such small landholdings that extra labour is necessary for subsistence. They are often not much better off than the agricultural labourer.

(3) and (4) The bulk of the population fall under the category 'agricultural labourer', that is, wage labourers on a day-to-day basis for the landowning peasants. Even households indicated under 'other labour' are dependent on agricultural work as a sideline. The Mualim family, for instance, supplies the village with its bean curd, but only Pak Mualim and the younger children are engaged in this production. Mrs. Mualim and the elder children are agricultural labourers. Another example is an elderly couple who, finding agricultural work too tiring at their age, live mainly on the income the wife receives as midwife. They are nevertheless also supported by their children who are agricultural labourers.

(5) Families depending wholly on work other than agricultural labour are: two rice merchants (middlemen) who buy rice from the farmers in the village and sell it further to wholesalers in Mojokuto; one household composed of grandmother and granddaughter who is supported by grandmother working as househelp to one of the more well-to-do families; another household composed of widowed mother and two children, supported by the mother working as *bakul* or itinerant trader, selling village goods to Mojokuto and vice-versa.

The secondary occupations of agricultural labourers are varied, including such work as petty trading, carpentry and handicrafts, or the raising of ducks for the sale of the eggs. Some villagers may even temporarily leave the village in search of odd jobs during the low season or *paceklik*. As has been noted earlier, wet-rice cultivation is labour intensive from the preparation of the land up to the planting, and again during the harvest. In the period that the plant is allowed to grow there is a pause in the labour activities. It is during this period that labourers are forced to seek work elsewhere.

An agricultural labourer receives from 100 to 125 rupiahs for a day's work. This is usually 6 hours, from 7 to 10 in the morning and from 1 to 4 o'clock in the afternoon. If the labourer is a woman she will receive 60 to 70 rupiahs for the same working hours. Men's labour is ploughing, harrowing and hoeing; women's labour is planting and weeding. To give meaning to these wages we will mention the prices of a few essential items in the Javanese household.

rice (poorest quality HYV rice)	70 Rps./kg
paraffin oil	20 Rps./lt
cooking/coconut oil	40 Rps./lt
soybean curd (cigarette box size)	5 Rps./piece

Rice should not be taken for granted as being the most common staple, only the richer families will eat rice three times a day. Paraffin is used both for light (lamps - there is no electricity in the village) and cooking, although the majority will use wood for the latter. It is clear that with these prices, even a full working family will find it difficult to 'make ends meet'.

If a landless family is lucky it may be given a *borongan* (the responsibility of all preparation of the land until the planting) or a *kedokan* (the planting and first weeding) by a farmer. For a borongan a man will receive 50 kilos of rice (paid at harvest) per 100 *ru* (1/7 ha.) of land that is under his responsibility. A kedokan will bring the labourer one-tenth of the product.

Several writers in describing the Javanese countryside have mentioned methods of sharecropping as the *maro* and *mertelu*, respectively the division into two and three.[14] (For the tilling of the land the tenant will receive either a half or a third of the product.) Such systems are dying out as of the Java of today.[15] In the past, however, these sharecropping systems, more favourable than the ones common today, have all been noted in Bangsal.

2.4 'Hullers'

In later years the employment situation has worsened in the village. The process of proletarization that has made the majority of the villagers landless, so far has only implied the formal subsumption of labour under capital. No changes in the methods of production have accompanied the process of differentiation and thus exacerbating the difficulties for the poorer villagers. Since 1969, however, with the introduction of a number of small rice mills, or 'hullers' as the villagers call them according to their English name, labour has come also to be *really* subsumed under capital in one particular domain.

Traditionally, farmers would hand-pound their rice before consuming it, or else the unhulled rice (or *gabah*) would be hand-pounded by the small itinerant rice trader and his family (plus outside labour) before it was eventually sold to the rice wholesaler in Mojokuto. The actual work of hand-pounding was done by women. The rice was put into a long wooden rice-pounder (made from the trunk of a large tree) and the women would pound it with a heavy piece of wood which was held vertically and then dropped, lifted and dropped in a rhythmic fashion. The work is very time-consuming. It usually takes three women one day to pound one *kwintal* (100 kg) of rice. The payment is 5 kg per kwt hand-pounded rice. Before 1969, all rice was hand-pounded in this way in Sarangmanuk.

In 1969, however, the first rice mill was constructed in the village of Bangsal and since then six others have been erected. Today, only a very small fraction of the total rice crop is hand-pounded. Thus a very valuable source of employment has been lost to the poor villagers. The richer peasants prefer to have the rice for home consumption hulled as the cost is lower than that of hand-pounding, namely 3 kg per kwintal hulled rice.

In spite of the heavy investments represented by the machinery and buildings of the hullers, hulling is cheaper than hand-pounding because of the greater production capacity of the former. In 1969 one unit of huller cost 345,000 rupiahs and in 1974 the average price was 800,000 rupiahs. The price varies of course with the size of the huller and the sophistication of the equipment. Generally the price ranges from 400,000 rupiahs, but a big huller complete with polisher would cost 1.8 million rupiahs. An average size huller can hull four tons per day and has the advantage of being able to operate 24 hours a day during the peak periods. Usually it is operated by four or five permanent workers.

The marketable rice surplus of the rich farmers is hulled for the same reason - the lower cost of hulling. However, if some of the rice-traders and women who earlier were employed in hand-pounding had lowered the cost of hand-pounding, it would have been of no avail. There is in fact an agreement between the huller operators and the Chinese rice-merchants in Mojokuto that only the 'white' hulled rice is to be accepted from the small rice-traders. The only part left of the total rice crop which is still hand-pounded is the rice directly used for consumption by the families of poor peasants and landless - rice more often than not received as wages in nature from work as day labourers or as harvesters, or else from the small peasants' own crop.

It is difficult to figure the total loss in income to the poor villagers due to the change in milling technique. The difficulty stems from the uncertainty as to the relative size of the total crop that is still being pounded. One would perhaps think that the payment in kind received by the poorer villagers as well as the part of the crop of the poorer peasants that is reserved for home consumption would be hand-pounded. In fact the situation is more gloomy. A large part of the rice received by the poorer villagers is converted into money to buy other necessities or cheaper kinds of foodstuffs such as corn, cassava and sweet potatoes. In relation to the former situation this means a net loss to the peasants who now must hull their rice in order to sell it. As has been noted earlier, the rice merchants will only accept hulled rice. Thus the poor peasants cannot profit from the use of their own labour which is without money value to them.

To indicate the loss suffered by the poorer villagers, we will only look at the net loss they have had in the fields of the well-off farmers' (those with over 1 ha. holdings) now hulling their total rice crop. The well-off farmers in Sarangmanuk hold a total of 15 hectares. With a pre-HYV average yield of 3 tons per hectare and a regime of general double cropping, the total yearly yield is 90 tons. As we noted earlier, the women used to receive 5 kg for every 100 kg of hand-pounded rice. Ninety tons of *gabah* (unshelled rice) becomes approximately 65 tons of pounded white rice. The total pay earlier received by the women hand-pounders, and hence their net loss, is thus

$$\frac{65 \times 5}{100} = 3{,}250 \text{ kilos.}$$

This amount, earlier distributed among a large number of landless villagers, is now shared between the huller operators and the rich farmers in a division of 1,950 kgs (three-fifths) for the former and 1,300 kgs (two-fifths) for the latter.

Considering the circumstances under which the majority of the villagers live, it is not difficult to understand that they try to profit from participating in the harvests where the traditional labour arrangements of *gotong royong* or mutual help has found a last refuge.[16]

2.5 The Traditional System of Harvesting

The traditional and still by far the most prevalent harvesting system in Java is characterized by the participation of all who want to join in the harvest and for their trouble receive a share in kind. Today, this share, or *bawon*, is usually one-tenth of what each has been able to harvest. Earlier, when it was the farmers who were interested in getting the extra help, shares were relatively higher.[17] An informant (over 50 years of age) remembers the time when harvesters received one-fifth of a share in Sarangmanuk.

Harvesting is done with a small hand-knife called the *ani-ani*, which cuts the stalks one by one at the top. Though efficient in the hands of the experienced worker, the ani-ani cannot be compared to more modern methods of harvesting or even to the simple sickle. It is said, however, that this is an obligation to the rice goddess, Dewi Sri, who must be treated with the necessary reverence. The myth has it that the rice plant originated from Dewi Sri. The goddess designated the use of the ani-ani and should any other implements be used it is said that she will then not bless the next harvest.

The social side of it is that the less well-to-do are thus enabled to profit from the produce of the ground. The ani-ani enables all to participate, women, children, the elderly. (We have seen instances where pregnant women as well as women with children tied to their backs participated in a harvest.) Professor Wertheim, writing on social change in Java in 1900-30, mentioned that a landowner would have been ostracized should he replace the ani-ani with a scythe.[18] A scythe would have been much more efficient but as the work would have been harder, this would eliminate job opportunities for a significant number of the villagers.

A farmer will usually give relatives and neighbours advance notice of when he will harvest, others will join in uninvited. Word will get around in the village that such-and-such a field will be harvested that day so that an impressive gathering can always be expected. The crowd of harvesters do not always have to be of the village. During the harvest season a great number of landless (usually from less fertile villages or where the rice crop is not grown the year round) roam the countryside in search of harvests in which they hope to participate.

The harvesters line the fields, moving inwards as they cut the paddy. The signal to begin is given by the owner who will try to control the harvesting by reprimanding the careless workers when there is too much trampling of the paddy. There is a great rush, for the more one cuts, the larger the share. We have seen up to 100 harvesters on a 100 ru field (1 hectare : 700 ru). Once the rice is cut the tempo slows down. There is now no longer a race to cut more than the others. The harvesters carry the paddy to the owner's house where his wife will divide each harvest into ten equal shares, one to the harvester, nine to herself.

The mass participation in the harvests, however, has the consequence of making the burden of the farmer a bit too difficult to bear. In the past, those who were better off were strongly encouraged to redistribute their wealth. One of the ways in which this is manifested is by the farmers providing a large share of their harvest to the villagers. But with more people in the fields, traditional bawon system is becoming more and more unprofitable for the farmers. It is inevitable that there are more losses - actual loss due to carelessness in the rush to cut as much paddy as possible, and loss due to stealing. We should also mention that there are in fact two phases of rice harvesting. The first phase, the real harvest, is when the harvesters take the paddy to the owner's house. After this harvest, however, there are still remnants of paddy that have been missed or dropped by the harvesters and a second group called *pengasak* are allowed to clean up the field. Unlike the first harvest, the pengasaks' paddy does not have to be shared with the owner.

To reduce their losses, farmers try to limit the number of harvesters in their fields. This, however, is much easier said than done. At one harvest, the wife of the farmer stood guard to ward off latecomers - arguing that as there were already too many harvesters in the field, their shares could not be very much. This proved little discouragement and as each pleaded, she gave in. More unscrupulous farmers admit only those who are of the village or personally known to him. Others, going a step further, allow only those who have taken part in the cultivation of the plant, that is the preparation of the land, the planting, weeding, etc.

To some extent, a farmer may receive a certain prestige by allowing everybody to join in his harvest and by giving large bawons. One such farmer, a neighbour of ours, would have been a successful candidate for the post of Kamituwo (head of a sub-village) had not the events of 1965 and its consequences occurred. (The man was a known communist sympathizer.) Whatever prestige he may gain is however, most often counterbalanced by his losses. The example described above is more an exception than the rule, for up to today, with nothing to gain, he is still known for his generous bawons. The social responsibility of the farmers is expanded because of the greatly increased number of landless, and although there is strong pressure to retain the tradition, the owner-harvester relationship is much more fragile than might be expected.

2.6 Tebasan

To free themselves from the traditional bawon harvesting system and the limits it puts upon the ability of the peasants to secure the crop for themselves, farmers are introducing *tebasan*.

The new tebasan harvesting system was to our knowledge first observed in December 1972 in Central Java by a research team from the Agro-Economic Survey of Indonesia.[19] Since then the new system has spread to ever new districts. In the village of Bangsal, tebasan was practised for the first time during the wet season harvest of 1974. A total of six persons in Bangsal was reported as tebasan operators, one of them was an inhabitant of Sarangmanuk and a close neighbour of ours.

The essence of the new tebasan system is the use of a practice 'legalized' under the old customary law or *adat*[20] for the purpose of limiting the number of harvesters and lowering the costs of harvesting. Both traditionally and today, tebasan stands for the method of selling a crop just before harvest for a clean cash sum. Traditionally, however, such a transaction did not call for a change in the system of harvesting. The latter was done by all those who wished to participate and they were given bawon shares by the new owner of the crop. Secondly, traditional tebasan was reserved for exceptional cases and was frequently connected with usury and the immediate need for cash on the part of the seller of the crop.[21]

What happens under the new tebasan system is the following: As already stated above, the farmer sells his crop rights to another man shortly (a week or so) before the harvest day. The buyer is usually a man who has specialized (at least to some extent) in acting as a middle-man between the farmer and the market. This *penebas*, or buyer, gives an agreed cash sum to the farmer for the crop. The money might be paid in advance or after the actual marketing of the rice, financial risks being divided between the two depending on the agreement or the circumstances.

In selling his crop rights, the farmer relieves himself of the headaches and responsibilities connected with the harvest. For his part, the penebas handles the harvest and sells the rice.

The penebas is ideally and usually not of the village, and as a stranger he cannot be considered to have responsibilities towards the local poorer villagers. On harvest day, he comes to the farmer's field with a band of client harvesters from his own village. The number of harvesters will effectively be limited to 5-20 per 100 *ru* depending on the harvesting tool being used, the sickle or the ani-ani. The penebas will be in an easier position to keep the local villagers from joining the harvest as he is seen as having a justified claim to a profit. (Being a penebas is after all *his* way of making a living.) Still, tensions run high and violent clashes occur. It is our opinion that the indignation among the poorer villagers is very strong indeed, and that so far, only the lack of appropriate organizations can explain the absence of open conflict.

Tebasan has brought about a very important change in introducing the sickle instead of the ani-ani as the harvesting tool. The sickle is more efficient than the ani-ani and the productivity of labour is thus increased. On the other hand this change has a further limiting effect on the number of harvesters as work with a sickle is more arduous and thus reserved for the younger and more able. Also the second or *ngasak* harvest mentioned above is eliminated, the sickle cutting the paddy only a few inches above the ground and not leaving anything but the stubs.

The tebasan harvesters do not receive a traditional bawon share in natura but are paid in cash according to the quantity cut by each harvester. When the harvest is over, the paddy is loaded in sacks into the *cikar* (ox-cart) of the penebas and transported to his house. Here, a weighing scale is used to measure the exact amount of each harvester's paddy.[22] He is then paid accordingly at 2 rupiahs per kilo harvested paddy. In relative terms this payment is radically lower than what is received under the bawon system. With a payment of 2 rupiahs per kilo harvested paddy and a price of 70 rupiahs for a kilo of rice in the market (see above), it means that to obtain one kilo of rice, a harvester must cut 70/2 = 35 kilos of paddy. Conversely, under the bawon system, with a payment to each harvester of one-tenth of the amount of paddy harvested, a harvester need only cut 10 kg to obtain 1 kg for himself. Thus the 'real wage' of harvesting undergoes a substantial reduction when the transformation is done from *bawon* to *tebasan*.[23] The ensuing lower cost of harvesting means higher incomes for the penebas as well as for the farmer. On the other hand, the total share received by the individual tebasan harvesters need not decrease, it may even increase as fewer harvesters are needed to harvest the same area.

Unlike the bawon system when all villagers could join in indiscriminately, in tebasan each individual harvester's participation has the character of a favour bestowed upon him by the penebas. The penebas prefer to engage the same people as his harvesters, usually from his own village and with whom he has a relatively close relationship. Being dependent upon the penebas for the privilege of employment, the tebasan harvesters' relation to the former is the relation of *clients* towards their *patron*.

3. INVOLUTION OR SOCIAL DIFFERENTIATION

In this last section, we will discuss *tebasan* under the general perspective of rural change. What are the implications for social relations in the village community from the changes occurring in one particular sector of the economy, that of harvesting? To answer this, we have to consider the changes occurring both in the light of the particular agricultural and historical background of Java and Bangsal as well as from the standpoint of the process of commercialization and the impact of the market on the peasant mode of life.

The dominant view of social relations in Java as formulated by Clifford Geertz has it that they are expressions of an 'agricultural involution'.[24] According to this view, the predominant trend has been 'the durability of the post-traditional rural economy', meaning that instead of sharper opposition in the village centred on land-ownership, tenure systems and tenancy relationships have grown more intricate and complicated 'in the effort to provide everyone with some niche, however small, in the overall system'.[25]

We have tried to show, to the contrary, that there has been a tendency towards increased differentiation through the simultaneous and complimentary processes of accumulation and expropriation as a result of the growing commercialization of agriculture. This has led to a situation in Bangsal where 80 per cent of the village population is dependent on work on other peasants' land because the former have lost the control of the basic means of production, land.

It is true that there are a great number of 'tenure systems' and 'tenancy relationships'. For Bangsal we have mentioned *maro, mertelu,* as well as systems of *sambatan, gotong, royong, borongan, ngedok,* in addition to wage-labour. However, we have also noted (1) the virtual disappearance of mutual help or sambaṭan, (2) the predominance of wage labour in relation to share-cropping, as well as (3) a tendency of a worsening in the conditions under which share-cropping arrangements are made (the disappearance of maro and mertelu, i.e. of 1:1 and 1:2 crop-sharing; the reduction of ngedok and bawon from a fifth to a tenth fraction). Thus, over time, 'tenancy relationships' are not growing more complicated, but are rather becoming more uniform, with wage-labour as the standard. The 'intricacy' of tenancy relationships, in the first place, is due to their being *combinations* of traditional relations with a justification in customary law or *adat* and more modern ones arising from the impact of the market and money relations on the village economy. Finally, as to the 'effort to provide everyone with some niche . . . in the overall system', we may say that the introduction of tebasan and hullers on the contrary amounts to a virtual *eviction* of the poorer villagers from their very 'niches'!

3.1 Commercialization

What is referred to above as 'the growing commercialization of agriculture' has to do with the spread of commodity production in the countryside. When products are said to be produced as commodities what is meant is that they are produced as exchange-values, that is as products that can be bought and sold. Objects in themselves are external to man, and consequently alienable by him. In order that this alienation may actually take place, however, it is necessary for men to treat each other as private owners of those alienable objects. The exchange of commodities thus implies a mutual recognition of men as private proprietors. Consequently, the spread of commodity production is tantamount to the spread of private property to ever new domains.

The expansion of commodity production in Java has been a long and drawn-out process in which we can mention as landmarks: the introduction by the Dutch in the late nineteenth century of land taxes to be paid in money; the decline of the peasant handicraft industry and the spread of foreign products; the need to acquire money for daily necessities; the rise of a landless class which has to acquire even rice through the market.

The medium by which commodities are exchanged is money. We thus get the formula C - M - C (Commodity - Money -

Commodity) signifying the sale of one product (for example rice) in order to buy another (for example clothes). The formula C - M - C expresses the state of affairs in which the use-value of commodities is still dominant, that is, rice is treated like an exchange value only because a peasant needs to obtain other useful articles, like clothes as in this case. As long as this state of affairs reigns, there is a natural limit to the accumulation of wealth in the hands of individuals. To be a rich peasant then means having a lot of useful articles, most commonly rice, for which the rich peasant's family has only a limited need beyond which the rice can be distributed to the poorer villagers as the very sign of wealth.

In the case where money economy has penetrated a society, however, the formula can run like this: M - C - M', indicating that money serves as a means to secure commodities with the sole purpose of getting more money. (The formula M - M', money becoming more money, indicates usury and has become quite widespread in the village.) This opens up the possibility for wealth, like land (to the degree of this having become a commodity itself that can be owned and alienated by private individuals), to be concentrated in the hands of individuals. This is why the pre-capitalist village economy 'cannot withstand the disintegrating forces of trade and commercial development, the stealthy invasion of money economy'.[26] This is also why the earlier egalitarian Sarangmanuk could develop into a village of social differentiation based on landed wealth.

3.2 Communal Restraints

On the other hand, what has been referred to by Geertz as the 'durability of the post-traditional economy' can explain the relative slow pace by which the process of differentiation and individualistic rural change has taken place in Java, and in Bangsal in particular. Even if clearly differentiated in terms of land ownership today, it remains true for Bangsal as well as for Java in general, that 'village society did not bifurcate . . . into a group of large landlords and a group of oppressed near-serfs'.[27] *The process of social differentiation was combatted within the framework of the Javanese village through communal restraints put on the actions of individuals.*

Under the impact of Dutch agrarian colonialism, the pre-colonial peasant communities were remodelled from within. In Java the villagers were deprived of their best land, and until 1870 were forced to furnish work on the colonial enterprises, in particular the sugar factories. After 1870, land was rented from the peasants, but the earlier system continued its pressure on the village economy. 'So great were the demands on the landholder', states Furnivall, 'that landholding was no longer a privilege but a burden which occupants tried to share with others'.[28] Under the circumstances of colonial oppression, communal solidarity called for a levelling of inter-village differences to preserve the fragile balance between man and land.[29] The answer often was a communal, regular and periodic distribution of cultivated fields among the villagers.[30]

In the district, communal landholding was earlier quite widespread.[31] In Bangsal, land tenure always seemed to have been individual. This, however, does not preclude communal restraints on the actions of individuals. In a penetrating article on the peasant communities in Java and Mexico, Eric Wolf has seen their corporateness to reside in a systematic attempt at redistribution of wealth among the members of the community.[32] In Mexico, religion became 'the balance wheel of communal economics'.[33]

> Each year, religious participation wipes out considerable sums of goods and money; each year, part of the surplus of the community is consumed in offerings or exploded in fireworks to please the saints. The system takes from those who have, in order to make all men have-nots . . . Since it levels differences of wealth, it also inhibits the growth of class distinctions based on wealth.[34]

In Java, the religious *slametans* traditionally given at frequent intervals had a similar function. Both in Java and in Mexico, differentiation based on wealth is partly counteracted by a large *ceremonial fund*.[35]

The *slametans* are only part of a larger system of Javanese customary law or *adat*. The essential of the adat is the right of disposal or *hak pertuanan* of the community.[36] The community as a group has rights in the land, or in the case of *bawon*, in the produce of the land. The group regulates the rights and claims of each member in such a way as to obtain for all, their share of the common benefits to be derived from the land.[37] Ideally and traditionally the group controls the use of land among its members, the latter as individuals being devoid of any power to alienate the land. But even in the case of the existence of private property in land, the redistributive practices of slametan and bawon indicates that the community has not entirely lost the control of the products of its labour.

One ought not to exaggerate the uniqueness of the Javanese rural system and to see in it only an exotic 'communalism'. From European history we remember the strong communal traits of feudal agriculture, traits that reigned until the turn of the last century in some regions. In fact European land tenure represented a compromise between common land property (i.e. in pastures and forests) and private tenure in land (individual peasant plots). From an economic point of view, each village under this system was a self-sufficient territorial community or *Markgenossenschaft*. The common rights prevailed first of all . . . in the commons or *Algemeine*. The forests were sources of wood, construction materials, a place for hunting and the collecting of berries. The meadows were primarily pastures and sources of fodder for the cattle. Here, the arable fields were, however, also subject to communal restraints. One could say that the fields became common lands after the harvest, at the moment when they were no longer fields but had become meadows. The villagers even had a right to the remains from the harvest and the stubble as well (i.e. gleaning rights, etc.). Marc Bouloiseau is therefore completely justified in saying that 'les droits du proprietaire s'étaignaient donc après la première recolte'.[38] In the present case of Java, one could say that the *adat* prescribes that the rights of the proprietor are evaded even *before* the harvest and that the rights of the community assert themselves in the claim of the villagers to a part of the harvest, *bawon*. The difference in the manner in which the common rights are asserted in Europe and Java stems from the differences in the very nature of agriculture in the two areas. In Europe, the common rights were mainly *negative* rights, the rights of all to free enjoyment of the commons.[39] This is due to the peculiar European combination of field agriculture based on family labour and the exploitation of pastures and forests. European agriculture is thus *continuous in space* (fields - meadows - forests) *and in time* (fields becoming pastures). Asian wet-rice agriculture, however, *is continuous in time* (rice field the year round) *and discontinuous in space* (rice fields versus unexploited jungle, although in the Java of today the jungle has disappeared).[40]

In the case of *bawon,* the peasant owner of the land does not truly own his rice crop. The harvesters according to adat have a right both to participate and to receive a part of the crop. The farmer here is not yet in a position where he can treat the crop as a commodity, as an object of private property alienable at will. With the spread of commodity production, this limitation will increasingly be felt as a nuisance by the rich.

> Every prosperous person has to share his wealth right and left; every little windfall must be distributed without delay. The village community cannot easily tolerate economic differences but is apt to act as a leveller in this respect, regarding the individual as part of the community.[41]

Clearly such a system is a barrier in the way of accumulation. Consequently, this can only take place 'where it has become possible for the peasant to escape the demands placed on him to underwrite with ceremonial expenditures the traditional social ties with his fellows'.[42]

The rise of modernistic Islam in rural Java from 1910 onwards might be seen as one attempt by peasants to end their ceremonial commitments as these latter have a strong tie with the peculiar syncretist and only nominally Muslim Javanese peasant religion.[43] Typically, the 'penebas' in Sarangmanuk complained to us about the strength of *adat* among the villagers. He opposed it to *hukum negara* or the 'Code Civil' which as he quite correctly pointed out, did not include any clause which limited the private property rights of individuals. Pak Gatot, the penebas, was himself the son of the richest farmer in the village. Earlier he had joined the Jemaah, a highly this-worldly Muslim sect repudiating slametan and even the necessity for devout Muslims to undertake at least once in a lifetime a pilgrimage to Mecca (indeed an economically wasteful and unproductive venture). Pak Gatot has earlier been involved in a host of entrepreneurial projects: acting as a middleman between the many producers of ducks' eggs in the village and a buyer from town; operating a shop selling daily necessities to the villagers; constructing in 1969 the first small huller or petrol driven rice-mill in Bangsal.[44]

The importance of the introduction of *tebasan* as an example of rural change is that much greater because it is in the *harvest* that the traditional labour arrangements 'has found a last refuge'.

The changes in the relations of production that have already occurred have not involved the villagers 'en masse', and thus have been easier to accept. A peasant who earlier has exchanged labour with his fellow villagers and who one day finds himself landless will perhaps go on working on other peasant's land. The only difference is that as a landless he does not any longer exchange labour. Rather, he exchanges his labour power for a wage paid in kind but most commonly in money. Otherwise, no changes in the methods of production have taken place; ploughing, harrowing, planting and weeding is done today in the same manner as described by Raffles around 1810 in his *History of Java*.[45] Further, the changes in the relations of production have occurred with the tacit understanding that a part of the rice crop belongs to the workers in the form of the bawon.

With tebasan, a challenge is made to the majority of the villagers in the attempt to lower the costs of harvesting. A change in the method of production is also attempted in the substitution of the ani-ani by the sickle. This amounts to an effort to change a way of life. We cannot simply regard the cultivation of rice as a way of producing foodstuffs. Traditionally the cultivation of rice is the very core around which the whole village world turned. The various phases in the productive cycles are accompanied by rituals, slametans and myths as to how to do the *right things*.

Nowhere is this seen clearer than in the case of the ani-ani. The ani-ani is not a tool among other agricultural tools. It is given to the peasants of Java by the rice goddess Dewi Sri, and is to be used to please her. Deviation from the blessed pattern will bring bad luck. This does not mean that the use of the ani-ani solely rests on prejudice. On the contrary, one can easily see that it has a lot of advantages when compared to the sickle - it is easily handled, careful and accurate. The traditional rice varieties in Java are fragile, so that the use of the sickle can cause serious losses of mature grains falling to the ground. (A traditional Javanese peasant would, however, express the negative aspect of grain losses by saying that the goddess is crying.)

Clifford Geertz seems to consider the reaping method through the use of the ani-ani, 'the stalk-by-stalk not to say grain-by-grain cultivation', as one more instance of agricultural involution.[46] For our part, we see the use of the ani-ani as stemming more from the general nature of rice agriculture.[47]

As Wittfogel has pointed out, with the invention of artificial irrigation, socially working man had found a new 'nature-machine', leading to garden-like intensification such as rainfall agriculture does not know.[48] Production in irrigated rice agriculture depends on the carefulness of the labourer. Wet-rice cultivation is characterized by a sort of man's negative and indirect action on the plant. There is so to speak no brutal contact in space, nor any overlap in time with the object. The use of, say, a mower and the accompanying vigorous movements would not, as it were, be very conducive to this garden-like agriculture. On the contrary, the ani-ani 'fits' into the pattern. A particular technology like that of the ani-ani is further accompanied by corresponding movements, myths and customs, and the change of a tool cannot be seen in isolation from the totality in which it has its meaning. The change of tool is therefore tantamount to a change of a way of life, bringing in its train important consequences for the whole collectivity. This can easily be seen in the transformation from *bawon/ani-ani* to *tebasan/sickle*. From this can be grasped perhaps, why 'simple' technical changes might be accompanied by fierce resistence and 'inertia' by the collectivity in question. As A.G. Haudricourt puts it:

> Chaque technique comporte donc l'emploi et l'acquisition de gestes. Par l'étude de l'outil, de sa forme, de la manière de le tenir et de l'utiliser, nous rejoignons ainsi l'homme non pas un homme abstrait, . . . mais un homme vivant dans un certain milieu et accoutumé à tout un ensemble d'habitudes et d'attitudes qui caractérisent, comme l'outillage lui-même, le groupe humain auquel il appartient . . . Changer d'outils - *[*for instance from the ani-ani to the sickle*]* - c'est non seulement adopter un nouvel instrument de travail, mais c'est aussi souvent le bouleversement de tout un système, de tout un rythme de travail; on comprend mieux des lors certaines résistances collectives ou individuelles.[49]

For instance, the Badui in the highlands of West Java, who live in a sea of wet-rice agriculture, still have not adopted the use of the hoe, the plough, the water-buffalo, and irrigation agriculture. They consider it dangerous to abandon slash-and-burn (*ladang*/swidden) agriculture and the digging-stick.[50]

Among the villagers in Bangsal, it is of no wonder that the strongest resistance against change is to be found among the poor and the landless. As to the 'agents' of change, they seem to be the not-too-big peasants, those who are not dependent on participating in bawon for their living and yet are not in a position to engage in usurious crop-lending. The rich peasants and landowners, on the other hand, seem rather reluctant to adopt tebasan, at least in its present shape. The rich peasants owe a large part of their income to the fact that they can sell a surplus of rice at high prices in between harvests.[51] They are hence not interested in parting with their rice at harvest time when the prices are lower.[52] Should it be possible to lower the costs of harvesting without the farmer's having to sell his whole crop (for example by acting as penebas on his own land), however, it is clear that these rich farmers would then not be so reluctant to adopt the practice. Is it an 'inherent' tendency in the tebasan system which points in that direction?

Earlier we said that agricultural labour relations in Bangsal were characterized by the formal submission of labour under capital, i.e. the production of absolute surplus-value. This production distinguishes itself from the earlier system of production only in a formal sense. This is, for instance, the case of an independent peasant who becomes a day-labourer on his own land. There exists an economic relation of domination from the fact that the capitalist consumes the labour power and thus supervises it and directs it. Between the owner of the conditions of labour and the worker there is a purely monetary relationship, a relationship of buying and selling. But there is no innovation in the process of production itself, which goes on in the same way as earlier.

It is our contention that the introduction of tebasan will eventually lead to the formal subsumption of labour under capital in a new domain, that of harvesting. Further, with the introduction of hullers, one can speak of perhaps the first instance in Javanese peasant agriculture of the *real* subsumption of labour under capital; in this case we can speak of the production of relative surplus value. As in the case of hullers, we think that in tebasan the tendency is in the direction of the workers being paid a time wage, i.e. a daily or half-daily wage as such as it is with ordinary agricultural labour in Bangsal. The worker might even be paid an hourly wage, the price of the working hour being the quotient of the value of a day's labour power, divided by the number of hours of the average working day. The total number of workers is reduced in both cases and in contrast to the destructive consequences of overwork, here we find the sources of the suffering of the labourer to be from his insufficient employment.[53]

It might seem a little far-fetched to read such a tendency into tebasan, as tebasan labourers are paid according to the quantity cut by each one, in principle just like the bawon harvesters. As we noted earlier, nominally tebasan is a way of selling a crop which has some legitimacy in the Javanese adat or customary law. The traditional tebasan, however, did not imply a harvesting method different from the bawon system. From the way that tebasan is actually conducted, it becomes clear that we must look outside the realm of adat in order to find precedents to the new way of rice harvesting. *Such precedents can be found: in fact, the way of harvesting 'palawija' (all crops other than rice), is clearly a model for 'tebasan'.*

Palawija particularly refers to those crops that are grown during the dry season from May to October, including such crops as maize, soya, onions and cassava. These crops have been introduced in Indonesia from the sixteenth century onwards, however, they did not become widespread before the turn of the century. In this century their importance has increased greatly. Maize and cassava are grown both for subsistence as well as for marketing, while onions and soya are typical high-risk cash-crops. They all have one important thing in common if compared to rice: their commercial treatment. Their very introduction in the first place can be seen as a response to the necessity to meet new monetary demands (increased taxes, etc.). Maize, which is very common in the district of Mojokuto, has for a long time been harvested under a system very similar to that of tebasan. A farmer sells his crop to a contractor or wholesaler. The latter comes to the farmer's land on harvest day bringing with him his own hired workers and an ox-cart or even a truck to transport the corn. The workers cut the corn by using *sickles* and *they receive ordinary wages (usually on a daily basis)*. In the similarity between this harvesting system and tebasan, we have perhaps the best illustration of how rice has become a commodity and can now be treated as just another cash-crop.

In our view, what happens here is the tebasan farmers *employing* 'the traditional form of production, . . . a form "known and understood by all", *to organize new relations of production'*.[54] Writing in quite a different connection about the integration of former independent 'primary communities' into the Inca 'Asiatic mode of production', Godelier has eloquently defined the phenomenon referred to above in the following terms:

> Donc, d'une facon générale le nouveau mode de production prenait *appui* sur les rapports de production . . . existants pour les bouleverser. Il y a donc là une mécanisme d'extension de ces rapports au-délà de leur sphère d'origine, de fonctionnement originaire.[55]

What is happening with the introduction of tebasan is the use of one element in the Javanese customary law to introduce new relations of production in harvesting which have no basis in that same law. Our thesis that there is a tendency in the direction of more and more labour becoming wage-labour is strengthened by the fact that one commonly employs the sickle to cut the rice. The rise in productivity implicit in the change of harvesting tool from ani-ani to sickle will benefit the owner of the crop most if the harvesters are not paid for their labour (as is the case of the harvesters receiving a fixed share of the crop regardless of the tool) but for their labour-power. In this latter case, the labour of the harvesters will be the property of the crop-owner. Further, labour-power is most commonly paid a time-wage. The use of sickles thus has meaning to a crop-owner if it reduces the time for which he has to hire harvesters.

So far, however, the process described above is only in its initial stages.[56] Still we feel we have shown that instead of tenure systems growing 'more intricate', tenancy relationships 'more complicated' and co-operative labour arrangements 'more complex',[57] economic relations are becoming more and more uniform and simple with wage-labour as the standard.

3.3 The Immediate Causes for the Introduction of Tebasan and Hullers

Finally we have to answer the question of why tebasan and hullers have been introduced just *now* instead of, say, twenty years ago. We have mentioned above that in the 1930s, a farmer who tried to introduce the sickle in the harvest would have 'ostracized himself' (Wertheim). The process of commercialization that we have discussed at length is, after all, only a *necessary precondition* for the introduction of tebasan and hullers. In addition we have to look briefly into the immediate causes, which we will limit to three: *the political factors*, the *green revolution*, and the *appearance of new products*.

(1) *Political Factors*. After the 1965 abortive coup d'état, the political situation in Indonesia has changed dramatically. Under the Sukarno regime the Indonesian Communist Party (PKI) was the largest communist party in the non-communist world.[58] Far from pursuing a radical policy of agricultural modernization, the party in the countryside represented a conservative force, often defending

the old communal institutions. Any attempt to modernize agriculture and to introduce labour-saving devices was effectively combatted by the peasant organizations of the Communist Party, the Barisan Tani Indonesia.

As a result of the political events at the national level in 1965, and as a consequence of the repercussions at the local level in that same year and later on, it has become possible for the landowners to escape the demands placed on them to underwrite with social expenditures the traditional ties with their fellows,

(2) *The Green Revolution*. The technology of the 'green revolution' implies that rice now is produced as a commodity. The industrial inputs of fertilizers, insecticides, etc., mean that the role of capital inputs is more important than before. The BIMAS credit further must be paid back, and this means that a relatively large part of the crop has to be immediately marketed to get the needed money. The higher yields obtained with the new High Yielding Variety rice types also induce the farmer to try to get as big a share of this surplus as possible, for after all, what is the use to the farmer of obtaining higher yields if it is only immediately spread among a large number of people?

The HYV rice are often not grown for the consumption needs of the farmer's family, the varieties (and the PB variety in particular) being considered inferior in taste and even 'unfit for humans', as one peasant puts it. Frequently, the bigger peasants would grow good-quality rice for their families'needs in one plot, the rest of the land being set aside for the HYV rice. In this case, the distinction between rice as a subsistence crop and as a cash-crop appears openly.

The HYV rice is more fit for the use of the sickle. It is more sturdy than the traditional Java-rice. With the very new varieties c-4 and 'pekdok' (the latter being directly sown by strewing and not needing to be transplanted from a seedbed as earlier), the sickle is almost indispensable. These varieties are very short and one has to bend lower in order to cut them. Often they are cut by a team of two men, one holding several stalks together as a bundle and the other cutting them with the sickle.

The traditional aversions against the use of a harvesting tool other than the ani-ani for fear of Dewi Sri is also weaker in the case of the new varieties. These latter being of foreign origin, it is said, Dewi Sri doesn't really care if the sickle is used to harvest them.

(3) *New Products*. In the wake of the political changes at the national level after 1965, a whole new economic policy

different from that of Sukarno's radical nationalism has been inaugurated. Heavy foreign investments have been made in various sectors of the national economy and this new policy is felt as well in the countryside. In Bangsal, for instance, a Japanese company has taken over the sugar factory earlier owned by the Dutch, using it for processing jute (*rami*).[59] Together with foreign investments there has been a flooding of the market by new foreign products. In many respects this has completely changed the life-style of at least a small well-off section of the village population.

As an illustration can be mentioned that even after the National Revolution, 1945-9, in Sarangmanuk only two persons owned a bicycle. Today there are more than 50 Hondas, Yamahas and other Japanese-manufactured motor-bicycles in Bangsal, all since 1965. In short, with the new products there also arose the need for them. One can hardly exaggerate the impact of the new wants on village life. A motor-cycle costs 400,000 rupiahs, compared to the most expensive status symbol earlier, the bicycle, which costs 20,000 rupiahs (not to speak of the daily wage rate of 60 to 120 rupiahs as noted earlier). Watches and transistor radios are rather common among the well-off peasants, and the landlords even compete among themselves as to who has the largest number of Mitsubishi minibuses, each one costing several million rupiahs.

The new tebasan system makes it possible to satisfy the wants for the new products through a *redistribution of income from the poorer bawon harvesters to the landowners*. As an example we can mention that after the first tebasan harvest in Sarangmanuk, the landowner bought himself a motor-cycle, while Pak Gatot, the penebas, bought a new casette-player complete with stereo loudspeakers, amplifier and, since there is no electricity in the village, a car battery to provide the needed power!

More than 65% of the total population of Indonesia is employed in the primary sector. For the enormous majority of peasants and agricultural labourers among Java's 90 million inhabitants, the participation in the harvest has for a long time been indispensable if they are to avoid outright hunger as a permanent way of life. The fast-spreading tebasan system and the introduction of hullers dramatically worsens the economic situation of the majority in radically reducing both the number of harvesters and the pay given, and also in limiting their work opportunities.

Faced with the challenge in their own village for the first time in the 1974 wet-season harvest, the inhabitants of Sarangmanuk reacted with both confusion and indignation. An attempt at boycott at harvest-time was made, but its effect was limited with an abundance of free farm-hands around. In a way the villagers seemed to hope that tebasan was only a passing event and that the new 'fashion' would somehow blow over.

In this article we have stressed the difficulties facing the many poor villagers in Java as a consequence of the introduction of more rational agricultural techniques. We must not forget, however, that the changes have come about largely as a result of the national programme of the Indonesian governmental authorities for economic development. In this latter perspective, the fact must not be lost sight of that the earlier situation of 'shared poverty' meant a crippling of the possibilities for economic growth. The real tragedy in Java is not that the peasants suffered, and it may even seem that they have got off relatively lightly. Geertz has written, 'the tragedy is that it, *[the peasantry]*, suffered for nothing.'[60] Formerly the total social product was spread out over a multitude of hands, leading to general impoverishment and precluding savings, not intestments, in the economy, and thus also eventually growth. The present development points to an expanded market economy in that commodities are now produced and bought that formerly existed as natural products consumed by the producers themselves. The ruin of the small producers, it must not be forgotten, does not imply a shrinkage of the home market. On the contrary, a decline in well-being is compatible with an increase in the amount of money in possession. This is so because a relatively greater part of the means of subsistence is now to be acquired in the market. On the other hand, in order that real economic take-off is to come about, it is necessary for the well-off peasants to invest their greatly increased wealth in production projects, and not to waste it on conspicuous consumption. Whether this will actually happen, it is too early to judge, but in this lies the kingpin as to whether real economic growth in agriculture in Java will take place. Thus a heavy historic responsibility is weighing on the shoulders of the village entrepreneurs in Indonesia in the time ahead.

NOTES

1 This essay is a revised and extended version of a paper by *Lien Pekih Aass*, "Harvesting Methods and Rural Change. A Case study of a Javanese Village".

2 *Bangsal* is the fictitious name given to our village by the M.I.T. group. We thought it simpler to continue the use of the name.

3 *Dewey, A.*, Peasant Marketing in Java. New York 1962; *Geertz, C.*, The Religion of Java. New York 1960; *Geertz, C.*, The Social History of an Indonesian Town. Cambridge 1965; *Geertz, C.*, Agricultural Involution. The Processes of Ecological Change in Indonesia. Berkeley 1970; *Geertz, H.*, The Javanese Family. New York 1962; *Jay, R.*, Javanese Villagers. Social Relations in Rural Modjokuto. Cambridge 1969.

4 *Statistical Pocketbook of Indonesia, 1971* (Jakarta, 1971), p. 24.

5 Limiting ourselves to a discussion of economic issues in this study, we will not elaborate further on the religious schism in the village. The religious conflict between the orthodox Muslim villagers (*santri*) and the majority who are only nominally Muslim, is a very harsh and bitter one. This conflict, not at all unrelated to the general socio-economic and political cleavages in Java, we hope to describe closer in a later study.

6 There are over 14 useful plants in our hosts' compound: fruit trees such as the banana, papaya and mango trees, coconut palms, roots such as cassava and sweet potatoes, sugar cane, and various other vegetables such as egg-plant, *bayem* (a type of spinach), peppers, as well as other plants used as spices and medicine.

7 According to a pre-war study by G.J. Vink, there was an average pre-harvest labour-use of 151 man-days per hectare, *Vink, G.J.*, De grondslagen van het indonesische Landbouwbedrijf. Wageningen 1941.
The Agro-Economic Survey of Indonesia found the average to be 284.5 man-days per hectare for the HYV rice, *Agro-Economic Survey of Indonesia*, Research Note no. 8, Bogor 1973.

8 *Angladette, A.*, Le riz. Paris 1967.

9 *Nyantri* is the verb form of *santri*, religious pupil, which today has the connotation of one who is strongly religious. Earlier this word apparently had another meaning.

10 For the most part, households are made up of the nuclear family, with a good number being three generation house-

holds. The exceptions are households made up of widowed mothers or fathers with their children, or nuclear families plus househelp and relatives in need.

11 The legal title of the land rests with the state.

12 *White, B.,* The Economic Importance of Children in a Javanese Village. December 1972 (mimeo.).

13 Harvesting was traditionally reserved for women.

14 *Geertz, C.,* Agricultural . . . and *Jay, R.,* Javanese . . .

15 In Sarangmanuk there was one case of *mertelu* (1:2) sharecropping carried out between siblings. *Utami, W., & Ihalauw, J.,* Some Consequences of Small Farm Size (in: Bulletin of Indonesian Economic Studies, 9:2, 1973), notes that in the area they studied (Kabupaten Klaten in Central Java), the *mrapat* (1:3) sharecropping system is the most common method of tenure in the villages.

16 *Gotong-Royong* is further still widespread in house-building, weddings, etc.

17 *Burger, D.H.,* Rapport over de desa Pekalongan in 1868 en 1928 (Economische beschrijvingen I, 1928). Professor Burger in this study noted that in Pekalongan (Central Java) in 1868, the *bawon* was between 1/3 to 1/5. In 1928 this had gone down to 1/6-1/8 or even 1/12 in the surrounding villages.

18 *Wertheim, W.F.,* Social Change in Java, 1900-30 (in: Wertheim, W.F., East-West Parallels, the Hague 1964).

19 *Agro-Economic Survey of Indonesia,* Research Note no. 11, Bogor 1974. *Collier, W. & Wiradi, G. & Soentono,* Recent Changes in Rice Harvesting Methods (in: Bulletin of Indonesian Economic Studies, 9:2, 1973).

20 *Haar, B. ter,* Asas-asas dan susunan hukum adat(Jakarta 1960), p. 129.

21 The most widespread of usurious crop practices, however, is *ijon* (from green), where a creditor takes security in the debtor's crop while it is still green.

22 We noticed from our observations that the process of weighing is accompanied by the *penebas* grossly cheating the inexperienced peasants.

23 The difference 1:3.5 indicated is levelled out a little as the paddy (unhusked rice) received as *bawon* has to be dried and hulled before consumption/cooking.

24 *Geertz, C.,* Agricultural . . .

25 Ibid., p. 82.

26 *Boeke, J.H.,* Economics and Economic Policy of Dual Societies (Haarlem 1953), p. 27.

27 *Geertz, C.*, Agricultural . . ., p. 97.
28 *Furnival, J.S.*, Netherlands India (Cambridge 1937), p. 140.
29 *Wolf, E.*, Closed Corporate Peasant Communities in Meso-america and Java (in: Southwestern Journal of Anthropology, 13, 1957).
30 *Haar, B. ter*, Asas-asas . . ., p. 93.
31 *Jay, R.*, Javanese . . .
32 *Wolf, E.*, Closed . . .
33 *Wolf, E.*, Sons of the Shaking Earth (Chicago, 1959), p. 216.
34 Ibid., p. 216.
35 *Wolf, E.*, Peasants (Englewood Cliffs 1966), p. 7.
36 *Haar, B. ter*, Asas-asas . . ., p. 16.
37 Ibid., p. 89
38 *Bouloiseau, M.*, Communautés rurales et droits collectifs avant et pendant la révolution (in: L'abolition de la 'féodalité' dans le monde occidental, tome 1, Paris 1971).
39 '. . . les usages forestiers tiennent particulièrement à coeur aux paysans.' Ibid.
40 The concentration on labour-intensive rice cultivation makes the common rights to be mainly *positive* ones, i.e. the rights of all to a share in the total finished product.
41 *Boeke, J.H.*, Economics . . ., p. 34
42 *Wolf, E.*, Peasants . . ., p. 16.
43 The millenarian and communal peasant movements early in this century attacked Islam for being 'capitalistic' in its laws of inheritance according to which private property can be inherited.
44 This sect can be seen as a Javanese version of the ethos of capitalism that Max Weber has seen incarnated in the early Protestantism in Europe.
45 *Raffles, T.S.*, The History of Java. London 1817.
46 *Geertz, C.*, Agricultural . . ., p. 101.
47 It has a long history in Java and is mentioned in *Raffles, T.S.*, The History . . .
48 *Wittfogel, K.A.*, Die Theorie der orientalischen Gesellschaft (in: Zeitschrift für Sozialforschung, 7, 1938).
49 *Haudricourt, A.G. & Delmarre, M.J.-B.*, L'homme et la charrue, (Paris 1955), p. 33.
50 *Gourou, P.*, L'Asie (Paris 1971), p. 99.
51 The difference in the cost of rice at harvest time and in the low season can be very substantial. The PB variety (unhulled) cost 5,000 rps/kwt in December 1973.

In March 1974 the price dropped to 3,500 rps/kwt. Often the villagers are forced to borrow cash during the low period and pay back in rice at harvest time. A loan of 2,500 rps at *paceklik* (worth 0.5 kwt of rice) has to be paid back at harvest with one kwt. In general, interest rates are never less than 5% per month and usually higher.

52 An interesting parallel is given by van der Kolff in his study of the introduction of the *ngedok* system mentioned above. In the first decade of our century *ngedok* was a new form of tenancy. Van der Kolff writes: 'It was particularly the less well-to-do peasants who were favoured by the system (i.e. *ngedok*). It relieved them from the necessity of providing for those called in to assist with a meal.' On the contrary 'the more wealthy preferred to continue using the old system (i.e. of providing workers with a meal and a right of a part in the harvest), because they had the necessary help available at home and also an abundance of victuals'. *Kolff, G.H. van der,* The Historical Developement of the Labour Relationships in a Remote Corner of Java as They Apply to the Cultivation of Rice. New York 1957.

53 The agricultural workers have responded by threatening to raise the daily wages for agricultural labour to compensate for the loss from not receiving *bawon* any longer. However, the very fact that labour is now in even greater abundance than earlier does not put them in a favourable position.

54 *Godelier, M.,* Horizon, trajets marxistes en anthropologie (Paris 1973), p. 90. A similar case is found in the change from mutual labour exchange *(sambatan)* to wage labour, where the latter was justified with reference to the former and *adat* as implying an exchange of equivalence. The only difference was said to be that while in the former case two individuals would exchange labour, in the latter case, labour was exchanged with its equivalent in kind or money. *(Kolff, G.H. van den,* The Historical . . .)

55 Ibid., p. 90.

56 Drs. S. Hardjosudarmo mentions that '*bawon* which earlier was in paddy is now beginning to be paid in money at the basis of the wage level for women which exists in the particular agricultural areas'. *Hardjosudarmo, S.,* Massalah tanah di Indonesia (Jakarta 1970), p. 90. It is interesting to note that the biggest landlord in Sarangmanuk (15 ha) who was not in favour of the present *tebasan* system himself

offered the harvesters a daily wage of 100 rps. His offer was firmly rebuffed.

57 *Geertz, C.,* Agricultural . . ., p. 82.

58 *Pauker, G.,* The Rise and Fall of the Communist Party of Indonesia. St. Monica: Rand Corporation, USAF Project 1969.

59 The jute is grown on the land held in *hak pakai* or 'right of use'. In return the peasants receive a fixed rent, the sum being fixed by the government.

60 *Geertz, C.,* Agricultural . . ., p. 143.

BIBLIOGRAPHY

Agro-Economic Survey of Indonesia, Research Note no. 8, Bogor 1973.

Agro-Economic Survey of Indonesia, Research Note no. 11, Bogor 1974.

Angladette, A., Le riz. Paris 1967.

Boeke, J.H., Economics and Economic Policy of Dual Societies. Haarlem 1953.

Bouloiseau, M., Communautés rurales et droits collectifs avant et pendant la révolution (in: L'abolition de la 'féodalité'dans le monde occidental, tome 1, Paris 1971).

Burger, D.H., Rapport over de desa Pekalongan in 1868 en 1928 (Economische beschrijvingen I, 1928).

Collier, W. & Wiradi, G & Soentono, Recent Changes in Rice Harvesting Methods (in: Bulletin of Indonesian Economic Studies, 9:2, 1973).

Dewey, A., Peasant Marketing in Java. New York 1962.

Furnival, J.S., Netherlands India. Cambridge 1937.

Geertz, C., The Religion of Java. New York 1960.

Geertz, C., The Social History of an Indonesian Town. Cambridge 1965.

Geertz, C., Agricultural Involution. The Processes of Ecological Change in Indonesia. Berkeley 1970.

Geertz, H., The Javanese Family. New York 1962.

Godelier, M., Horizons, trajets marxistes en anthropologie. Paris 1973.

Gourou, P., L'Asie. Paris 1971.

Haar, B. ter, Asas-asas dan susunan hukum adat. Jakarta 1960.

Hardjosudarmo, S., Massalah tanah di Indonesia. Jakarta 1970.

Haudricourt, A.G. & Delamarre, M.J.-B., L'homme et la charrue. Paris 1955.

Jay, R., Javanese Villagers. Social Relations in Rural Modjokuto. Cambridge 1969.

Kolff, G.H. van der, The Historical Development of the Labour Relationships in a Remote Corner of Java as They Apply to the Cultivation of Rice. New York 1957.

Pauker, G., The Rise and Fall of the Communist Party of Indonesia. St Monica: Rand Corporation, USAF Project 1969.

Raffles, T.S., The History of Java. London 1817.

Statistical Pocketbook of Indonesia 1971. Jakarta 1971.

Utami, W. & Ihalauw, J., Some Consequences of Small Farm Size (in: Bulletin of Indonesian Economic Studies, 9:2 1973).

Vink, G., De grondslagen van het indonesische landbouwbedrijf. Wageningen 1941.

Bibliography

Wertheim, W.F., Social Change in Java, 1900-30 (in: Wertheim, W.F., East-West Parallels, The Hague 1964).

White, B., The Economic Importance of Children in a Javanese Village. December 1972 (mimeo.).

Wittfogel, K.A., Die Theorie der orientalischen Gesellschaft (in: Zeitschrift für Sozialforschung, 7, 1938).

Wolf, E., Closed Corporate Peasant Communities in Mesoamerica and Java (in: Southwestern Journal of Anthropology, 13, 1957).

Wolf, E., Sons of the Shaking Earth. Chicago 1959.

Wolf, E., Peasants. Englewood Cliffs 1966.

LAND AND LABOUR IN WEST LOMBOK: NON-INVOLUTIONARY CHANGE

Ingela Gerdin

INTRODUCTION

Lombok is one of those densely populated islands with wet rice cultivation that make up Inner Indonesia. Clifford Geertz, contrasting Inner and Outer Indonesia,[1] holds forth that there has been a process of agricultural involution going on in the Inner Islands. This process he characterizes as

> increasing tenacity of basic pattern; internal elaboration and ornateness; technical hairsplitting and unending virtuosity . . . tenure systems grew more intricate; tenancy relationships more complicated; co-operative labour arrangements more complex - all in an effort to provide everyone with some niche, however small, in the overall system.[2]

Though the argument is primarily based on data from the parts of Java where the so-called Cultivation System was enforced by the Dutch colonial government in the nineteenth century, Geertz argues that today 'the sharpness of the line between "inner Inner Indonesia" and "Inner Indonesia" generally has been thoroughly blurred. What was once a local pathology is now an epidemic disease'.[3] Lombok would be one of the 'less involuted areas', still the same process would be discernible there according to Geertz.

Using data from Lombok, A. Polak has tried to test Geertz' hypothesis on agricultural involution by determining whether or not there has been rising productivity per hectare through the application of more intensive labour methods while yield per capita has remained fixed or declined. He concludes that 'pertinent facts unearthed constitute far too shaky a foundation upon which to build with confidence'[4] - a conclusion that seems to hold for the Javanese case too.[5]

The present study takes a somewhat different point of departure: major changes of property and labour relations taking place on the West Lombok scene during the last century are outlined and the present-day situation is examined more fully in terms of land control and labour relations in the agricultural sector.[6] I am arguing that in the densely populated plains of West Lombok there has not been an increasing complexity of forms but rather a shift from certain forms of land tenure and labour relations to other forms. There has not been a process of involution but rather a progressive process of change where land and labour have become commodities, and instead of niches being created for everyone, there has been a separation of the producer from the means of production and a more precarious situation for those, who have no land of their own.

1. *PRE-COLONIAL WEST LOMBOK*

The island of Lombok is situated just east of Bali and is of approximately the same size as Bali. Though rather small, both of the islands housed several kingdoms in pre-colonial times. These kingdoms were not clear-cut geographical entities with defined borders but rather areas of influence that were constituted by control of specified groups of peasants and ties of allegiance between noble houses.

At the beginning of the eighteenth century, one of the major Balinese dynasties had managed to gain a footing in the western part of Lombok and gradually extended its influence until it had the acknowledged suzerainty over the indigenous Sasak dynasties in the eastern and northern parts of the island. Balinese lords with their retinues settled in the plains of West Lombok, an area which at that time was 'still forest', i.e. not within the firm influence of any previous ruling houses. It is said that the irrigation system and the fertile *sawah* complexes of West Lombok were constructed under Balinese supervision, Sasak labour force being brought there from other, more densely populated parts of the island.[7] The construction of the irrigation system was a public work carried out by and for the community with the ruling dynasty as organizer, but generally depicted by indigenous sources as the sole accomplishment of the ruling dynasty.[8] The king as a reincarnation of Wishnu was considered to be the spiritual embodiment of fresh water, i.e. water that could be used for irrigation. The ruling houses were the sponsors and organizers of ceremonies for promoting the overall fertility, and they controlled and co-ordinated the irrigation through special officials who supervised the constructions and the distribution of water. In 'exchange' for irrigation water, each cultivator had to give a small amount of rice to the ruling dynasty, the amount of rice being proportional to the calculated amount of water used. This fee was termed *suwinih* or *panumbas toya*,[9] the last term literally meaning 'water purchase'.

Sasak and Balinese traditional world views depict water, land and all other resources as ultimately belonging to the gods,[10] and the gods are essentially the same as the most elevated ancestors. The living held rights in land[11] as members of certain descent-lines. Actually, there were a series of rights pertaining to land, and Dutch scholars studying Indonesian land tenure have worked with a distinction between *beschikkingsrecht,* i.e. rights of disposal, and *bewerkingsrecht,* i.e. rights of cultivation or utlilization.[12] M. Gluckman, studying land tenure in Africa, reformulated these concepts as 'estates of administration' *(beschikkings-recht)* and'rights of production' *(bewerkingsrecht),* where 'administration' covers the powers to allocate the land further, to control and regulate its use and to defende it against trespassers. Gluckman has chosen the concept of 'estate' to 'bring out . . . the close connection of land-holding with status'. He distinguishes between primary, secondary, tertiary, etc, estates of administration, in order to be able to account for series of allocation of land.[13] Thus, in a chain of distribution of administrative rights, such as from ruler to official to headman, the ruler holds the primary estate of administration, the official the secondary and the headman the tertiary estate. This terminology is easily applied to a discussion of certain series of rights and will be used in the account below. But I will also make a distinction between sovereignty, i.e. political relations of superiority-subordination, and property relations, i.e. 'rights held by persons/groups against other persons/groups with regard to land'.[14]

In the latter half of the eighteenth century, some two-thirds of the cultivated land in West Lombok fell within the estate of administration of the supreme ruling house, and was cultivated by peasants with hereditary rights of production who had to perform labour services and deliver products to their lords.[15] Besides this category of land, termed *druwe dalem,* there were also secondary estates of administration attached to high offices, and produce from some land was set aside as revenue for lower offices and for maintenance of irrigation constructions, temples and mosques. Although much of the land was administered by the supreme house, other houses or descent-lines also had estates of administration *(druwe jaba).* The native terms for these estates, *druwe dalem* and *druwe jaba,* might be translated as a 'property of the inside' and 'property of the outside' where 'inside' and 'outside' refer to whether the rights to land and labour fell directly within the jurisdiction of the supreme ruling house or were allocated outside it, as secondary estates of administration.

Inside versus outside (centre versus periphery) is a notion of a hierarchical relationship common in Balinese and Sasak culture, also having implications of superior versus subordinate position and higher versus lower rank. The supreme house was the sovereign of other ruling houses, and holders of *druwe jaba* were supposed to assist in the military undertakings of the holder of *druwe dalem*, to pay a formal tribute to his ceremonies and at least theoretically to get permission from the supreme house, if they wanted to pawn or alienate *drewe jaba* rights.

Since the distinction between *druwe dalem* and *druwe jaba* was dependent on the political relations between houses, it was not defined once-and-for-all. If a subordinate house became more powerful, it might claim an independent status and thus a primary estate of administration so that *druwe jaba* would be converted to *druwe dalem,* and the reverse process also took place, as was the case for the Sasak dynasties in East Lombok after the Balinese take-over of supreme power. The only case of a once-and-for-all defined secondary or lower estate of administration would be that of a commoner house that had been granted rights of administration, since commoner houses could never aspire to a ruling position in the same way as noble houses.[16]

Thus, the distinction between *druwe dalem* and *druwe jaba* was one of relative sociopolitical position of the holders of the estates - but not one of different rights to the produce from the land. The holders of *druwe dalem* and *druwe jaba* had rights of disposal not only over land but also over people - as the Balinese phrase it: they 'owned' land and they 'owned' people. The holder of such an estate of administration had the right to appropriate a stipulated amount of produce from the land (i.e. surplus product) and could also demand labour and special services from the peasants *(heerendiensten),*[17] usually not specified in duration of time but in type of tasks: maintenance of palaces and temples, preparations for ceremonies sponsored by the holder of the estate. The supreme ruling house also directed *heerendiensten* to public undertakings such as maintenance of roads and of state temples.

The peasants held inalienable and hereditary rights of production in land and could never be ousted unless there was a failure to deliver the stipulated amount of tribute to the holder of the rights of administration or a major crime was committed. Neither could the producer break loose from land except by permission from the ruling house and the estate-holder, that is to switch from one estate to another. Ideally, the producer was inseparable from the means of production.

Rights of production were hereditary but only in the direct descending patri-line. When a peasant, holding rights of production, died without leaving male descendants, the disposal of these rights went to the holder of the estate of administration who could redistribute them as he wished. But the holder of the estate of administration still had rights to their labour, only now they worked directly for his household and received their means of subsistence from the supply of this household.[18]

If rights of production formerly held by a peasant reverted to the estate of administration, because the peasant lacked direct descendants who were entitled to inherit them, the holder of the estate of administration could redistribute these rights to another producer. Usually, the rights of production were redistributed for good and became the hereditary and inalienable rights of the producer, and in this way land and labour as an inseparable unity were reproduced. But there were also instances where the holder of the estate did not redistribute the rights of production for good but had his land worked by share-croppers with no permanent rights to use the land *(tanah pengancil)*.

There was a kind of bidding system, where the one who offered to deliver the largest amount of rice to the landowner would get the share-cropping contract.[19] The contract was a personal, temporary agreement between the landlord and the share-cropper, and could be terminated by either party as soon as one year of cultivation had passed. There were not necessarily any other ties or loyalties between the landlord and the share-cropper, and when the contract ceased, neither party could make any claims on the other (in contrast to the state of things in the estates of *druwe dalem* and *druwe jaba*, where the estate-holder had the right to the labour of the former peasants but also the obligation to support them). Contrasted to *druwe dalem* and *druwe jaba*, *tanah pengancil* represented a first step in a process of dissolution of the unity of land and labour.

In the contracts pertaining to *tanah pengancil*, no *heerendiensten* or other services were included, but the landowner's share of rice was higher than that for irrigated ricefields in the estates of *druwe dalem* and *druwe jaba*. It seems that it was primarily those who 'owned' many people, and therefore controlled more labour than could be channelled into ceremonies, temple and palace constructions etc., who were interested in transforming *druwe dalem* or *druwe jaba* into *tanah pengancil*.[20] A surplus of rice could be sold, and there was a large export of rice from Lombok. A substantial part of the incomes from the selling of rice was used for purchase of 'modern' weapons - the rivalry between different ruling houses and dynasties led to an armaments competition in small scale, and the presence of the Dutch in the archipelago further necessitated armament. Long-distance trade also brought luxury goods such as silk and European liquor to the courts and other rich houses - Lombok was known for the extravagant life led by many a rich household. Since trading activities were despised and contradictory to the Balinese and Sasak view on wealth as an automatic effect of concentration of power (to primarily seek wealth would more or less imply a non-power position), the indigenous ruling houses were not apt to do the trading themselves. But ruling houses still made profits on trade by customs and contracts on shares of the profit made by foreign traders (Chinese, Arabs and Bugis as well as Europeans) who were granted trading rights in the realm. All export and import trade was strictly controlled by the houses in power and the freedom of movement of the foreigners was circumscribed so that they were more or less confined to the ports and had to use middlemen for trading with the local population.[21] Though the foreign traders never entered the local market places themselves, their activities must have had effects on the internal trade. But even if products were bought and sold, neither land nor labour were yet full-fledged commodities. True, rights in land could be alienated, but only with consent from those who held superior rights of administration and ultimately by the supreme ruling house in that hierarchy of rights. The only officially accepted reason for alienating land rights was need for resources to carry out death ceremonies for deceased family members - a concern not only for the descendants of the deceased but also for the whole community, since not yet cremated souls were seen as potentially dangerous, threatening order, prosperity and fertility.

In the 1890s, the majority of the peasants still had hereditary rights of production. It remains an open question as to whether the rivalry between different houses and dynasties in combination with large-scale trade giving the possibility of selling rice and buying foreign goods would have increased the frequency of short-term share-cropping contracts of the type applying to *tanah pengancil* at the expense of the dominant estates of *druwe dalem* and *druwe jaba*. In 1894, the Dutch invaded Lombok and, after three months of heavy fighting, managed to defeat the ruling dynasty burdened at that time with a severe civil war on its hands.

2. COLONIAL WEST LOMBOK

After the Dutch take-over, the land of the former supreme ruling house was confiscated and declared Crown land *(staatsdomein)*, with the villages as 'owners' of the land (a regulation that never had any practical consequences). The peasants holding rights of production in these *druwe dalem* lands would still have hereditary and inalienable rights. *Druwe jaba*, on the other hand, was declared the private property of those holding rights of administration in such land, and could be bought, sold and pawned - thus, at least legally, it was a commodity that could be circulated without any of the former restrictions. While the hereditary rights of production held by peasants working *druwe dalem* land were acknowledged, the status of those working *druwe jaba* land but not holding the rights of administration over that land was left unclear: the Dutch legislation did not treat the question of whether this category had hereditary rights of production or only temporary contracts (though it seems that the Dutch inclined towards the second alternative).[22] In effect, this question was left to be regulated by the holders of the rights of administration. In the thirties, Dutch sources indicate that peasants working *druwe jaba* land had only temporary rights of production[23] - i.e. the same situation as that in the former *tanah pengancil* - but how this change took place is unfortunately not documented.

At the turn of the century, the distribution of *druwe jaba* and *druwe dalem* in West Lombok was measured.[24] (see Table 1)

TABLE 1.

Type of land	Total measured (hectare)	*Druwe dalem* (percentage)	*Druwe jaba* (percentage)
Irrigated rice fields *(Sawah)*	23,466	65.5	34.5
Dry land *(Kebun & tegalan)*	6,072	76.5	23.5

Whereas the former supreme ruling house had merely appropriated surplus products from *druwe dalem* land, the Dutch levied a land tax from both types of domains. The tax on irrigated land was the most important source of revenue for the colonial state[25] and even if some of it was used for irrigation constructions and other public works, a surplus was constantly drawn from the island. Most public works were carried out by use of *heerendiensten*, though, and did not encumber the state funds. *Heerendiensten* were obligatory until 1929, when an ordinance was issued stating that people could buy themselves free from these labour services - they were indeed exhorted to do so.

The more well-off groups to a large degree did buy themselves off from these duties, whereas poorer groups were not in a position to do so. By this measure the colonial government wanted to make labour more efficient by employing wage labour (Dutch officials complained that by using *heerendiensten*, the situation often developed into a social gathering rather than an occasion for work as the day went by).[26] That this system could be realized indicates that at the time a considerable number of people were willing to sell their labour-power in spite of the contempt held for this type of wage-labour in traditional Balinese and Sasak world views. Indeed, a large landless group had developed because of the inheritance rules applying to *druwe dalem* land where rights of production were indivisible even if there were several potential heirs.[27] Whereas *druwe jaba* land was divided between the heirs, *druwe dalem* land was passed on from father to eldest son or to the closest male relative, if sons were lacking. In the early thirties, the Assistant Resident of West Lombok remarked that on the one hand the restrictions placed on *druwe dalem* also restricted the possibilities for land accumulation on a few hands and kept land distributed among the peasants, but that on the other hand the type of inheritance resulted in a considerable part of the rural population not having any rights in land at all.[28]

Even if the law forbade transactions of *druwe dalem* land, the law could be evaded, though with difficulties, and some holders of rights of production in *druwe dalem* land were only nominally holding these rights. For example, some types of contracts officially classified as 'share-cropping contracts' - which were allowed - were in reality nothing but pawning or alienation of rights. The so-called share-cropper had forwarded a sum of money to the holder of rights of production, and the produce of the land was to go fully to the share-cropper as interest on the loan. This 'share-cropper' could in his turn let the land in share-cropping, and the rights of production could not be reclaimed by their former holder as long as the money was not paid back. When the Dutch government lifted the prohibition on buying and selling *druwe dalem* land in 1935 the frequency of land transactions registered by the government increased drastically.[29] and so did prices on some of the land because of clandestine alienation. Through this measure, *druwe dalem* peasants became legal holders of land as private property (while *druwe jaba* peasants had already become mere share-croppers), and all cultivated land (except land serving as revenue for certain offices and institutions) had legally as well as in practice become a commodity.

3. WEST LOMBOK IN THE 1970s

Today, labour as well as land, tools, and cattle are bought and sold. In the plains of West Lombok, land is the scarce asset in agricultural production. No land is left unused, and the fertile, densely populated plain is neatly chequered by irrigation canals and rice-fields. Roads and paths wind through this man-made landscape, where dark green spots of lush vegetation indicate villages and gardens. Most housing ground and cultivated land is private property, and in agriculture land is by far the most expensive production factor. Buying, selling and pawning land are frequent and common procedures. In a sample of 36 land-owning households, 23 households had bought or sold land, and of 80 landless households, there were 22 cases where the household itself or the parental generation had sold land. By contrast, only one of the present landowners had started from a position where he held no land of his own, and my informants unanimously state that it has become increasingly difficult to acquire land for someone starting from scratch. According to official records of ownership of irrigated land, compiled by A.M. Hartong[30] from village statistics (all villages of Lombok), approximately one-third of the population is landless, and land is distributed as shown in Table 2.

TABLE 2.

Size of holdings (ha)	Number of units
0.1 - 0.99	104,333
1.0 - 1.99	37,465
2.0 - 2.99	10,075
3.0 - 3.99	2,496
4.0 - 4.99	1,410
5.0 -	1,746

My own survey of 127 Balinese households in the village of Pagesangan and a survey of 40 Sasak households in the village of Kuranji give a somewhat different distribution. The relative amount of landless households is higher and that of smallholding peasants lower. Before giving the figures, I will provide some background data.

Pagesangan is a fairly large village of 10,000 inhabitants grouped in 15 *kampung* (wards), 6 Balinese and 9 Sasak ones. The village is situated only 3 km from the commercial and administrative centre of Lombok, but though there are frequent commercial contacts with town, agriculture is the most important sector of economic activities. Here, a survey was taken of two Balinese *kampung* that were considered to be neither excessively rich nor extremely poor.[31] For comparative purposes, 40 households in a purely Sasak village 4 km south of Pagesangan were surveyed. As this village was situated further away from town, very few people would ever go to town to trade or to look for temporary jobs, and almost 100 per cent of the 3,300 inhabitants were mainly working in the agricultural sector.

In Table 3, the distribution of irrigated land according to the surveys and to official figures for all Lombok is given.[32]

TABLE 3

Size of holdings	Percentage of households		
	Pagesangan	Kuranji	Total Lombok
No land	71.5	55	33.3
0 - 0.9	14.0	35	44.1
1 - 1.9	4.0	-	15.7
2 - 2.9	4.0	5	4.6
3 - 3.9	2.0	-	1.0
4 - 4.9	2.5	2.5	0.6
5 -	2.0	2.5	0.7

Both of the surveys show a higher percentage of landless households and a lower percentage of smallholders (less than 2 ha) than do the official figures.[33] There are several reasons for this. The first one, that comes to mind, is that land might be less equally distributed in the area where the surveys were taken than in other parts of Lombok. Indeed, in a few remote areas, where land is not a commodity and where there are strong restrictions on land transactions, almost every household has some land. Moreover, in the dry south of the island, almost all of the villagers have land, too, due to the special circumstances there: rainfed, not very fertile, *sawah*, periodic crop failures and no other opportunities for work make it virtually impossible to live in that area if not owning land or having other resources. But this is not the whole truth. The official figures are based on two sources: An estimate of the number of landless households is made by the village officials, while the distribution of land between different households is drawn from the registration of landownership carried out in connection with the intended land reform 1963. At that time, the guidelines for the reform were already laid down, and it was ruled that nobody in this densely populated area was allowed to hold more than 7 ha *sawah* land. This often led people owning more than the stipulated amount of land to try to register part of their land in the name of close relatives or other trusted persons. Another factor that will make distribution of land appear as more evenly spread than it in fact is, is that villages with their surrounding fields are the administrative units, and a person holding land in several village areas will be registered as holding several land-holding units, one in each village.[34]

Before proceeding with the conditions of work, I will present Table 4, describing the households on the basis of the type of economic activity they mainly depend upon. I say 'mainly', since many households are involved in more than one type of economic activity of importance; for example day labourers often engage in petty trade, and rich peasants in large-scale trade in rice and other agricultural products and may sometimes receive a substantial portion of their 'income' from these secondary activities. But even if many households are engaged in several types of economic activities, this is different from a situation of 'work spreading' as described by Geertz.[35] Table 4 illustrates a situation where a majority of the households may be said to live in poverty, but this does not imply that the poverty is 'shared' in the Geertzian sense.

In Table 4 the term 'peasant' is used to denote owners of land who actively participate in cultivation at least as managers of the production process, while the term 'landlord' is used for those landowners who let all their land in share-cropping.

Generally, the households in the 'poor peasant' category below must have additional sources of 'income'; share-cropping,

TABLE 4

Main 'occupation'	Percentage of households Pagesangan	Kuranji
Rich peasant/landlord having more than 4 ha *sawah*	3.9	5.0
Peasant having 2-3.99 ha *sawah*	6.3	5.0
'Self-sufficient' peasant having 0.5-1.9 ha *sawah*	11.0	7.5
Poor peasant having less than 0.5 ha *sawah*	7.1	27.5
Sharecropper	4.7	17.5
Owner of one or two heads of cattle (used for ploughing)	3.2	2.5
Day-labourer	49.6	35.0
Petty commodity producer (carpenter, tailor)	4.7	-
Butcher/trader	1.6	-
Employed labourer	1.6	-
Priest	1.6	-
Civil servant (teacher/ clerk/police)	4.7	-

petty trade or wage-labour, in order to be able to sustain themselves. Around one hectare of *sawah* would be just sufficient for maintaining an ordinary household[36] according to the accepted norm - and there is a definite norm for 'sufficiency' or minimal acceptable standard of living, denoted by the word *sangu*. Perhaps the best translation of the word *sangu* is 'enough': enough to eat each day, to hold the necessary life-cycle ceremonies at a moderate level etc., but not more, mere *sangu* does not allow for splendour.[37] People are almost unanimous in pointing out households which have or have not *sangu* or have more than *sangu*, but members of a rich household will modestly refer to themselves as 'having just about *sangu*'. In the Javanese case, Geertz says that 'rather than haves and have-nots, there were, in the delicately muted vernacular of peasant life, only *tjukupans* and *kekurangans* - "just-enoughs" and "not-quiteenoughs"'.[38] In the Lombok case, this type of statement is true if one considers only what people say about themselves but not what they say about others.

Usually, when a peasant holds more than 2-3 ha *sawah*, he will have to rethink the management of the production: whether to let out part of the land to a sharecropper or to employ more wage labour. Having more than a certain amount of land the peasant is simply faced with this situation that appears first during the wet monsoon season, when rice is the only crop grown in the irrigated fields. Rice is a labour-intensive crop, and the necessary co-ordination of the irrigation of the fields means that labour-intensive peaks will fall within the same limited period of time for all fields, whereas during the *polowijo* season a variety of crops is grown, which allows for timing of peak and slack periods in a more flexible way. The location of the land (whether the fields are scattered or not, or whether the fields are all in the vicinity of the landowner's residence) and the size and composition of the household will of course influence the decisions.

The 'rice season' can thus be said to be a 'bottleneck' for peasant household management of larger holdings of *sawah*. The rich peasant can either give up management of parts of his land altogether and let out the *sawah* in share-cropping or some other form of tenancy, or he can keep the control of the land and employ 'co-managers' during a limited period or throughout the year. A 'co-manager' of the former type, called *pembantu* (lit. helper, assistant), is usually employed to work a certain amount of land and to co-ordinate cultivation on that land only during the 'rice season'. The landowner provides seeds, tools, cattle for ploughing etc., while the *pembantu* contributes with his labour and is given a certain amount of rice for this, usually some 100 kg of rice for working 1/2 ha - but often the amount is not explicitly stipulated and the *pembantu* receives 'whatever the landowner will give'. This expression shows on one hand the dependence of the *pembantu* on the owner of the means of production, but on the other hand it is also an appeal for generosity and plays on social reputation. The *pembantu* does not control the means of production, and when the 'rice season' has passed he has nothing more to do with the land, if it does not please the landowner to let him cultivate the plot (usually then half of the crop goes to the landowner and half of it to the *pembantu*). Having a *pembantu* instead of a share-cropper on one's land leaves the secondary crops to the disposal of the landowner - in ordinary share-cropping contracts, the secondary crops[39] all go to the sharecropper.

A rich peasant may also extend his household as a unit of production by tying one or more outsiders to it as assistants. This institution is called *pengangon* (from the verb *ngangon* which means 'to use'). A *pengangon* and usually his/her immediate family are directly reproduced by the peasants: they are provided with the basic necessities of life such as food, clothes and also life cycle ceremonies. The landowner can draw freely upon their labour and appropriate any surplus labour over and above the labour spent on the necessary physical and social reproduction of the *pengangon* (and perhaps his immediate family). Basically, the *pengangon* is in the same situation as that described above for a family having lost its rights of production during the time of the Balinese rule, being provided for by the house holding the estate of administration. One difference is, though, that peasants and former peasants in pre-colonial times were tied for life but the *pengangon* status today can be changed by his own decision, or more usually, by the provider. To have a *pembantu* or a *pengangon* taking care of the production on one's land gives much higher economic returns to the landowner, returns that could be used for further accumulation of land.

As seen from the Table 4 there are considerably more day-labourer households than share-cropper households, especially in the census from Pagesangan but also in the census from Kuranji. The *pembantu* households have been listed under the category of 'day-labourer', since a *pembantu* does not control any means of production, must sell his labour power and is not continually employed throughout the year. The share-cropper, though not owning his means of production (at least not land) is still controlling them during the production process.

Share-cropping contracts in this area are of a kind where the landowner gets a previously fixed amount of rice once a year, after the rice harvest, the same type of contract as described in the Dutch colonial reports. Presumptive share-croppers bargain for the opportunity to cultivate the land, and the one who dares to promise to deliver the most rice to the landowner will get the contract. Nowadays, the amount of rice to be delivered (the *pajeg*) tends to approximate the amount of rice produced on the land during the 'rice season'. But the share-cropper gets the secondary crops cultivated, be this *polowijo* or rice grown during the dry season. The landowner provides no seeds, tools or cattle - even if the share-cropper would rent cattle for ploughing from the landowner, he would do it on the same terms as he would from anybody else. The share-cropper makes the decisions of production and takes the risks (the only exception being when there is a disastrous failure of the main rice crop, when the landowner is called to inspect the crop and usually allows for reduction of the *pajeg*). For someone with little or no land and no employment outside the agricultural sector, share-cropping is a comparatively favourable way of making one's living.

To give an example of the economy of share-cropping, let us assume that someone is a share-cropper on 1/2 ha *sawah* and that he has to deliver 250 *ikat* (sheafs) of rice, each weighing 5 kg, altogether 1,250 kg. Let us further assume, that the land yields 1,500 kg of rice, since our share-cropper does not grow the new varieties of rice, being afraid not to be able to repay fertilizers and insecticides. Furthermore, he does not own any cattle. (The situation sketched is a fairly 'normal' one.)

In order to keep costs of production low, he will do as much of the work as possible himself assisted by his household members. He prepares the seedling nursery, and sows 25 kg of rice, which is enough for planting 1/2 ha of *sawah*. Hiring cattle for ploughing will cost him 250 kg of rice, to be paid at harvest time. For planting he will probably employ some day-labourers, but his outlay for this will not amount to more than a sum of money equivalent to some 10 kilo of rice. Weeding, checking the regulation of water and guarding the ripening crop are tasks that can be carried out by his own household, but at harvest time, 1/11th of the rice harvested will go to the harvesters, and 1/200th of the sheaves tied will go to those who carry out that task. The landowner, who lives 3 km away from the land, expects the *pajeg* to be delivered at his ricebarn by his house, and the share-cropper, relaxing as no plague has befallen his rice crop, does not carry the rice there but hires horse, cart and wagon and pays 1/200th of the rice transported for this. Thus, his costs of production are (reproduction of his household not included):

seeds	25 kg
hiring cattle for ploughing ..	250 "
planting	20 "
harvesting (1,500 kg:11)	137 "
tying sheaves (1,363:200)	7 "
transportation of the *pajeg* (1,250 kg) to the landowner ..	6 "

This amount, plus the *pajeg* of 1,250 kg adds up to 1,695 kg or 195 kg more than the land yields in one crop of rice - and this is still calculated as if the share-cropper and his household had not eaten, bought tools, clothes and other necessities, performed any rituals or entertained any guests.

But the crops grown under the dry season are all for the share-cropper in the sense that he does not have to deliver any part of them to the landowner. For the sake of simplicity, let us assume that the share-cropper will grow one more crop of rice (the assumption is a quite feasible one). Once more, he is lucky that the crop is not infested by any plague, and the yield is 1,250 kg. Subtracting the costs of production (439 kg, since there is no *pajeg* to be transported) and the loss remaining from the first crop grown leaves 641 kg rice for the share-cropper's household, plus the returns from the third crop, which may be, for example, soybeans, cucumber or sweet potatoes but probably not tobacco, a crop with high return when marketed at the right time but also with high costs of production. If his household has six members, two adults and four children (between the age of 2 and 14 years), at least the equivalence of 7 kg of rice a day will be needed for the reproduction of that household at the level of *sangu*. After the second rice crop grown, there is still less than the needs of the household to be filled (1,914 kg) which is probably not covered by the third crop. This household will have to find additional sources of income, such as petty trade, day-labour, etc. (and, of course, the situation is especially difficult if the household has had to borrow money or rice at the usual high rate of interest).

Still, a day-labourer's household is in a less favourable situation. Assuming the members of a household of six persons would get employment altogether for 720 man-days (one person 360 days, one person 240 days and an adolescent 120 days), this would not give more than around 1,200 kg of rice (unpounded rice, as has been used in the preceding calculation). This would be below the level of *sangu* and there would hardly be any additional sources of income.

It even happens that a share-cropper can lend some money to the landowner, and if he can do so, not only are the further payments of *pajeg* reduced proportionately - if the loan equals two thirds of the price of the total amount of rice in *pajeg*, only one third of the *pajeg* has to be delivered until the money is paid back - but the share-cropper cannot be ousted from the land until the money is paid back. This practice thus reinforces the share-cropper's control of the land in a long-term perspective.

A small peasant and a share-cropper both control their means of production, but whereas a peasant does so continually, the share-cropper may be ousted after the period of one or more years since he is not the owner of the land. The peasant does not pay any ground-rent, but the share-cropper has to deliver ground-rent to the landowner for getting the rights of production. As a production unit, the small-holding peasant household and the share-cropper household have more in common however than the share-cropper household and the *pembantu* household. If a rich peasant leaves land in share-cropping, an economy of small producers is extended and any processes of polarization of landownership (accumulation versus loss of land) are at least slowed down.

The conditions of rice cultivation especially are such that at peak seasons labour from outside of the peasant or share-cropper household has to be employed. Formerly, there was an elaborate network of labour exchange between kinsmen and neighbours, a practice still prevalent in some of the remote areas of Lombok. Today, in the plains of West Lombok the cultivator almost exclusively employs 'free' labourers - 'free' in the negative sense of the term. The day-labourers are 'free' from any rights to the land they work on, they are 'free' from any continuous employment and make a poor living, often well below the level of *sangu* , working for wages when their labour is wanted. Quite contrary to Geertz' statement that co-operative labour arrangements have grown more complex, these arrangements have by and large been replaced by wage labour.

There are wages in money as well as in kind. Money wages could be either in the form of getting a certain amount of money for a certain amount of time worked, usually counted per labour-day, or wage according to amount. In the former case, wage for a normal working day (six hours) will usually amount to a sum of money for which approximately 1.5 kg of rice can be bought, i.e. somewhat more than what is needed for a single person to have *sangu* (dependants not counted) - *if* that person had the opportunity to be continuously employed which is usually not the case. In the latter case, (wage according to amount), the returns vary for fast and slow workers, of course, but tend to be the equivalent of something between 1-2 kg of rice per working day. Wage in kind is often calculated on a 'share-basis': the worker gets 1/11th of the rice harvested, 1/200th of the sheaves tied, 1/3rd of the wood cut, and so on. This type of agreement on stipulated percentages to the worker and the owner is called *bagai hasil*, which means 'share the yield'. In form, *bagai hasil* agreements look very much like share-cropping arrangements. What, then, is the crucial difference between the positions of the day-labourer and the share-cropper in the production process? In both cases, surplus labour is appropriated by the owner of means of production through monopoly on crucial production factors such as land. But whereas the day-labourer sells his labour power for a sum of money or a part of the produce, the share-cropper acquires the rights of production for a certain period by delivering a stipulated amount of the produce to the landowner. In the former case, labour is alienated during the production process, whereas in the latter, it is not. As holder of the rights of production, the share-cropper is in a position where there are opportunities to appropriate surplus labour from day-labourers, and at the same time he is yielding surplus product to the landowner. The *pembantu* is in these respects in the same position as the day-labourer, the most apparent difference between their work conditions being the duration of time employed.

CONCLUSIONS

The use of wage labour in agricultural production is a prevalent practice today, but as late as in the 1930s, most of the considerable number of landless people in the villages made their living as share-croppers and hired labour was seldom used in the agricultural sector according to official sources.[40] This latter statement is confirmed by the memories of my elderly informants:

> Pak Komang, a rich peasant in his sixties, was planning to plant as much as 2 ha of his *sawah* with tobacco, a crop which requires many extra hands, and reflected on the state of things formerly and now: 'Tobacco eats much labour, that is true, but it gives much money too. Today, it is easy to cultivate tobacco because we employ day-labourers, but formerly, when I was a child, things were different. My father never cultivated more than a little tobacco for our own use. He was still backward and was so afraid to give out money and pay wages that he did not dare to employ day-labourers as we do today. I think one should not be afraid of giving out money when one knows that it will eventually return and bring its children *[= interest, more money]* along too.'

In the late thirties, 36 per cent of all irrigated land in West Lombok was cultivated by share-croppers according to official figures[41] and in the heavily populated plain of that area, where there was (and is) no room for swidden agriculture, the figures were even higher. In the irrigation districts *(subak)* where most of the land held by the inhabitants of Pagesangan and Kuranji is situated, irrigated land in share-cropping amounted to as much as 56 per cent. Comparing these figures from the surveys drawn from Pagesangan and Kuranji, one can note a considerable difference: out of the 77.35 ha in that census, only 16.68 ha were in share-cropping, which amounts to approximately 21.6 per cent. Now, these figures can only be used as rough indicators of declining share-cropping practices, since they are not strictly comparable (the Dutch figures from 1938 are based on two whole districts comprising 2,575 ha whereas the surveys only cover less than 80 ha, for example). Also, some of the land classified as let out in share-cropping in the official Dutch records of 1938 might in practice have been alienated instead, although the prohibition on transactions of *druwe dalem* land had already been abolished at that time. Still, it does not seem probable that these factors could account for more than a double percentage (56 per cent) in 1938 as compared to 1973 (21.6 per cent).

Furthermore, considering that there was a large number of landless people in the rural area, that very little hired labour force was used in agriculture and that village industry was insignificant, it would be plausible to assume that share-cropping was really a more widespread practice at that time than it is today. Share-cropping in this area means *majeg*, agreements over at least one year where a specified amount of rice has to be delivered to the landowner. Nowhere in the detailed Dutch reports on organization of work and contracts in the agricultural sector is the practice of *pembantu* mentioned as an institution of importance, but 'ordinary' share-cropping is pointed out as the overwhelmingly frequent kind of agreement. At least in the thirties, it seems that hereditary rights of production has been replaced by a bargaining between presumptive share-croppers for temporary rights of production as the practice is today. When *druwe dalem* rights were still valid (before 1935), share-croppers in *druwe dalem* land, at least, could not get hereditary rights of production, and this seems to have been the state of things for share-croppers on *druwe jaba* land, too.

This kind of temporary agreements in terms of products but not labour services was to be found, though not frequently, during the time of Balinese rule *(pengancil)*, but the dominant form was that of the producer having hereditary rights of production in land, indeed being tied to land. From this time until today, there has been a progressive process of separation of the immediate producer from his means of production. During the period of Dutch rule, not only did land become a fully-fledged commodity, but share-cropping in the form of temporary agreements (where the share-cropper acquired the rights of production for a limited time in exchange for a part of the produce) more and more replaced the form where the producer was tied to the land. Still as late as in the thirties, wage labour was seldom used in agriculture, whereas today this is common practice (wage labour often being a substitution for sharecropping). The progressive separation of the producer from the means of production is a trend found in many societies, and wage labour (i.e. the producer selling his labour-power) is the last step in this process. Definite changes of land tenure and shifts in labour relations have taken place, but it can hardly be said that these changes were of the kind where 'tenure systems grew more intricate; tenancy relationships more complicated; co-operative labour arrangements more complex'.[42] When use of wage labour became the predominant practice, the complexity of labour relations was reduced as compared to former co-operative labour arrangements and labour exchange between neighbours and relatives.[43] Mutual obligations between kinsmen or neighbours are minimized in the agricultural sphere through the employment of day-labourers who will receive the same amount of wage for the same task irrespective of their relations to the employer.

But the organization of agricultural production in Lombok today is not exclusively characterized by wage labour, as there are also instances of e.g. share-cropping and petty commodity production, and the combination of different forms gives agricultural production its own peculiar character. The co-existence of several different forms may superficially make the situation look as a case of involution; as if tenancy relations and labour arrangements had in fact become more complex. But a combination of distinct forms is not the same as an 'over driving of an established form in such a way that it becomes rigid through an inward over elaboration of detail'.[44]

Old forms have been replaced and established forms have acquired new functions rather than having become involuted. An example of the latter is the *pengangon* institution, which today enables some peasant households to extend the use of wage labour at the expense of share-cropping arrangements. Although the *pengangon* institution is just an extension of the peasant household, it is a means for creating larger production units at the expense of small-scale, household-based production. Quite contrary to the process of fragmentization of landownership that should be characteristic for a process of involution,[45] the shift from share-cropping arrangements towards the employment of wage-labour accentuates processes of concentration of land in fewer hands.

But even if the organization of agricultural production cannot be said to be involuted, some of the notions concomitant with the concept of involution can be found in Balinese and Sasak (and, possibly, Javanese) ways of representing the organization of production. Labour arrangements, for example, are generally discussed in terms of distribution of resources rather than in terms of labour, taking the notion of private property as a starting-point. Those who are in the position to employ day-labourers or have their land worked by share-croppers are said to help the day-labourer or share-cropper by providing opportunities for them to earn their living, (or 'providing niches, however small, in the overall system'). Share-cropping is viewed as an especially generous way of letting someone get a piece of the economic pie, as allowing the share-cropper to step into the production process so that he can benefit from the land. Neither the employment of wage-labour nor share-cropping is represented in terms of appropriation of labour but in terms of access to resources. This is feasible in a situation of chronic underemployment where land is the scarce, and thus valued, production factor.[46] Land and other resources are private property and represented as 'belonging' to certain persons, who 'redistribute' these resources to other persons, who work the land and get some 'share' of the produce. Of course, in a situation of underemployment, those who do not control means of production but can get the opportunity to work for some return are favoured compared to those who do not get this opportunity. In this perspective, a share-cropping contract is certainly attractive for a pauper - he is said to be given help by the land-owner so that both of them will get something out of the land *('sama2 dapat')*. This is phrased as 'giving land','giving help'or 'giving wage' by the Indonesians themselves and as 'giving work'[47] (sic!) or 'shared poverty' by Geertz. Both views emphasize access to resources such as land but neglect the other side of the coin, i.e. labour - and the appropriation of labour. In this perspective, there is no exploitation of man by man within the framework of the village. Neither was there in Sukarno's picture of the Javanese peasantry as consisting of millions of *Marhaen;* petty producers controlling their own means of production, where the extreme 'pettyness' was stressed. This, by the way, comes quite close to Geertz' conception of fragmentization and shared poverty. Notions concomitant with the concept of involution are certainly to be found in indigenous as well as Western representations of organization of production in Inner Indonesia - or should we say misrepresentations?

NOTES

1 *Geertz. C.,* Agricultural Involution. The Processes of Ecological Change in Indonesia (Berkeley & Los Angeles 1963), pp. 12-15.

2 Ibid., p. 82.

3 Ibid., p. 128.

4 *Polak, A.,* Agrarian Developments on Lombok. An Attempt to Test Geertz' Concept of Agricultural Involution (in: Tropical Man, 5, 1972), p. 38.

5 See e.g. ibid., pp. 31f, and *Aass, S.,* Chayanov and Java: A Discussion of Chayanov's Micro- and Macro Theory of Peasant Economy (Lillehammer: Institutt for Driftslaere og Landbrugsøkonomi 1976, mimeo.) pp. 33f.

6 Fieldwork in Lombok was done for 8 months in 1972-3 and for 14 months in 1975-6 and was sponsored by the Scandinavian Institute of Asian Studies, the Swedish Council for Humanistic Research and the Bank of Sweden Tercentary Fund (through the Mobilization Project at the Department of Peace and Conflict Research, University of Gothenburg).

Historical data are mainly drawn from Dutch colonial reports, and have been interpreted in the light of field experiences and indigenous manuscripts. In many of these reports, juridical aspects (e.g. land tenure) are treated at the expense of actual practices (e.g. land use) which gives a somewhat 'legalistic' flavour to the first part of the essay. Almost no written sources are to be found for the period 1940-70.

7 *Cool, W.,* With the Dutch in the East (London 1897), p. 175; *Noyoka,* Pelajaran sejarah Bali (Den Pasar 1975), pp. 31f; *Teeuw, A.,* Lombok. Een dialect-geografische studië ('s-Gravenhage 1958), pp. 13-15.

8 See e.g. the myth of Dane Mang Poleng in *Collectie Korn,* bundel 241 (KITLV).

9 *Roo de la Faille, P. de.,* Studië over Lomboksch adatrecht (in: Taal-, Land en Volkenkunde van Nederlandsch-Indie, 's-Gravenhage 1918), pp. 146-9.

10 Compare *Belo, J.,* Bali: Temple Festivals (Seattle 1953), p. 1.

11 The expression 'rights in land' is used as a shorthand expression for 'rights held by persons/groups against other persons/groups with regard to land'. As P. Bohannan points out: 'Rights is a concept we use when social relationships are of primary consideration. There is, thus, a man-man unit to be considered as well.' *Bohannan, P.,* Land, Tenure and Land-Tenure (in: African Agrarian Systems, ed. by D. Biebuyck, London 1963), p. 102.

12 These concepts were taken from the study of *Vollenhoven, C. van.,* De indonesier en zijn grond, Leiden 1919.

13 *Gluckman, M.,* The Ideas in Barotse Jurisprudence (Manchester 1972), pp. 89-93.

14 *Bohannan, P.,* Land . . ., p. 102.

15 Main sources on land and labour, when not otherwise stated, are: *Rapport over de regeling de agrarische toestanden op Lombok* (in: Adatrechtbundel, 1, 1910); *Eerde, J.C. van,* Het grondbezit op Lombok (in: Verslagen der algemeene vergadering van het Indisch Genootschap 1904); *Liefrinck, F.A.,* Slavernij op Lombok (in: Tijdschrift voor Indische Taal-, Land- en Volkenkunde, 42, 1900, pp. 508-38); *Roo de la Faille, P. de,* Studië . . .

16 The main Dutch studies on traditional land tenure were carried out just after the conquest of Lombok by the colonial power. In these studies, a sharp distinction is drawn between *druwe dalem* and *druwe jaba* since one of the aims of the Dutch investigations was to establish the exact extension of the land that belonged to the supreme ruling house and could be taken over by the Dutch as *domeingrond*. They actually froze a fleeting relationship into a clear-cut line of classification.

17 The Dutch term will be used, since there is, to my knowledge, no single indigenous term applicable to these labour services.

18 Means of subsistence included not only means for the physical reproduction but also expenses for life cycle ceremonies, which were essential for the maintenance of the proper relationships to the ancestors. Jane Belo's statement on Balinese conceptions could be applied to traditional Sasak views as well: 'The relationship, then, between living inhabitants and the dead souls, the ancestral gods who are the true owners of the land, is a close one. As the years roll around members of an ancestral line will die, and be born again, so that in the unending cycle of reincarnation it is the ancestral line which continues to hold the apportioned lands, and the individual members merely return from time to time to "ask for rice".' (Belo J., Bali . . ., p. 1) If rights of production ceased, the former peasants had to "ask for rice" via another descentline, i.e. that of the holder of the rights of administration who also sponsored the ceremonies for maintenance of relations to the ancestors.

19 *Tanah pengancil* consisted of irrigated rice fields only, whereas *druwe dalem* and *druwe jaba* applied to all kinds of land.

20 Roo de la Faille mentions only members of Balinese ruling dynasty as holders of *tanah pengancil, Roo de la Faille, P. de,* Studië . . ., p. 164.

21 *Eck, E. van,* Schets van het eiland Bali (in: Tijdschrift voor Indische Taal-, Land- en Volkenkunde, 22, 1875), pp. 332-43; *Zollinger, H.,* Land- en Volkenkunde van het eiland Lombok (in: Tijdschrift voor Nederlandsch-Indië, 1847), p. 341.

22 See e.g. *Memorie van overgave, Resident Eschbach, 1905,* (KIT), p. 36.

23 See e.g. *Landrentemonografie, West Lombok, 1938* (Priv.), p. 83.

24 *Kraan, A. van der,* Selaparang under Balinese and Dutch Rule (diss., Australian National University, Canberra 1976), p. 178.

25 The Australian historian A. van der Kraan has estimated the percentage of the rice crop (main rice crop) that had to be paid in land tax for irrigated land:

Period	Mean value of percentage paid as tax
1914-1920	21.2
1920-1930	17.9
1930-1940	26.4

(Source: *Kraan, A. van der,* Selaparang . . ., pp. 211-32.)

Today, land tax is not very high (and never was after independence). In the plains of West Lombok it amounts to some half kilo rice *(padi)* per acre as a mean value over the last ten years.

26 See e.g. *Memorie van overgave, Controleur Vissers, 1933* (KIT).

27 The inheritance rules had been the same during pre-colonial times, but it seems that there was still room for agricultural expansion at that time.

28 *Memorie van overgave, Assistent Resident Bosselaar, 1934* (KIT).

29 In 1929, i.e. before the prohibition on transactions of *druwe dalem* was lifted, there were 357 registered cases of selling land and 57 cases of pawning land for *all* West Lombok. In 1936, the first year when transactions of *druwe dalem* were legal, there were 609 cases of registered land sales and 76 of pawning land in only

one of the five districts of West Lombok. *Landrente-monografie, West Lombok* . . ., p. 79.

30 *Hartong, A.M.,* Het adatrecht bij de Sasakse bevolking van Lombok (Unpubl. report, Katholieke Universiteit, Nijmegen, 1974).

31 Of the remaining four Balinese *kampung*, two are considered to have approximately the same economic status, one poor since there were some 90% landless day-labourers, and one rich - the latter was made up by a single large kin group *(sidikara)* with a core of wealthy families but many poor households as well. The Sasak *kampung* were generally deemed to be poorer than the Balinese ones, although the man owning most land (more than 100 ha, it was said) was a Sasak.

32 Irrigated cultivation is the most important sector not only because there is more *sawah* than *kebun*, but also because *sawah* cultivation is labour-intensive and high-yielding.

33 Land is more evenly distributed in Kuranji than in Pagesangan. This may be a bias in the sample of households, but may also have to do with differences in processes of accumulation and loss of land. Much land in the Kuranji area is owned by absentee landlords (many of them residing in town) and poor peasants will have a chance to cling to their tiny plot of land if they can work as share-croppers as well. The difference between the two situations is one of degree and not of kind, though. It may be noted, that there are no reasons to assume that there is as increasing fragmentization of landholding in any of these cases, as very small units are not viable in the long run and tend to be alienated and incorporated into larger units.

34 See also *Polak, A.,* Agrarian . . ., p. 26.

35 According to Geertz 'a man will let out part of his one hectare to a tenant - or two or three - while at the same time seeking tenancies on the lands of other men, thus balancing the obligations to give work (to his relatives, to his dependants, or even to his close friends or neighbours)'. *Geertz, C.,* Agricultural . . ., p. 99. I have not encountered any such case in Lombok. And if someone 'will rent or pawn his land to another for a money payment and then serve as a tenant on that land himself' (ibid., p. 99) this is not because of obligations to kith and kin but simply because of shortage of money.

36 Household size is fairly uniform throughout the surveys: there is, for example, no significant difference in size between a household holding 0.5 ha of land and one holding 3 ha (mean size 6.1 and 6.9). The few very rich households having considerably more than 4 ha of irrigated land are usually larger (one extremely large household included 18 persons) and on the other extreme, day-labourer households tend to split up more quickly so that the mean size is somewhat smaller (4.2).

37 Having just *sangu* does not imply a household-based subsistence economy, though. Some secondary crops, such as tobacco, red pepper and sugar cane, are mainly cash crops, others (e.g. cucumbers and maize) are not, but not even rice can be said to be a crop grown for subsistence only. Only a small part of the rice cultivated on the land of rich peasants can be consumed by their own household. The surplus is stored in wait for the prices to rise, and often these stores are increased by purchase of rice when the price is low. Many a poor cultivator has to sell most of his crop immediately after harvest, when prices generally are low, in order to pay debts, and will have to buy rice later in the year. (Prices are usually low at harvest time, but the cultivator is even worse off if he has to sell his crop when still standing in the field *(ngijon)*, a quite common, though illegal, practice. The cultivator gets only about half as much for his crop as he would if he sold it after harvest, but is forced to accept this in order to cover his and his household's immediate needs.) Many households end up with a cash crop even if the original intention was to cultivate for subsistence.

38 *Geertz, C.*, Agricultural . . ., p. 97.

39 During the dry season, land is not allowed to lay fallow and usually two crops are taken. Common crops are soybeans, tobacco and red pepper, crops that are also exported from the island. Maize, cucumber, sweet potatoes, sugar cane and various kinds of beans are grown mainly for home consumption. Rice may be grown once more during the dry season nowadays, a practice that was forbidden during the time of the Balinese kingdom. In fact, during the years 1975-6, the government started a regime of planting which ruled that a certain amount of land *had* to be planted with rice during the dry season in order to try to make Lombok self-sufficient in rice.

40 *Memorie van overgave, Assistent Resident Bosselaar . . .; Landrentemonografie, West Lombok* . . ., p. 95.

41 Ibid., p. 83.
42 *Geertz, C.*, Agricultural . . ., p. 82.
43 For discussion of traditional obligations and labour relations, see *Polak, A.*, Agrarian . . ., pp. 34-41.
44 This is the definition of involution given in *Geertz, C.*, Agricultural . . ., p. 82, but when discussing the involution of organization of work, Geertz does so in terms of combination of different forms (e.g. Ibid., pp. 99f).
45 Ibid., pp. 128f.
46 See *Block, M.*, Property and the End of Affinity (in: Marxist Analyses and Social Anthropology, ed. by M. Block, London 1972, pp. 203-28).
47 *Geertz, C.*, Agricultural . . ., p. 99.

BIBLIOGRAPHY

MANUSCRIPT SOURCES

1. *Koninklijk Instituut voor de Tropen, Amsterdam (KIT)*
   Memorie van overgave, Resident Eschbach, 1905.
   Memorie van overgave, Controleur Vissers, 1933.
   Memorie van overgave, Assistent Resident Bosselaar, 1934.
2. *Koninklijk Instituut voor Taal-, Land- en Volkenkunde, Leiden (KITLV)*
   Collectie Korn, bundel 241.
3. *Private Collection (Priv.)*
   Landrentemonografie, West Lombok 1938.

LITERATURE

Aass, S., Chayanov and Java: A Discussion of Chayanov's Micro- and Macro Theory of Peasant Economy. Lillehammer: Institutt for Driftslaere og Landbrugsøkonomi 1976, mimeo.

Belo, J., Bali: Temple Festival, Seattle 1953.

Block, M., Property and the End of Affinity (in: Marxist Analyses and Social Anthropology, ed. by M. Block, London 1972, pp. 203-28).

Bohannan, P., Land, Tenure and Land-Tenure (in: African Agrarian Systems, ed. by D. Biebuyck, London 1963, pp. 101-15).

Cool, W., With the Dutch in the East (London 1897).

Eck, E. van, Schets van het eiland Bali (in: Tijdschrift voor Indische Taal-, Land- en Volkenkunde, 22, 1875).

Eerde, J.C. van, Het grondbezit op Lombok (in: Verslagen der algemeene vergadering van het Indisch Genootschap 1904).

Geertz, C., Agricultural Involution. The Processes of Ecological change in Indonesia. Berkeley & Los Angeles 1963.

Gluckman, M., The Ideas in Barotse Jurisprudence (Manchester 1972).

Graaf, H.J. de, Lombok in het 17e eeuw (in: Djåwå, 1941, pp. 43-61).

Hartong, A.M., Het adatrecht bij de Sasakse bevolking van Lombok (Unpubl. report, Katholieke Universiteit, Nijmegen, 1974).

Kraan, A. van der, Selaparang under Balinese and Dutch Rule. Diss. Australian National University, Canberra, 1976.

Bibliography

Liefrinck, F.A., Slavernij op Lombok (in: Tijdschrift voor Indische Taal-, Land- en Volkenkunde, 42, 1900, pp. 508-38).

Nyoka, Pelajaran sejarah Bali. Den Pasar 1975.

Polak, A., Agrarian Developments on Lombok. An Attempt to Test Geertz' Concept of Agricultural Involution (in: Tropical Man, 5, 1972, pp. 18-45).

Rapport over de regeling de agrarische toestanden op Lombok (in: Adatrechtbundel, 1, 1910).

Roo de la Faille, P. de, Studië over Lomboksch adatrecht (in: Taal-, Land- en Volkenkunde van Nederlandsch-Indië, 's-Gravenhage 1918, pp. 131-77).

Teeuw, A., Lombok. Een dialect-geografische studië. 's-Gravenhage 1958.

Vollenhoven, C. van, De indonesier en zijn grond. Leiden 1919.

Zollinger, H., Land- en volkenkunde van het eiland Lombok (in: Tijdschrift voor Nederlandsch-Indië, 1847, pp. 177-205, 301-83).

THE PROBLEM OF KINSHIP: WOMEN'S LABOUR AND RELATIONS OF PRODUCTION IN THE NEW GUINEA HIGHLANDS

Magnus Lindgren

This essay takes as its starting-point the problem of descent in Melanesian social structure. I will try to show that descent in the New Guinea Highlands cannot be understood as a distinct phenomenon isolated from more basic social processes. Therefore my aim is wider than the rather narrow problem of descent in Highland New Guinea, and the essay can be seen as a contribution to the more general discussion about the role of kinship in primitive societies, that is the interrelationship between kinship, ideology and relations of production.[1] My conclusion is that descent in the New Guinea Highlands is a property relation functioning as an ideology which serves to legitimate and hide relations of inequality and exploitation in the process of the material and social reproduction. A second aim, which is related to the first one, is to question the approach in kinship studies that regards kinship attitudes as a function of the kinship system itself.[2] Also here I argue that it is more appropriate to look at the social relations of production, rather than viewing kinship as an autonomous system that can be explained in its own terms.

The discussion about descent in New Guinea was initiated already in the 1950s by van der Leeden's book on the people of the interior of Sarmi in the then Netherlands New Guinea.[3] Their society was described as 'loosely structured', a term interpreted as a tendency towards bilineality which was regarded as the result of the small size of local groups leading to an emphasis on the nuclear family and the brother-sister tie. According to Barnes, what distinguishes New Guinea local groups from descent groups is that non-agnates are numerous in them and that it is hard to detect any differences in status between agnates and non-agnates because the latter become assimilated to the local agnatic core.[4] It seems that a male has a choice whether he will adhere to the local group in which his father is an agnate or to some other group to which he can trace non-agnatic connections. Therefore it is a misapplication of the descent concept developed by Fortes to describe such local groups as descent groups. Barnes' solution is that recruitment is by patrifiliation and not by descent. That is, a genealogy is not a necessary requirement for group membership. As filiation always is bilateral, one can claim membership in both the father's and the mother's group, though patrilocality is the norm. In his book on kinship among the Mbowamb, Andrew Strathern takes a similar standpoint saying that it is the local group that is the important unit in the Highlands and that filiation gives access to it.[5] To sum up this view, a man holds rights of membership in a local group if he can show that his father has been a member of it, and not because of a descent relation to a specified ancestor. To me this seems a doubtful standpoint as filiation is the fact of being the child to a parent and as such cannot give rights in the corporate property of a descent group. A descent group is not constituted by filiation but by the fact that its members are related to a common ancestor. Descent has its foundation in the politico-jural domain, while filiation stems from the domestic domain. Thus it is wrong to use the concept of filiation to explain recruitment to political and corporate groups. And the fact remains that the local groups with which we are concerned are descent groups in as much as they possess a corporate property, ancestral land, which is the basis for ancestor worship and political action. I think that the concepts of descent and filiation have acquired a reified meaning in the discussion. Anthropologists have developed general principles for the recruitment of political groups from how people in one part of the world conceptualize their groups and from the statistical composition of such groups. And then it becomes a kind of problem when Melanesians do not adhere to the anthropologist's definition of descent. Filiation and descent are good examples of analytical concepts that have become principles with an independent existence.

The view regarding descent as a principle of recruitment has produced some peculiar results. Agnation has become a statistical phenomenon and consequently one has attempted to measure the degree of patrilineal descent. Meggitt's book on the Mae Enga is a well-known example.[6] Agnation is defined as effective patrilineality and patrilocality, and Meggitt proposes that the degree of agnation is inversely related to the availability of land. To me the whole discussion seems rather confused and I do not think that one has fully realized what it is one intends to explain. Exactly what is it that the mentioned hypothesis attempts to account for? It seems to be nothing but the ratio of non-agnates to agnates in local groups. The conception of descent as a principle of recruitment leads to the view of agnation as a statistical phenomenon. But of course agnation is not a statistical phenomenon, for if it was, it would be the outcome of historical particularities, as the actual ratio of non-agnates to agnates in a given local group is the result of the historical circumstances in that particular case. Thus one would be able to measure agnatic descent in percentages, but it sounds somewhat senseless to say about a local group that it is, for instance, 65 per cent agnatic.

But what is agnation if it is not the ratio of non-agnates to agnates? Other anthropologists have regarded descent as a method of classifying groups and individuals. This is the view held by Glasse,[7] Sahlins[8] and others. According to Sahlins descent is a principle for the arrangement and alignment of political groups. This is because completely different descent groupings may be made up of the same agnatic descent material. Strathern has suggested that food can constitute the mediating link between non-agnatic members and the ancestors on whose land they permanently reside.[9] Non-agnates and by means of kinship completely unrelated persons are converted into full members of the descent group through the process of continuously eating food grown on the ancestral soil. Thus Melanesian kinship is achieved kinship and the mediating link to the ancestors may be of two kinds. On the one hand we get a descent relation mediated by means of genealogies, and on the other descent mediated by non-genealogical means, like for instance food and ceremonies. This view is based on indigenous concepts of shared ancestral substance and it helps us to better understand how Melanesians conceptualize the relation between people, land and ancestors. But I fail to see that it is really capable of *explaining* this relation as it leads us to account for ideology in ideological terms. Among Melanesists there is a marked tendency to make a sharp distinction between the ideology of kinship and the realm of action of kinship. In terms of this distinction one can make a cultural study of kinship (i.e. norms) as opposed to a social study of kinship (i.e. actual behaviour).[10] Scheffler has found this view useful when dealing with the cognatic structure of the Choiseulese.[11] Making a difference between *cultural or ideological constructs* and the social processes they may regulate or validate, he labels the former *descent-constructs* which then refer to indigenous formulations of genealogical connections between persons and their ancestors.[12] The distinction is supposed to account for the observed and much discussed discrepancy between the ideology and composition of Melanesian descent groups. I cannot see much analytic value in the distinction. It is nothing but the simple recognition of the well-known fact that people do not always behave like they purport to do. Consequently Scheffler comes across problems difficult to surmount when he shall relate the descent-constructs to actual behaviour, that is social processes in his terminology.

I agree with Scheffler and others in regarding descent as an ideology by which people and groups of people are classified and that it is difficult to support a definition of descent as a principle of recruitment. Then, how shall we best explain this ideology of descent in the New Guinea Highlands? Can we explain it by referring to a presumed discrepancy between norms of behaviour and actual behaviour in the way Scheffler does, or do we have to analyse the indigenous concepts so as to find out what people really mean when they talk about descent? The first strategy leads to a kind of dualism, and we are left without concepts to account for the relation between ideology and action. Maurice Bloch has argued that the tendency in recent kinship studies to separate ideology and action is a misleading approach because what anthropologists usually call ideology is actually a type of behaviour and not a set of immaterial ideas.[13] On the other hand, the approach that takes the native's point of view to investigate what Melanesians think about descent rests on the idea that the problem of descent in New Guinea is a problem of our definition of descent. Of course, if we regard descent as an ideology it is important to know what this ideology is and not automatically take over an 'African' model. But if descent is an ideology by which people conceive of their relations to each other and to the land they live on, it is wrong to take this ideology for granted and regard it as the true representation of the relationship. Because as ideology descent never represents this relation but *mis-represents* it. To limit oneself to indigenous concepts is to explain ideology in ideological terms. The ideological approach has shown us that Melanesians do apply a consistent view of descent if we regard it as ancestral substance which can be transmitted to individuals in a variety of ways of which genealogy is one and food another. In the following I will try to show that descent is an ideological misrepresentation of the most fundamental relations between men and their environment. Thus we have to start with the objective social relations which provide the raw material for the ideology.

We will see that the ideology of descent misrepresents the relations between Man and Nature and therefore we first have to consider these relations, that is the social relations of production. Which are the relations of production in Highland New Guinea? An important feature of most New Guinea Highlands groups are the strained relations between the sexes. Of course there is a wide variation from one society to another, but generally speaking, in most contexts, men are considered superior and women their inferiors. I do not argue that sexuality shall be taken as the basis for the male dominance. Quite on the contrary, as Maurice Godelier has pointed out, sexuality serves as the ultimate ideology for the justification of the male dominance.[14] It is also known that the dominance of males over their women is confined to certain categories of women. If the relation between a man and his wife is characterized by dominance, violence and avoidance, the brother-sister tie is a very close and intimate relation best described by reciprocity and mutuality.[15] The women a man has authority over and over whom he may exert violence are the females in the sphere of alliance, that is his wife, daughters, brothers' wives and their daughters. Godelier relates the male dominance directly to the importance of kinship in these societies. The women reproduce life itself and this reproduction is regulated by kinship relations which also correspond to the social structure. To give birth to children is to reproduce the social structure. Thus it is logical to expect that the males who control the society at large also must have a firm control over women. I will refrain from criticizing this point of view here. Instead I will look at the positions of men and women in the sphere of production. The male domination may be related to the division of labour in Highlands societies. Generally it can be said that males provide the land while women are responsible for labour. This does not imply that men do not work, but their labour is mainly confined to the clearing of new fields and related activities which often are carried out *collectively* by them. In other words they *transform nature and reproduce the land* whereas the women plant, weed, harvest the tubers, prepare food and bring up pigs. Thus most female tasks are carried out *individually* and do not interfere with nature in the same obvious way as do male occupations. Moreover, what is important is that women supply most of the surplus labour. They are the 'bottlenecks'[16] in the production of a surplus. From Leopold Pospisil's account of Ekagi (Kapauku) agriculture we know that weeding is the limiting factor in Highlands agriculture.[17] It sets the limits to the extent of garden production and thus there is a close correlation between the number of females in a household and the area of garden land cultivated. While sweet-potatoes are the everyday food which reproduces the society materially, pigs are the most important surplus item used to reproduce the social structure. Thus the women control the production of pigs in two ways. They are the limiting factor in the production of pig fodder, and, as Rappaport has shown, they are the first to feel the diminishing return of increased labour when the pig herd grows and a physical strain builds up on them as they have the task of managing the herd.[18]

Before we consider the relations of production between the sexes, that is how women's labour is appropriated, it would be instructive to compare the Highlands situation with Bloch's analysis of the Merina of Malagasy.[19] Among the Merina the environment and the techniques of exploitation are factors in the devaluation of human labour in the process of production which in turn leads to a misrepresentation of the Man/Land relationship as ancestral land. Production becomes a matter of control of land, not a question of labour. New Guinea Highlands horticulture is very different from the irrigated rice cultivation of the Merina, but my argument is similar to Bloch's. In the Highlands new land in the form of fallows or forest is continuously brought under cultivation. And we have seen that men have the task of clearing the new land. In the Highlands this leads to a devaluation of female labour - 'men clear the gardens and we are able to eat' as a Mbowamb woman told Marilyn Strathern.[20] I think that we already in the division and organization of labour can find the germ of an agnatic ideology. Men provide the labour for the reproduction of land, that is the corporate property. And given a system where land is the main source of identification for local groups, that which gives a man access to the group, it is fairly reasonable to expect an ideology in which lines of males are seen as the reproducers of both land and society, that is patrilineal descent. Consequently agnation becomes an ideological misrepresentation of the objective fact that women contribute the largest part of the labour which reproduces society both materially and socially. Moreover, I think that my argument may provide an explanation of why it is so easy to change one's group membership in Highlands societies. The criterion of membership in the local group has often been said to be working and living together, rather than a rigid descent criterion.[21] Agnation is so to say the ideological over-valuation of male labour and a man may become an agnate when taking part in male activities and *contributing male labour*, that is living and working together with the other men of the local group. So far the line of my argument is as follows:

1. In the type of horticulture we find in the Highlands, land must be continuously reproduced to allow for the local group to exist.
2. Men provide the labour for the reproduction of land. This is often done collectively.
3. Women work individually and provide most of the labour for the material and social reproduction of society.
4. The first two conditions taken together are given an ideological misrepresentation in agnation which is a devaluation of women's labour pointing out men as the sole reproducers of local groups and the whole society.
5. The conversion of non-agnates into agnates and members of the local group is made possible by the agnatic ideology which represents men as the ones reproducing the group.

We see that kinship in these societies is a property relation and thus belongs to the superstructure. Therefore it is impossible to give an explanation of it without first having investigated its relations with the infrastructure. It becomes obvious that the problem of descent and locality disappears if we consider it in the light of the fundamental relations of production.

My conclusion is consistent with Barbara Bradby's recent reanalysis of Godelier's data on the production of salt currency among the Baruya.[22] She comes to the conclusion that exchange transactions between men in the Highlands depend on a non-valorization of women's labour. In a society where female labour is devalued men to not need to take into account their wife's labour when exchanging objects produced by men and women together.

The surplus produced by women is used in contexts of ritual and ceremonial importance. That is activities that serve to reproduce and recreate the social structure. Such activities include life-cycle rituals like the contracting of marriages and death payments, as well as compensation payments, and redistributive pig feasts and exchange-cycles of the *moka* kind. If it is a feature of the division of labour that women produce pigs and some other surplus items, exchange becomes a way to appropriate this surplus labour, that is a relation of production. Control over women is economically important as men depend on them for pig-rearing and gardening. I think the necessity to appropriate women's surplus may offer an explanation of the male-female relationships in the Highlands. A man relies on his wife, unmarried sisters and daughters for the supply of a surplus. We have seen that there are two kinds of male-female relationships, a positive and a negative one. The former we find between a man and his sisters and the latter between a man and his wife and daughters. As a man appropriates his wife's surplus labour it is clear that the husband-wife relation is symptomatic of this contradiction within the minimal production unit. This relation contrasts with the brother-sister tie which is of the positive and intimate kind. A man does not rely on his sister as a provider of a surplus to the same extent as he is dependent on his wife and daughters. Of course he may get food from her rather frequently, but as she is expected to marry out she is no permanent member of the brother's production unit. The control over her is handed over to the brother-in-law. Moreover, when a man is in most need of the women's surplus, that is when he is married and has started his own family, his sister is already out of his control as she then has become a member of her husband's group. But in her position as unmarried daughter, a woman is a provider of surplus to the father's unit. Thus it is important for him to exert control over unmarried daughters and we can expect the same kind of relationship between a father and his daughter as the one prevailing between a husband and his wife.

Kinship attitudes cannot be interpreted as properties of elementary structures of kinship if with elementary structures we mean independent and fundamental structures.[23] We see that the elementary structures dissolve into even more fundamental and independent relationships, that is the social relations of production. The kinship attitudes we find in these societies are more a function of the appropriation of labour than dependent on the kinship system itself. The prevailing attitudes of kinship in Highland New Guinea form a native model of the mode of production and therefore one will explain ideology in ideological terms when treating them as elementary and irreducible structures.

I will now consider the mother's brother-sister's son relation which is of utmost importance for the operation of exchange systems in the region. Melanesian ideas of procreation show a balance between the paternal and maternal principles, though there are exceptions (e.g. the Trobriands). This phenomenon is not a unique feature for the region, but what makes it important is its relevancy for descent group membership and exchange relations. It is widely recognised that the mother's brother has some sort of claims on his sister's children. Claims that are paid off by exchanges and payments to him and his clan. This relationship is one of the essential elements in the ceremonial exchange cycles like the *moka*.[24] Roy Wagner provides an account of the Daribi concept of procreation and descent.[25] The Daribi, living on the fringes of the Eastern Highlands of New Guinea, conceive of a child as a result of the combination of a maternal and a paternal substance. Each clan has its unique substance deriving from the founding ancestor. A man gets his maternal substance, i.e. the paternal substance of the mother's brother's clan, from his mother. He shares it with his brothers and sisters but cannot transmit it to the next generation unless he becomes a resident member of his mother's brother's clan. As he in this way is connected with the maternal uncle's clan the latter has claims on him, because from the uncle's point of view he is an agnate who happens to reside elsewhere. These claims last for the whole life of the nephew and must be continuously paid off by exchanges with the uncle's clan. Otherwise the sister's son will be recruited to the latter. We find similar ideas among, for instance, Mbowamb[26] and Siane.[27] Even if it is an exaggeration to argue that it is a universal condition in the majority of Highlands societies that children are recruited to their father's clan by means of payments, as actually seems to be the case among the Daribi, it is important to note that there is a recognition of the nephew's rights in the corporate property of the mother's brother's lineage and consequently that property rights may be passed on by females. These ideas may be regarded as a consequence of the agnatic ideology which represents men as the ultimate reproducers of society, so that both sisters and their children are regarded as the property of the local descent group. An alternative explanation is to regard them as the outcome of the close brother-sister bond in as much as the sister's offspring also have close ties to their mother's brother. But here we must be cautious so as not to resort to the native model of descent and kinship. We have just established that patrilineal descent and the male-female relationships in a sense are ideological constructs as they misrepresent the objective social relations of production. But what is peculiar with the brother-sister bond is that it is not subject to the dominant male-female ideology. Instead it is a recognition of the fact that women *qua* sisters have inalienable rights in the means of production of their natal patriclan, and that they may confer such rights to their offspring. As Meggitt has shown in his book about the Mae Enga the ideology of patriliny sometimes may come into conflict with these rights of the nephews in the lineage land.[28] It is typical that such conflicts become manifest when the localized patrilineages are threatened as a result of population pressure, or rather when the corporate property, the foundation of the male ideology, is threatened by overpopulation. In such situations restrictions are put on such land rights that have no ideological sanctions. This is a confirmation of Fortes' idea that complementary filiation has its basis in the domestic domain whereas descent is a political principle. However, it is more clarifying to say that descent has ideological origins and that complementary filiation is non-ideological as it expresses the ultimate dependence of men on their women. The main structural contradiction in these societies is between the ideology of patriliny and the objective social relations of production. These latter recognize the women's rights in the clan property and their rights to pass it on to their children. The difference is that the recognition of these rights is not in terms of ideology, but stems from the women's position in the sphere of production. Hence the sometimes conflicting idioms of kinship in the Highlands.

What bearing does our analysis of the avuncular relationship have for an understanding of exchange relationships? Valerio Valeri, in a discussion about Polynesian kinship systems, contrasts them with systems found in Melanesia.[29] The former, he says, give a continuity between local groups whereas the latter introduce a *discontinuity* between such groups. My conclusion is that the discontinuity is a product of the patrilineal ideology which emphasizes the identification of the local group with its territory. But the local discontinuity is not absolute in as much as there are opportunities for political alliances between like groups. The basis of this limited continuity is the exchange relations which often have their origins in the avuncular relationship. An absolute discontinuity which is implied by a rigid adherence to the principle of patriliny in matters concerning property is counterbalanced by the exchange relationships. But this alternative idiom for relations between groups which would be able to introduce a political continuity is itself subject to the dominant ideology as long as men are the ones making the exchanges. The exchange transactions become a way to appropriate women's surplus labour and reproduce the whole agnatic structure and ideology. The contradiction is between the rights of men and sisters to transfer property to their respective offsprings but as long as agnation is a dominant ideology, exchange relations have as their effect the recruitment of children to their father's clan and the rights of women to confer property on their offspring are never structurally recognized. The role of surplus is the recreation of the agnatic ideology and not to give women equal rights in property and people.

To sum up our discussion so far, the division and organization of labour combined with certain features of Highlands agriculture give rise to an ideological misrepresentation of labour in the form of patrilineal descent which is an overvaluation of men's labour. The different forms of exchange constitute relations of production in which women's labour is appropriated for the sake of reproducing the agnatic group ideology. Here we come across a major difficulty in a materialist analysis of primitive societies. It seems that kinship which at the first stage of our analysis appeared as ideology in some way becomes a part of the infrastructure when we consider the relations of production. These are so to say a consequence of the dominant ideology at the same time as they reproduce this ideology. In Godelier's words this is an example of how kinship may function as relations of production.[30] But such a view which regards relations of production as contained within the dominant ideology makes it difficult to construct a dynamic theory of society capable of explaining social change, as has been pointed out by Bloch in a recent article.[31] But from several accounts of New Guinea Highlands societies we know that there are occasions when women openly oppose the male dominance and that women also may be represented in a way that gives justice to their role in the sphere of production.[32] Thus there are ways available for them to question the social structure, and consequently the relations of production are not fully contained within the ideology. I cannot offer an ultimate solution to the problem here but it is clear that kinship has different roles to play at different levels in a society. When organizing the minimal unit of production kinship has apparent non-ideological functions to fulfil, that is reproduction in the sense of material reproduction and the creation of new life. At another level we have seen that such units can be bound together by co-operative efforts, like for instance the communal labour men do when clearing new land. We are still at an infrastructural level but as kinship in this way can unite groups of different levels it may also provide the relations for political dominance and exploitation. Therefore kinship relations within the minimal unit of production become dominated by kinship relations of higher levels, which in the New Guinea Highlands is expressed in the aggressive male-female relationship. But at the same time the biologically and materially reproductive functions of women within the family may provide the tools for criticizing the dominant ideology and the relations of production.

The Problem of Kinship

The ideological functions of kinship and its impact on the relations between the sexes become clearer if we consider the Dani of the Indonesian province of Irian Jaya.[33] The division and organization of labour follows the same pattern as in other Highlands societies. Despite this the Dani have a very undeveloped system of patrilineal descent which if it can be characterized as a descent system at all certainly is not an agnatic ideology in the sense we have used the term. Furthermore, Dani males are not at all aggressive towards their women, nor is there avoidance between spouses or any ideas about pollution. Sometimes the Dani are even described as uninterested in sex. The reasons why the Dani have not developed a male supremacist ideology, I think, are to be found in the exogamic system and its implications for the exchange relationships. Where most Highlanders are organized into localized and exogamic descent groups, the Dani have non-localized moieties and sibs. Thus among the latter exchange between *local* groups is not a way to appropriate women's labour, whereas the general Highlands pattern makes use of exchange as a relation of production which is both dependent upon the existence of agnatic local groups and reproduces such groups and their ideology. This does not mean that Dani women are not exploited or that exchange here is not a relation of production. What it implies is that the ideological rationale for exchange is not the reproduction of local patri-clans, but the recreation of a non-localized moiety system. Consequently there is no devaluation of women's labour. The relations of production are essentially the same as among other Highlands groups but the dominant ideology is another one. This shows that the kinship system may change and the relations of production persist.

NOTES

1 See for instance *Bloch, M.,* Property and the End of Affinity (in: Marxist Analyses and Social Anthropology, ed. by M. Bloch, London 1975); and *Godelier, M.,* Horizon, trajets marxistes en anthropologie. Paris 1973.

2 *Lévi-Strauss, C.,* Structural Anthropology (London 1968), pp. 31-54.

3 *Leeden, A.C. van der,* Hoofdtrekken der sociale structuur in het westelijke binnenland van Sami. Diss. Leiden 1956.

4 *Barnes, J.A.,* African Models in the New Guinea Highlands (in: Man, 62, 1962, pp. 5-9).

5 *Strathern, A.J.,* One Father, One Blood. Descent and Group Structure among the Melpa People. London 1972.

6 *Meggitt, M.J.,* The Lineage System of the Mae Enga of New Guinea. Edinburgh 1965.

7 *Glasse, R.M.,* Huli of Papua: A Cognatic Descent System. Paris 1968.

8 *Sahlins, M.,* On the Ideology and Composition of Descent Groups (in: Man, 65, 1964, pp. 104-7).

9 *Strathern, A.J.,* Kinship, Descent and Locality: Some New Guinea Examples (in: The Character of Kinship, ed. by J. Goody, London 1973).

10 Ibid.

11 *Scheffler, H.W.,* Choiseul Island Social Structure. Berkeley & Los Angeles 1965; and *Scheffler, H.W.,* Ancestor Worship in Anthropology: Or, Observations on Descent and Descent Groups (in: Current Anthropology, 7, 1966, pp. 541-8).

12 *Scheffler, H.W.,* Ancestor . . ., p. 543.

13 *Bloch, M.,* Placing the Dead: Tombs, Ancestral Villages and Kinship in Madagascar (London 1971), pp. 218 ff.

14 *Godelier, M.,* Le sexe comme fondement ultime de l'ordre social et cosmique chez Baruya de Nouvelle-Guinée (in: Cahiers de Centre d'Etudes et de Recherches Marxistes, CERM, 128, 1976, p. 1-44.

15 Ibid., pp. 7-8.

16 *Bloch, M.,* Property . . ., p. 207.

17 *Pospisil, L.,* Kapauku Papuan Economy. New Haven 1963.

18 *Rappaport, R.,* Pigs for the Ancestors: Ritual in the Ecology of a New Guinea People. New Haven & London 1967.

19 *Bloch, M.,* Property . . .

20 *Strathern, M.,* Women in Between. Female Roles in a Male World: Mount Hagan, New Guinea (London & New York 1972), p. 159.

21 *Lepervenche, M. de,* Descent, Residence and Leadership in the New Guinea Highlands (in: Oceania, 38, 1967-8, pp. 134-58, 163-89).

22 *Bradbury, B.*, Male Rationality in Economics - A Critique of Godelier on Salt Money (in: Critique of Anthropology, 3:9 & 10, 1977, pp. 131-8).

23 *Levi-Strauss, C.*, Structural . . .

24 *Strathern, A.J.*, The Rope of Moka: Big-Men and Ceremonial Exchanges in Mount Hagen. Cambridge 1971.

25 *Wagner, R.*, The Curse of Souw: Principles of Daribi Clan Definition and Alliance in New Guinea, Chicago & London 1967.

26 *Strathern, A.J.*, One Father . . .

27 *Salisbury, R.F.*, New Guinea Highlands Models and Descent Theory (in: Man, 64, 1964, pp. 168-71).

28 *Meggitt, M.J.*, The Lineage . . .

29 *Valeri, V.*, Le fonctionnement due système des rangs à Hawaii (in: L'Homme, 12, 1972, pp. 29-66).

30 *Godelier, M.*, Horizon . . .

31 *Bloch, M.*, The Past and the Present in the Present (in: Man, N.S 12, 1977, pp. 278-92).

32 See for instance *Godelier, M.*, Le sexe . . .; and *Strathern, M.*, Women . . .

33 For an account of Grand Valley Dani Society, see *Heider, K.G.*, The Dugum Dani. A Papuan Culture in the Highlands of West New Guinea. Chicago 1970; and *Peters, H.L.*, Some Observations of the Social and Religious Life of a Dani-Group (in: IRIAN. Bulletin of Irian Jaya Development, 4:2, 1975, pp. 1-197).

BIBLIOGRAPHY

Barnes, J.A., African Models in the New Guinea Highlands (in: Man, 62, 1962, pp. 5-9).

Bloch, M., Placing the Dead: Tombs, Ancestral Villages and Kinship in Madagascar. London 1971.

Bloch, M., Property and the End of Affinity (in: Marxist Analyses and Social Anthropology, ed. by M. Bloch, London 1975).

Bloch, M., The Past and the Present in the Present (in: Man, N.S. 12, 1977, pp. 278-92).

Bradbury, B., Male Rationality in Economics - A Critique of Godelier on Salt Money (in: Critique of Anthropology, 3:9 & 10, 1977, pp. 131-8).

Glasse, R.M., Huli of Papua: A Cognatic Descent System. Paris 1968.

Godelier, M., Horizon, trajets marxistes en anthropologie, Paris 1973.

Godelier, M., Le sexe comme fondement ultime de l'ordre social et cosmique chez Baruya de Nouvelle-Guinée (in: Cahiers de Centre d'Etudes et de Recherches Marxistes, CERM, 128, 1976, pp. 1-44).

Heider, K.G., The Dugum Dani. A Papuan Culture in the Highlands of West New Guinea. Chicago 1970.

Leeden, A.C. van der, Hoofdtrekken der sociale structuur in het westelijke binnenland van Sami. Diss. Leiden 1956.

Lepervenche, M. de, Descent, Residence and Leadership in the New Guinea Highlands (in: Oceania, 38, 1967-8, pp. 134-58, 163-89).

Lévi-Strauss, C., Structural Anthropology. London 1968.

Meggitt, M.J., The Lineage System of the Mae Enga of New Guinea. Edinburgh 1965.

Peters, H.L., Some Observations of the Social and Religious Life of a Dani-Group (in: IRIAN. Bulletin of Irian Jaya Development, 4:2, 1975, pp. 1-197). Translated from Dutch.

Pospisil, L., Kapauku Papuan Economy. New Haven 1963.

Rappaport, R., Pigs for the Ancestors: Ritual in the Ecology of a New Guinea People. New Haven & London 1967.

Sahlins, M., On the Ideology and Composition of Descent Groups (in: Man, 65, 1964, pp. 104-7).

Salisbury, R.F., New Guinea Highlands Models and Descent Theory (in: Man, 64, 1964, pp. 168-71).

Scheffler, H.W., Choiseul Island Social Structure. Berkeley & Los Angeles 1965.

Scheffler, H.W., Ancestor Worship in Anthropology: Or, Observations on Descent and Descent Groups (in: Current Anthropology, 7, 1966, pp. 541-8).

Strathern, A.J., The Rope of Moka: Big-Men and Ceremonial Exchanges in Mount Hagen. Cambridge 1971.

Strathern, A.J., One Father, One Blood. Descent and Group Structure among the Melpa People. London 1972.

Strathern, A.J., Kinship, Descent and Locality: Some New Guinea Examples (in: The Character of Kinship, ed. by J. Goody, London 1973).

Strathern, M., Women in Between. Female Roles in a Male World: Mount Hagen, New Guinea. London & New York 1972.

Wagner, R., The Curse of Souw: Principles of Daribi Clan Definition and Alliance in New Guinea. Chicago & London 1967.

Valeri, V., Le fonctionnement du système des rangs à Hawaii (in: L'Homme, 12, 1972, pp. 29-66).

MARRYING THE ANCESTORS: MARRIAGE STRATEGIES OF THE SURENESE NOBILITY IN LOMBOK

Sven Cederroth

In this study[1] I shall discuss traditional Sasak marriage. My intentions are to show how the ranking system and the intense concern with ancestors as well as some other features of the old cosmology determine the way marriages are contracted. I will also try to show how an élite uses this marriage system to further its own interests and maintain its traditional privileges.

1. MARRIAGE IN SUREN

Traditionally, marriage was, and in some parts of Lombok still is, the occasion for a big and expensive feast; it can be said to be 'the big feast' in the life cycle of the individual.[2] With the growing importance of orthodox Islam, and a more and more strict adherence to the prescribed Islamic marriage formula, this feast as an occasion for exhibition of wealth and conspicuous consumption gradually becomes de-emphasized. The data concerning marriage presented below are all collected in a north Lombok community where this process of change has barely begun, and are thus in conformity with the old traditions.[3] However the wind of change is blowing rapidly over Lombok these days, and for the past two years or so all procedures concerning marriage and divorce have to be carried out according to a formula prescribed by the religious office, which among other things means that all marriages and divorces have to be registered.[4]

In fact, today, traditional Sasak have to undergo marriage ceremonies not less than three times in order to be completely married. Three days after the elopement they celebrate *tobat kakas* by which ceremony a temporary permission to have sexual intercourse is acquired. The permission so obtained is valid until subsequent ceremonies *sorong serah* and *tobat sah* can be held. According to *adat*[5] the marriage is thereby legal and no further ceremonies are required, but nowadays the authorities also demand that all Muslims shall perform a marriage ceremony *(nikah)* which is in agreement with the moslem law *(fiqh)*. This is done in Suren between the first and second marriage according to *adat*.

My concern here is exclusively with the traditional *adat*-based marriage as the innovations introduced from outside are weakly integrated into the society and looked upon by the community members as mere formalities. The *nikah*, is, however, not without serious financial implications. The cost varies between 5,000-10,000 rupiahs (US$ 12-25) which is a considerable amount of money for a poor peasant who earns perhaps 200-300 rupiahs (50-75 cents) per day.[6]

When a young boy falls in love with a girl, he will start to court *(meleang)* her. He goes to visit her at her parents' home in the evenings, where he will be served coffee or tea and have a chance to talk to the girl. He will visit her perhaps once a week, often bringing some small gifts for her parents, such as betelnuts or some tobacco. A popular girl may have many boys courting her at the same time, without indicating whom she prefers. This courting may sometimes go on for several years, but will in most cases be terminated within six months to one year.

Thus, courtship may involve face-to-face communication between the boy and the girl. But frequently the boys make use of a *jeruman*, a sort of go-between, to express his feelings towards the girl. Anyone can act as a go-between, but mostly a boy chooses a close friend. If this friend is a member of the girl's family, complications may arise later when the obligatory discussions following a successful elopement are undertaken between the families *(ngeraosin saji krama)*. The go-between is often given favours of some kind in exchange for his services, and he (or she) can moreover use his position to solicit presents, saying that the girl wants it, while in fact he keeps it to himself. If the girl really receives the goods, (for instance a towel or cloth), and keeps them, this is taken as a sign that the boy's feelings are reciprocated, and that he can start to prepare for the elopement. If, for one reason or another the marriage does not take place, those gifts must be returned.

When the girl and the boy have agreed to elope, a suitable day has to be chosen. This is done according to a system of calculation called *dewasa* where each day, month and year in a 8-year cycle has a certain given value *(naktu)*. These values are added together and the sum is compared to a formula which makes it possible to determine whether the day is auspicious or not for a certain activity.

The elopement, which must be carried out in strict secrecy, is the most critical phase of all the marriage procedures when the likelihood that something unexpected will happen is the greatest. Stories about the boy being surprised by his prospective father-in-law, or about the girl running away only to find herself hiding together with a stranger, and not with her fiancé, etc., are numerous and people love to talk about them. There are also cases, not at all uncommon, where the couple are pursued by angry members of the girl's family, threatening to stab the boy with their daggers *(keris)*. They say that in former times this happened frequently. Nowadays people in general do not care that much, but I shall describe what happened when an aristocratic girl eloped with an ordinary policeman, a case which will indicate that even nowadays it can sometimes be very dangerous to try to marry someone considered to be of higher rank.

After a successful elopement, the girl and the boy find themselves together for the first time in the house of some relative of the boy. They must stay in the hiding-place for three days, not being allowed to leave the house except for necessary walks to the river. As soon as possible after arriving at the hiding place, they are given *bedak krames* by an old woman. This is a mixture of cucumber and coconut oil with which they are rubbed all over the body. It is done in order to protect the couple and their offspring against all sorts of illness and other kinds of misfortune.

On the evening of the elopement, the father of the girl reports her disappearance to the headman of the ward *(keliang)*, who, after ensuring that her disappearance is real and that she is not just visiting a neighbour or a relative, concludes that she has eloped with a boy *(memulang)*. That same evening the family of the boy also reports to their *keliang* that their boy has married a girl named so-and-so, and that he intends to celebrate *tobat kakas* together with her three days later.

The next morning the boy's *keliang* in his turn informs the girl's family, and tells them that their daughter has eloped with a boy named so-and-so. If they do not accept the boy, this is now their last opportunity to search for the girl, and if they do so without finding her it means that the coming discussions about the elopement fine *(saji gama)* will be extremely complicated. If they do find her, this, at least formerly, means a state of war between the two families.

Assuming however that everything goes smoothly and no one is extraordinarily upset, the next phase is the celebration of the *tobat kakas*. This is a short, inexpensive ceremony, carried out in the hiding-place and attended only by members of the boy's family. Since it usually takes a very long time before the boy is able to pay his parents-in-law the agreed elopement fine, and since it is only after this payment has been made that the final legal marriage ceremony can take place, the *tobat kakas* can be seen as a sort of preliminary marriage, legalizing, at least temporarily, the union in the eyes of the community. After *tobat kakas* has taken place the newly-wed couple can return to ordinary life, although the boy still has to be careful to avoid the immediate kin of the girl, since the necessary reconciliation has not yet been carried out. They may now also have sexual intercourse, which they were not allowed to have as long as they remained in the hiding-place. The ceremony, *tobat kakas*, shows the same characteristics as the later marriage ceremony, but is less elaborate.

The time has now come for initiating a reconciliation. This starts with a discussion among the family of the bride about the size of the elopement fine. One or two representatives from the boy's family may also be present. The discussion is normally a short and undramatic affair, since all items that must be included are specified beforehand by tradition. The exact amount varies, sometimes very much, between different strata of the community. I will later discuss some implications of these differences, restricting myself at present to those items that are invariably included in the *saji gama*.

1 A specified amount of Chinese coins, *kepeng bolong* used until quite recently instead of the national currency in this area. If it is impossible to raise a sufficient amount, paper money may nowadays be substituted for these coins.
2 Some pieces of white cloth *(tembasaq)*.
3 A number of wooden spears with iron points *(tombak)*.
4 One or more water buffaloes *(wirang)*.
5 Spices, coconuts, firewood, ingredients for betel chewing etc. in sufficient amount.
6 A basket *(rombong)* containing about 2.5 kg rice and 244 Chinese coins *(ulun dedosan)*.
7 *Ajin gubug*. This is a sum of money for maintenance of the common property. The amount varies considerably in different parts of the village. For example in *gubug Lolon* it is fixed at 10,000 coins, while at *gubug Ketip* it amounts to 4,000, and in *gubug Karang Bajo* it is only 1,000 coins.

Various other items may be added, depending on the specific circumstances of the marriage concerned.

If the boy's family thinks that the amount decided upon is too high, or includes some items that rightly should not be there, they can protest and ask for a reduction. If this happens (which in fact it only rarely does) another discussion must take place to make the final decision about the amount of compensation to be paid by the bridegroom. Once a decision has been made and accepted by the other side, the boy should in theory pay the full amount eight days later. This time limit, however, is rarely observed and it often takes several years until everything is paid, and *sorong serah* the final marriage ceremony is celebrated. It also often happens that all items, except the most expensive ones, the water buffaloes, are paid quickly. The buffaloes are then delivered later. Not before this is done are all procedures concerning the marriage finished, and the couple are considered legally married.

When the big day finally comes, and everything is ready for the feast, an assembly takes place early in the morning. In the ward where the boy and his relatives assemble everyone is busy counting and arranging the things that will be delivered to the girl's relatives. Before long a colourful procession leaves. These are the representatives from the boy's side carrying with them all the items agreed upon in the earlier discussion between the two sides. The procession is headed by a spokesman, a *pembagun,* carrying an antique sword, a *keris pusaka* on his back, who like all the others, wears the traditional dress always worn on festive occasions. Everyone in the procession squats on the ground in front of the *berugaq,*[7] where all the family members of the girl have gathered. Remaining in this humble position the *pembagun,* speaks in very polite language, modestly devolving what he brings, and invites the other group to start inspecting. When this is done and no objections as to the amount and quality of the goods brought are heard, he enters the *berugaq,* followed by the man carrying *ulun dedosan,* the basket with rice and copper coins. The father of the bride takes the basket, reads a secret formula *(mantra)* and then opens it, breaking the ribbon tying the coins together. He then begins the distribution of the items. There are some rules determining the distribution. For instance the bride's mother and the witness *(wali)* will always get a fixed amount. The main division, however, is relative, depending on the amount of money and goods that are to be distributed, and the number of relatives who have assembled on the *berugaq.*

After this, the buffaloes are slaughtered by a religious official *(kiyai)*[8] and preparation for the common meal *(periapan)* starts. When this meal has taken place, usually late in the evening, it is time for *tobat sah,* the final marriage ceremony which confirms that the families are reconciled. In contrast to *tobat kakas* where only the boy and his relatives are present, both sides now send representatives to this ceremony which can take place on an ordinary *berugaq,* in *santren* at *penghulu,* or in the old mosque depending on the wishes of the families involved.[9]

In this ceremony some prayers are read by *kiyai* who also reads the Muslim confession of faith *(dua kalimah sahadat)* which has to be repeated by the bridegroom. He also has to reconfirm at this occasion his wish to take the girl he has eloped with as his legal wife.

Finally the *kiyai* takes 50 Chinese coins from the *ulun dedosan*, slowly counting them one by one in front of the bridegroom. The *keliang* from the bride's ward, sitting behind the bridegroom with a rattan cane in his hand beats him once with this cane, each time the *kiyai* counts one coin. Two ceremonial plates of food, which have been brought from the bride's house are used for a final common meal *(periapan)*.

Returning to the home of the bride, the bridegroom places himself on one of the *berugaq* whereupon the bride, bringing water from the house, washes his feet *(kaki gonggompaq)*. She then drinks three times and washes her face, also three times, using the same water. The bridegroom then tears off his shirt and headgear, which are snatched away by his wife who is then chased by her husband until they both disappear into the house.

2. MARRIAGE AND RANKING

After this general description of the procedure when contracting marriage in Suren, I will proceed now to discuss marriage in relation to the ranking system. As an introduction to this discussion I will present the following case, which took place during my stay in Suren.

> Badaruddin is a policeman, born in Bima (Sumbawa), but in 1972 when these events took place, working at the district police-station in desa Anjar, about 5 km from Suren. Up to the end of 1971 the police-station had been situated in Suren, and during his stay in that village, Badaruddin had met a noble girl named Denda Kertasari, daughter of Raden Sumbawali, *pemangku pedaleman,*[10] who was also responsible for upkeeping the local *adat (ketua adat)* as well as head of the council of elders *(tuaq lokaq)*. Even after he had moved away from Suren, Badaruddin continued to communicate with Kertasari, now mainly by means of letters. For this purpose he made use of a so-called *jeruman,* a girl-friend of Kertasari with whom she used to play. (At this time she was only 14 years old). According to Badaruddin, he had received six letters from Kertasari urging him to

elope with her, and one evening in September he had made his way to Suren and was waiting for Kertasari outside the fence surrounding *kampu* (see below) in Suren Timur. (Being *pemangku*, Sumbawali lived inside the *kampu*). When Kertasari finally came she was not alone but was accompanied by Denda Kartini, a girl who stayed in the house of Sumbawali in order to help his wife with housework. When she realized that Badaruddin and Kertasari planned to elope, she was afraid to go back alone and tell what had happened, and therefore ran away together with the others. A few minutes later, when the girls did not come back, Sumbawali realized that something had happened and ran to the alarm-drum *(kul-kul)*, close to the village office. Before long some 200 persons were out searching for the missing girls, but in vain. Badaruddin, who had also heard the beating of the drum, and understood what was going to happen, was hiding with the girls beneath a steep riverbank (the rivers in this area are usually dry most of the year). At about 5 o'clock in the morning they finally reached desa Anjar where they hid in a cave for a few hours, before reporting to Bapak Ayi, the chief of the police-station.

This was only the beginning, and many troubles still awaited Badaruddin. From now on, Sumbawali, supported by all the nobility in Suren, did everything possible to prevent the marriage. According to the *adat*, the person who has escaped with someone else's daughter has to report this within three days. This was done by *keliang* Dasan Lendang, the place where Badaruddin lived. As soon as the people in Suren knew with whom Kertasari and Kartini had escaped they held a meeting *(gundem)* in *kampu* Suren Timur, at which they discussed also the *saji gama*. They decided on the following items to be paid by Badaruddin:

1 1,000,000 Chinese coins.
2 44 white cloths.
3 44 spears.
4 13 water buffaloes.
5 *Ngalok Eka* 49,000 Chinese coins as a fine because he had used as *jeruman*, a member of *pedaleman*. (i.e. the *jeruman* was herself a member of Kertasari's family, and as such not allowed to support a marriage outside the range of the family.)
6 *Ngampah-ampah ilen pati*, 49,000 Chinese coins. This fine was applied in this case because Badaruddin had escaped with two girls at the same time.

7 *Dosan jeruman,* 10,000 Chinese coins. Another fine because he made use of *jeruman.*
8 *Terlambat selabar,* 12,000 coins. This fine was applied because they had received notification about the elopement too late.
9 *Lain keliang,* 1,000 coins. Fine applied since the girl's *keliang* was not the same as Badaruddin's.
10 *Ajin gubug,* 30,000 coins. This is the usual amount for Suren Timur (see above).

Badaruddin was thus supposed to pay all this because he had escaped with Kertasari, but in addition it was decided that he should pay *saji gama* also for Kartini although he had no intention of marrying her and did not want to *nikah* with her. According to the *adat* in Suren, however, he had already shown his intentions by allowing her to elope and he had thus to pay the *saji gama* for Kartini also. Another list, more or less like the one decided upon for Kertasari was therefore prepared which meant that Badaruddin was expected to pay altogether about 2 million Chinese coins and 24 buffaloes. Since he was not a rich man, owning no land or other valuables and subsisting only on his meagre salary as an ordinary policeman it was of course quite impossible for him to pay this amount. When Badaruddin sent two representatives of his to Suren to ask for *wali*[11] which is necessary to have when performing *nikah* in order to legalize the marriage according to Muslim law, he was met with a straight refusal: only after he had paid the full amount of *saji gama* would Sumbawali agree to send him a *wali.* Badaruddin tried not less than four times but without any success. Instead Sumbawali said that he did not recognize Badaruddin as husband of Kertasari, and demanded that she should be taken away from him and be kept by the village chief until *saji gama* had been paid. The village authorities, being obedient to Sumbawali as the highest chief of *adat* in the area agreed to this, but after a few weeks Kertasari disappeared again. She had run away for the second time with Badaruddin. Sumbawali's reaction was very harsh and Kertasari was before long taken into custody by the head of the district *(Camat)* himself. He decided, together with Bapak Ayi, the chief of Badaruddin, that something had to be done, and since they were both pious Muslims and therefore did not support Sumbawali's heretical interpretation of *wali*, they unanimously agreed that Badaruddin could use *wali hakim* for the *nikah* ceremony. *Wali hakim* is a sort of legal *wali* to be used when, for one reason or another, the normal procedure cannot be upheld. In this case some officials at the *kantor urusan agama* (office for religious affairs) in Gondang served as *wali*. This event took place on 27th October 1972 and the *nikah* was accepted by the official registering all marriages in the area *(P3NTR)*, who registered the marriage as usual. According to the Muslim law applied by these officials the marriage was now valid in the same way as an ordinary marriage, but according to Surenese *adat* it was still as invalid as ever, since none of the prescribed procedures had been adhered to.

Kertasari and Badaruddin thus finally could live together as man and wife, but their happiness turned out to be short-lived. Less than a month after *nikah* had taken place Kertasari left Badaruddin and went back to her family in Suren. What kind of pressures she had been exposed to before she took this step is impossible to say, but according to Badaruddin she was persuaded by means of black magic to leave him and he accused one of Sumbawali's relatives who lives in desa Anjar. Sumbawali also made accusations about the use of magic. According to a letter signed by Kertasari on 4th December, but obviously written by her father, Badaruddin had given her *senggeger* mixed with goat meat. This made her fall in love with Badaruddin and made her forget her duties towards her parents. All she could think of was how she would be able to meet with Badaruddin. But obviously this state of mental confusion was now gone, because she ended her letter saying that she did not love Badaruddin any more, and stated that if she should be forced to go back to him she would kill herself. Badaruddin tried several times to get into contact with his wife, and when he finally succeeded he asked her if she did not love him any more. She answered that she loved him, of course, but since he had not paid *saji gama* she was unable to come and stay with him.

Finally, since Badaruddin continued to regard Kertasari as his wife, each month sending her an allowance which was promptly returned to him by Sumbawali, the case was brought before the religious court in Maratam *(pengadilan agama)*. This court ruled that the marriage was indeed *sah*, i.e. it was a valid marriage. This decision, however, did not help Badaruddin regain his wife, who remained in Suren.

In the meantime, Badaruddin had met with another girl, whom he wanted to marry. Since 1st October 1975, Indonesia has adopted a new marriage regulation which, among other things, obliges all officials who want to take a second wife to get permission from the first wife. If she does not agree, he has to divorce her before being able to marry again. Badaruddin therefore sent a letter to Sumbawali, stating his wish to divorce Kertasari. Sumbawali, however, refused to sign the letter and give his permission to the divorce because, according to him, there had never been any marriage and he therefore could not agree to any divorce. Badaruddin is thus faced with, on one hand, the national law saying that he may not remarry until he has divorced his first wife and, on the other, the Surenese *adat* ruling that since there has never been any marriage there cannot be any divorce. According to Muslim law he is already married; according to the man who must sign the divorce papers he is not married.

2.1 The ranking system

This case raises several questions, and we shall start by examining the ranking system, since this provides the most obvious answer to the violent reactions from the nobility in Suren against this marriage.

Compared to the elaborated Balinese title system[12] the Sasak counterpart is somewhat simpler, but the basic principles are the same. As among the Balinese there are two major types of titles, discriminating people belonging to the nobility *(perwangsa)* from the common people *(jajarkarang)*, but in addition to this there is a further subdivision of titles among the nobility as shown in Table 1.

Table 1.

	Male title		*Female title*	
	Unmarried and childless	Married with children	Unmarried and childless	Married with children
Perwangsa	Datu	Mamiq	Datu Bini	Datu Bini
	Raden	Mamiq	Denda	Denda
	Lalu	Mamiq	Baiq	Mamiq Bini
Jajarkarang	Loq	Amaq	Leq	Inaq

There are numerous minor differences in this title system, and an exhaustive description would contain also several other titles, known only in parts of Lombok or perhaps only in a single village. The titles described above are, however, generally known throughout most of the island.

When the first child is born, the title as well as the names of the parents, are changed. Both parents will adopt the name of their child, and use this together with the second title above. If, for instance a commoner boy is named Sudinten, his full name will be Loq Sudinten, while his parents will be called respectively Amaq Sudinten and Inaq Sudinten. This tekonymy, which appears also among the nobility, serves to single out its bearer as a full, mature, member of the community, as opposed to those who have not yet any children themselves. A consequence of this system is of course, that a person's 'real' name will soon be forgotten and he will be remembered only as father *(amaq)* of his first child. Another consequence is that genealogies are difficult to keep. It frequently happened that informants could not remember the names of their own parents, while grandparents could rarely be identified by means of their birth names.

This title system is commonly referred to in the literature as a caste system. Without dwelling at length on the complicated question whether or not this is a true caste system, one may note that at least one of three characteristics[13] which are said to define castes is absent in this system. In India each caste (or sub-caste) is also occupationally defined, but this is not the case in Suren society. It is also worth noting that avoidance rules between different castes, which are a dominant feature of the Indian caste system, are not at all important in Suren. In daily life there are no specific restrictions preventing social intercourse between the ranking groups. Only at festive occasions are there certain prescriptions especially concerning food originally offered to the ancestors *(lungsuran)*. In my opinion, the best thing to do is therefore to avoid referring to this system as a caste system, thereby avoiding also other connotations commonly associated with the Indian caste system.

Although Suren formerly was the seat of one of the oldest (perhaps even the oldest) Sasak kingdoms there are no *datu* in the village today. The reason for this is unclear. It might well be that the Balinese killed the king and all his relatives when they conquered Suren or perhaps the king feared that this would happen and therefore fled with all his family. The Surenese themselves say that when the Balinese entered Suren, the king and his family took their refuge to the old mosque. When the Balinese tried to burn down the mosque, they found out that it was impossible. Although the mosque was and still is made only from wood and bamboo, it would not burn. When they, after this failure, made an assault against the mosque, they found it empty, the whole royal family had vanished. Until this day, the Surenese believe that their king is not dead, and that one day he will return.

The most prominent title bearers in Suren today are the group which claims right to use the *raden* title. They comprise perhaps 10 per cent of the total village population, but have long been, and still are, dominant in all important village affairs. There are only a few *lalu* in the village, and they consist of the former *raden* who have lost the claim to this title through repeated marriages with commoners who comprise the majority of the population.

There are in general no differences in wealth and living standard between the nobility and the commoners. Almost all the traditional rights of the nobility to make use of the labour power of the commoners and to acquire for themselves a certain part of the crop of their dependants (i.e. the commoners) have now been lost but they still retain a considerable though diminishing political influence in local affairs. The district headman as well as the village headman traditionally was chosen among the rank of the nobility, but in 1971 they lost the former office, which also meant that they lost most of their power outside immediate village affairs. When my fieldwork ended in 1976, they still kept their position in the village but faced the danger of losing the office of village headman in the elections scheduled for 1978.[14] If this happens, they will have lost the remaining part of their influence outside the ritual sphere. In many parts of the island this erosion of the traditional privileges of the nobility has gone much further than in Suren. In some areas, where the population is extremely influenced by orthodox Islam, the system has even been abolished altogether, on the argument that it is contrary to the egalitarian principles of Islam. Suren is one of the few remaining places where the nobility still keeps a measurable political influence, but in most parts of Lombok the title system is still more or less a factor as far as status is concerned.

This long-standing title system has bred the Surenese nobility with a feeling of natural superiority *vis-à-vis* the common people. They thus see their privileges as part of the natural order of things, and when they start to lose the more material parts of these privileges, they cling even more stubbornly to the immaterial, but easily visible signs of deference which are expressed among other things in language. The same word can in the local language be expressed in several different ways, and in this way can different degrees of politeness be connoted. A titleholder can demand to be addressed in a polite language, while being allowed to answer in a more rude language.[15] There are, of course, also many other ways in which this deference to titleholders can be expressed, for instance by means of gesture, or by deliberately adopting a humble stance and so forth. Marriage is, however, the main instrument used by the nobility when they try to maintain their alleged superiority.

2.2 The saji gama

A discussion of the Surenese marriage will find an obvious starting point in the elopement fine *(saji gama)*. Even an ordinary marriage between two commoners involves considerable costs, amounting to about 100,000 Rps (US$ 240). If Badaruddin actually had paid the elopement fine in his marriage with Kertasari this would have cost him more than 3 million Rps (US$ 7,200). If this is compared with a normal wage for a day labourer, which is 2-300 Rps (50-75 cents) one immediately understands the big difficulties the young men have to face when they shall pay the elopement fine. Fortunately enough, Suren is a rich village (at least according to Lombok standards) where traditional kin loyalties still are strong, and these two facts combined facilitate the collection of a fund for paying the elopement fine. There are extensive unused areas of land in Suren where an intended bridegroom can cultivate a cashcrop and in a short time earn a considerable amount of money. For this work he can count on extensive help from his relatives, who will also assist him later with all kinds of necessities for the marriage feast (for instance spices, coconuts, firewood, and above all rice). But despite these helps, it frequently happens that the bridegroom cannot meet his responsibilities within the prescribed time. In those cases, the marriage feast will have to wait, and this waiting time can sometimes amount to several years. An often sought solution in those cases is to divide the feast into two parts. A first feast will be held within the prescribed eight days, where all items except the water buffaloes are handed over. The bridegroom will then have a respite to collect money to buy those expensive animals, and when he has succeeded with this, a final feast takes place. Included in this is a *tobat sah* ceremony, which legalizes the marriage.

It sometimes happens, although very rarely, that the bridegroom neglects to pay for the water buffaloes included in the *saji gama*. This animal, when forming part of the *saji gama*, is known as *wirang* which can be approximately translated as 'disgraced', the implication being that the family of the bride continues to feel disgraced until the buffalo has been paid for. To slaughter a buffalo is thus necessary if the marriage is to be considered legally valid. I was told about one case where the bridegroom had for some reason failed to slaughter this buffalo. His daughters who are now grown up, are allowed to marry, but they cannot demand to have a buffalo slaughtered at the final wedding ceremony. Their father's neglect has thus to be paid for by them, to the extent that they are regarded as more or less illegitimate and therefore not able to demand the same treatment as a legitimate child. But also other members of that family feel themselves ashamed by this treatment, and one of the sons has therefore proposed that he in his forthcoming marriage shall pay one water buffalo extra as a substitute for the one his father never paid. In this way he intends to restore the reputation.

Manipulation of the *saji gama* is the main strategy employed by the nobility when they want to uphold their status, and we shall therefore proceed by examining this institution in some detail. The *saji gama* has sometimes been described as constituting a bride-price. In my view, however, it is misleading to call the *saji gama* bride-price and it is better described as a sort of elopement fine, the amount of which can vary according to the degree of emotional and cosmological disturbance caused by the elopement.

Polak discusses this question in a footnote,[16] but seems to be falling back on a definition in *Notes and queries on anthropology,* to conclude that the *saji gama* is in fact a real bride-price. The definition he uses goes as follows:

> Bride-price, bride-wealth, marriage payment, are terms used for goods, gifts or payments transferred by the bridegroom or his family to the bride or her family on the occasion of marriage.[17]

This suggests that the *saji gama* is a 'bride-price', but this classic definition has a further crucial element:

> It is not to be consumed in the course of the celebrations, nor is it handed to the wife: it goes to the bride's male kin (typically brothers) in order that they can themselves take a wife.[18]

Most of the items included in the *saji gama* are consumed during *sorong serah* celebrations, the same day as they are handed over. The few things not consumed (i.e. the Chinese coins, the spears and the cloths) are distributed among the bride's kin (not only male kin, her mother also receives a share) and between certain functionaries (e.g. the *keliang* in the bride's ward and the performing *kiyai*). It is thus only a small part of the *saji gama* that actually goes to the bride's kin, and it definitely does not provide them with any funds enabling them to take a wife for themselves.

The largeness of the *saji gama* depends on whether or not you belong to the nobility, and whether or not your marriage is within the same ranking category. Preferably the marriage should also be within the family (i.e. between first, second or third cousins) at least if you belong to the nobility. A cousin marriage will result in a considerably lower *saji gama*, than would be the case if the couple was unrelated. If, for instance, a man from the nobility marries an unrelated girl from *pedaleman*, *saji gama* will include among other things 650,000 Chinese coins and 7 buffaloes, while if marriage takes place between two members of *pedaleman*, being first, second or third cousins, *saji gama* will 'only' be 124,000 coins and 4 buffaloes. In a marriage between two commoners on the other hand, *saji gama* will normally amount to 2,000-4,000 coins and one buffalo. If this is compared to the list prepared for Badaruddin (see above), one cannot but be struck by the huge differences in the elopement fine between the various ranking categories. If the close kin of the bride feel that the marriage is undesirable they can easily prepare a very expensive list of items, in which they can also include various extra costs arguing that the bridegroom has committed one or more offences against *adat*.[19]

If despite all sanctions a noble girl insists on marrying a commoner man, she immediately loses her title, and will not be able to regain it if she later divorces. Her children, of course, also automatically lose all claims to any title. She will also be banished from her family.

> Inaq Chandrasari, a commoner from Karang Bajo, married a nobleman from Suren Barat, and together they had a daughter Denda Chandrasari (as we have seen, Denda is the title used by women from the nobility). When she had grown up she married a commoner from Karang Bajo and immediately lost her Denda-title. She was now called Leq Chandrasari (the title for commoner women who have not yet had any children) and she was also isolated from her family. After a while she divorced her husband and shortly thereafter remarried, this time with a nobleman from Batu Grantung. She did not, however, get her

Denda-title back and, moreover, she was still not accepted by her family of orientation.

This case illustrates the fact that a marriage between a noble girl and a commoner man is considered a much more severe violation against the *adat* than the reverse. If a man from the nobility marries a commoner girl, nothing serious will take place. He as well as their offspring are allowed to keep their title, although the children are considered to be of a not quite authentic nobility *(tember)*. If they in their turn also marry below their ranking category, the title of their children will fall one step, i.e. a *Raden* will have sons entitled *Lalu*, and the sons of a *Lalu* will be commoners. If they do not 'marry down' nothing will ever happen, and the original violation will by and by be forgotten. A hypergamous marriage is thus tolerated (as opposed to hypogamous marriages) but considered not quite appropriate. Thus when one of my best informants, a nobleman, married a commoner, he was forced by the disapproving attitude of his widowed mother towards her daughter-in-law, to move away with his wife, and build a new house close to the rice-fields.

As can be seen, *saji gama* is thus used as an instrument to prevent marriages between different ranking categories, and at least as far as the nobility is concerned also to stress that preferential marriage is within the range of third cousins. Besides the demand to marry within one's own ranking group, there is thus also a strong preference for endogamous marriages, and we shall soon proceed by examining this institution in some detail. Before going into this we must, however, take a brief look at another aspect of the marriage system which is also of great importance.

3. MARRIAGE BETWEEN GENERATIONS

The marriage system works also in another dimension, differentiating people generationally from each other in terms of older-younger. An important principle in the Surenese marriage system is the requirement to find a spouse within one's own generation. If a man marries a woman considered to be generationally older than himself this is a case of *salah basa* (lit. wrong language). In such cases there is an ambivalence concerning the appropriate term of address to be used and such a marriage is considered to be a severe violation against *adat*. It is said that formerly, during the time of the 'Raja Bali', a couple who had committed this sin were killed, and their bodies thrown into the sea. Nowadays, they are still discouraged from marrying, but if they persist, it will be enough if they pay the high fines added to the normal *saji gama*. There are at least two different kinds of *salah basa:*

1. *Bero*. In this case, which is considered to be the most serious one, the girl is generationally older than the boy, and using classificatory terms, it is said that in this case a child marries his mother *(anak mengambil ibu)*. Normally, 49,000 Chinese coins, 2 water buffaloes and 4 pieces of while cloth are added to the *saji gama*.

2. *Kero* This is the converse case, where the boy is generationally older than the girl, and it is said that a father marries his child *(ayah mengambil anak)*. The fine will be half that imposed in the case of *bero*.

Ensuring that one marries a generational peer even takes precedence over cousin marriage. Though inter-generational marriages are tolerated nowadays, people were always very ashamed when one came to talk about close relatives who had contracted *salah basa* marriages.

Within a generation similar principles are at work. The *adat* forbids a younger sister to marry as long as her older sister remains unmarried. Should such a marriage take place, a special fine called *pelengkak* and consisting of 5,000-10,000 Chinese coins is added to the *saji gama* Supplementing the prohibition against inter-generational marriages, we have thus also a rule stating that intra-generational marriages must take place in a proper order.

4. ENDOGAMOUS MARRIAGES

In Suren, both matri- or patrilateral[20] cousin marriages are preferred and no distinction is thus made between cross- and parallel cousins, who are considered equally desirable as marriage partners. There is, however, a striking difference between the nobility and the commoners concerning preference for first cousin marriages as opposed to second and third cousin marriages. Consider the following figures in Table 2 which are taken from my sample.[21] More distant relatives than third cousins are considered to be non-relatives, since almost nobody is able to trace his/her genealogical links any further than third cousins, and more distant relatives are thus for all practical purposes regarded as unrelated.

Table 2.

Marriages among the nobility

Between first cousins:	27 cases	40.3 per cent
Between second cousins:	18 "	26.9 "
Between third cousins:	15 "	22.4 "
Between non-relatives:	7 "	10.4 "
	67 "	100 "

Marriages between commoners

Between first cousins:	12 "	15.2 "
Between second cousins:	29 "	36.7 "
Between third cousins:	25 "	31.6 "
Between non-relatives:	13 "	16.5 "
	79 "	100 "

From the table above, we can see that among the nobility as well as among the commoners, marriages within the range of third cousins are the norm, amounting to resp. 90 and 84 per cent of all marriages recorded. But we can also see that the nobility differs from the commoners with regard to first cousin marriages, which are much more prominent among the former. Ideally, a first-cousin marriage is considered the most preferred union. Being closest to incestuous marriages, but without transcending the border line, it is endowed with sacredness. In such marriages an optimal amount of the spiritual qualities inherited from the ancestors is preserved and they are thus as close as possible to the ideal but forbidden union between a brother and a sister.[22] But being so close to incest, first cousin unions are also dangerous and therefore restricted to people with exceptional qualities, i.e. those belonging to the nobility. These risks taken into consideration, commoners tend to prefer second and to a somewhat lesser extent also third cousin unions, by means of which also a big amount of the heritage from the ancestors is preserved.

I will try to show that descent from a common mythical ancestor is what above all obligates people to stick to this system of cousin endogamy. This is so, because if in a bilateral situation the kinship ties are not constantly renewed by means of endogamous marriages, the descent group will within a short time be so dispersed that it will be impossible to recognize it as such any more. Another reason for this preference for cousin marriages, which is often mentioned by the villagers themselves, is that it facilitates negotiations about *saji gama*. It is true, that such marriages minimize the risk that conflicts will appear because of different rank and/or status between the two sides involved, but on the other hand complications directly related to the high degree of endogamy may arise. Consider for instance the situation given in Fig. 1.

Figure 1.

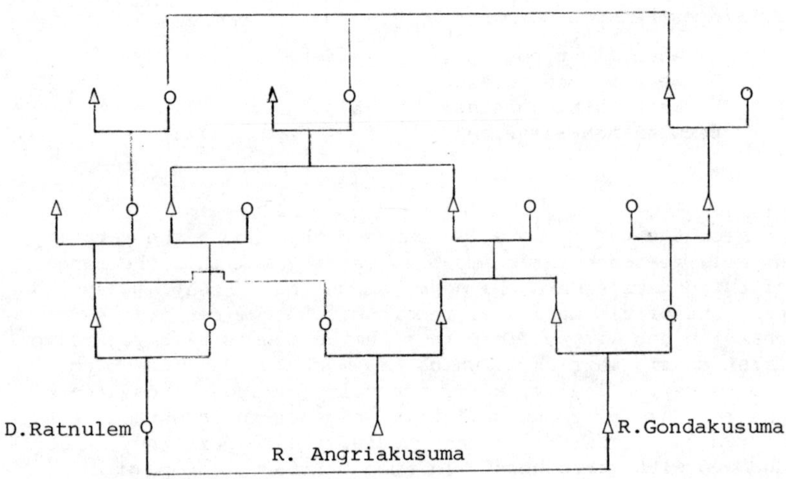

From this limited elaboration we can see that R.Gondakusuma is related to D. Ratnulem in several different ways (FBWiBD; FFBDD; FFMSiDSD; MFFSiDSD).

When discussing *saji gama* in the marriage between R. Gondakusuma and D. Ratnulem, R. Angriakusuma took part as a representative for R. Gondakusuma. Since he is as closely related to D. Ratnulem (MBD) as he is to R. Gondakusua (FBS), one may well wonder why he did not represent her side also. In this, as in other cases of the same kind patrilateral relations take precedence over matrilateral, and he thus represented only the side of the bridegroom. Since he himself found his position questionable he sat quiet all the time and did not take part in the discussions.

The rule requiring marriages to be endogamous, which among other things implies that the contracting parties are equal in rank is thus a strong rule, and most marriages in this society are in conformity with it. If, in spite of all sanctions, an exogamous marriage should take place, another equally strong rule comes into play. This rule states, that if the two parties are not of equal rank, the party of the bridegroom must be the higher ranking group. The opposite situation is, as we have seen, not tolerated. Even among nominally equally-ranked groups this rule finds application. It has for instance repeatedly been noted, that the *pedaleman* group try with every conceivable means to prevent their girls from marrying someone from the nobility who does not belong to *pedaleman*. Also in the case of *salah basa* marriages it can be seen that if the male side is the older (i.e. higher ranked) the violation is considered less serious.

5. ANCESTORS AND ENDOGAMY

Endogamy is valued in this society,[23] above all because the 'ancestral qualities' are thereby transmitted through the generations with as little loss as possible. These 'qualities' are seen to be inherited by both men and women i.e. they possess a male as well as a female aspect. The Surenese themselves distinguish between *turun wali* and *turun bibit*. A sibling group as a whole is said to be *turun wali* from the viewpoint of their father, but only children of his sons are *turun wali* in the next descending generation, while his daughter's children are said to be his *turun bibit*. In the first descending generation, the principle of the unity of the sibling group is thus upheld, while in the following generations a split occurs between descendants in the male and female line respectively.

A girl thus at the same time belongs to the *turun wali* group of her father and the *turun bibit* group of her mother, and the 'ancestral qualities' are transmitted to her from both groups. If these groups, because of former endogamy are coexistant, or highly overlapping, the 'ancestral qualities' will not be diluted, the blood will still be pure. If, on the other hand, former exogamous marriages have already diluted her blood, she will not be as close to the ancestors, i.e. she will not be as god-like as would otherwise have been the case.

The *turun wali* and *turun bibit* groups, representing respectively the male and female aspects and thus together the totality of the heritage from the ancestors, can if properly blended be viewed as a closed unit. The same set of qualities is then preserved within the unit, and with the prevalent notion of rebirth added, it becomes perfectly clear how the system works, and why each exogamous marriage is viewed as undesirable. If the marriage is not only exogamous, but also between different ranking groups, it is looked upon with increasing disgust, to the point of being intolerable as was for instance the case with the marriage between Badaruddin and Denda Kertasari, described above.

This said, account must also be made for the fact that the *turun wali* group is for all practical purposes the most important group. With the exception of daughters who have married into some other group, they live together in a single ward, and they form the 'ancestor group' to which also the married daughters (but not their children) must return when honouring the ancestors.

Ancestors are an important concern in this society. They are invited to participate in all main ceremonies, at which occasions they are offered different kinds of food *(ngengolang)* and it is believed, that if they are neglected in one way or another, they might get angry and cause misfortune. It is thus very important to placate them and show the necessary kind of reverence towards them. The process of becoming an ancestor begins immediately after death, culminating in the elaborate and very costly 7-day celebration *(nituq)* and ending with a big feast 1,000 days after death *(njiu)*.

Surenese society proper can be seen as composed of four endogamous ancestor groups, three of which consists exclusively of people from the nobility, and one whose members are all commoners. The three noble groups each possess a so-called *makam*, a sort of grave in which a mythical ancestor-founder of the group is believed to be buried,[24] and three of the groups (two nobility groups plus the commoner group) are also in possession of a *kampu*,[25] which is a place nowadays mainly used for gatherings of different kinds (e.g. discussions concerning *saji gama* take place here) and for the carrying out of certain ceremonies (e.g. *sorong serah*). Summarily, it can be said that these graveyards and gathering places serve to strengthen and enhance the unity of each group as opposed to the other groups. The graveyard is the point of origin for the whole group, and therefore the focus for common ancestor group rituals (e.g. *ngaji makam ngaturan ulaq kaja*), while *kampu* whose maintenance is common concern for the whole group, is also the place where the group acts as a separate decision-making unit. The descent group also lives together as a unit; a fact which of course further facilitates intercourse, thereby enhancing the possibilities of finding a spouse within the group.

The *pemangku*, living inside *kampu* is the official responsible for the maintenance of the graveyard and all ceremonies performed there, partly or wholly in honour of the ancestors in order to guarantee their blessings. The *kampu* can thus be looked upon as a sort of ancestor temple, and the ceremonies performed there and at the graveyard require participation of the women belonging to the group. Certain important functions (e.g. *inan meni* and *inan pedangan)*[26] are inherited from mother to daughter and may not be performed by anyone outside that specific family. Since an endogamous marriage permits the girl to take up permanent residence together with her ancestral group, the value of endogamy is thus further enhanced.[27]

Thus the requirement that the ancestors be rendered permanent worship, logically entails the Surenese preference for cousin marriage, as well as their insistence that marriages shall take place within the same ranking group and sometimes even excluding those members of the same ranking group who do not belong to one's own ancestor group. This is for instance the case with the *pedaleman* group who inflicts severe fines[28] if someone from one of the other nobility groups (with one exception, see below) wants to marry a girl belonging to the *pedaleman* group. The *pedaleman* place extremely high value on endogamous marriages. They not only impose outrageously high fines if an outsider tries to marry someone in the group, as in the case of Badaruddin and Denda Kertasari, but they do this in spite of the fact that the group contains several superannuated girls (in this case, aged above 20-25 years), who are unable to find a spouse within the group, and consequently must remain unmarried rather than being allowed to contract an exogamous marriage.

This high esteem in which the ancestors are held may also help explain the strong prohibition against marrying someone not belonging to your own generation, since to marry a person of an older generation would be to marry a potential ancestor.

Although, the ratio of 'family marriages' is very high in Suren, the descent group cannot be entirely self-sufficient in women, since however ideal from an ancestor-oriented point of view, this would not permit the forming of necessary alliances with other groups. Faced with this dilemma, the

Suren nobility acknowledge marriage with one of the other two groups as equal to marriage with members of one's own group. The *pedaleman* nobility thus frequently intermarry with the noblemen from Suren Barat. The latter group also contracts many marriages with the Karang Salah group, while marriages between this last mentioned group and *pedaleman* are very rare. This has historical reasons, since the Karang Salah group are descendants of the Surenese king, who once was defeated by an ancestor of the *pedaleman* group, and the old animosity between the two groups still persists to a certain degree.

6. RECONCILIATION AFTER ELOPEMENT

The purpose of the *adat* ceremonies is to restore again normal cosmological conditions after the violation of the natural, harmonious state of affairs, caused by the elopement. Only gradually, and by means of a carefully regulated procedure, is the offender again accepted as a full member in the society whose rules he has violated. The ancestral group of the girl needs her as a member in order to perform the necessary services towards the ancestors, and to transmit the heritage from the ancestors as purely as possible to future members of the group. They would therefore never willingly agree to her being taken away from the group. An elopement, without consent from her kin group, but with full agreement from the girl herself (if elopement takes place without her prior knowledge the girl may refuse to marry, in which case she is given back to her group) is thus necessary if a man shall acquire a wife, who does not belong to his own immediate kin.

But since most marriages, as we have already seen, are endogamous this cannot be taken as an explanation for the fact that the bride and the bridegroom have to elope, even if the marriage takes place within one's own kin group. An explanation has, I think, to be sought in the legal and moral ties which bind the girl to her natal family in such a way that they must be unfastened by means of an allegedly secret and violent act of elopement. The ties fettering the girl to her natal family depend partly on *adat* rules and partly on Islamic concepts, which combine to make any other solution impossible to fit into the world view of the Surenese.

Elopement has always, or at least as far back as we can go, been the normal way for the Sasak to contract their marriages but in addition to this, Sasak nobility in other parts of the island[29] used to arrange marriages between their children, while they were still small. In those cases an elopement was not necessary. This practice can be directly related to the title system which in the central parts of the island worked somewhat differently from that of Suren. The most important difference was that a man from the nobility immediately lost his title and became a commoner if he married a commoner girl. Since the number of people belonging to the nobility also was much smaller in these areas than was the case in Suren, there was an obvious risk that the nobility should be eliminated if they could freely follow their own preferences when choosing a marriage partner. In Suren, on the other hand, where there was no such threat, it was not necessary to interfere in such a restrictive way. Instead the somewhat softer, but still mighty force of *adat* was applied in order to prevent too many undesired marriages. Elopement, therefore came to be preserved in this area, also among the nobility, and today this institution is so deeply instilled that people cannot conceive of any other ways of contracting a marriage. Since it is the *adat* to elope, everybody has to elope irrespective of how closely they are related to each other, and irrespective of whether it is already widely known that they intend to marry. In all those cases, without exception, a fake elopement has to be staged. If, on the other hand, the elopement involves a more severe violation against the cosmological order (e.g. if the two sides involved belong to different title groups) the affair is real enough, and sometimes as we have seen even rather dangerous. In the latter case the procedures necessary for reconciliation are also more extensive and costly. Only at the final *tobat sah* ceremony, which sometimes can take place several years after the elopement is a complete reconciliation achieved when the bridegroom receives 50 blows from a rattan cane. This practice is interpreted by Prof. Moh Koesnoe[30] as a punishment for illicit sexual intercourse which has taken place in the time interval between *tobat kakas* and *tobat sah*. This punishment, which is based on the Muslim law *(fiqh)* is known as *radjam*. As he himself also admits, this punishment is to be found in no other place in Indonesia,[31] and even in Suren it appears in a completely distorted form, and not even its proper name has been preserved. The *radjam* punishment in its original form meant that the two sinners were stoned to death, or alternatively, if the persons involved were in some ways insane, or otherwise irresponsible for their deeds, they were flogged and then expelled. In Suren nothing of this happens. The 50 blows which are very gentle, do not even hit the boy, but are aimed only at the straw mat behind him.

Moreover, it is only the boy who receives any punishment. The girl is not punished at all. In my view, it is therefore more appropriate to see in this institution something other than an application of the Muslim *radjam* punishment. I think that the slaps are to be regarded as confirmation on the final reconciliation received through the payment of the *saji gama*, and the acceptance of this payment by the girl's family. By suffering this very symbolic punishment, the boy acquires again the status as a worthy member of the community, and the wrath he brought down upon himself when eloping with the girl is at last forgotten.

In an ideal situation, marriage takes place between equals, or alternatively, between a couple in which the men's group is higher ranked. What actually happens, however, is that the wife-taking group by means of an elopement act, places itself above the wife-givers, who in order to save their honour are forced to make a big show where they denounce the claims and demand compensation. The marriage ceremony then, symbolically reverses the ranking implied by the elopement and places wife-givers above wife-takers. The ritual meal which takes place immediately after the bridegroom has received his slaps, symbolizes that the disturbance of the cosmological order caused by the elopement is forgotten, and that a state of equality is again reached.

7. *CONCLUSIONS*

In this exposition of the Surenese marriage, we have thus found that the marriage is used by the nobility as a sort of last line defence in their fight for maintaining traditional privileges. They deny anyone but close relatives the right to marry their daughters and to achieve this goal, they impose high elopement fines on any outsider who tries to marry into their circle. The ideological foundation for such endogamous marriages is to be found in an ancestor-centred cosmology according to which it is of utmost importance that 'the thread connecting the living with the ancestors shall not be broken'. This happens every time an exogamous marriage takes place, since the ancestral qualities then will be transmitted to the children in one line only. This fits very well with the intentions of the nobility, who by reference to this cosmology can stop anyone who wants to attack their status and privileges. In most parts of Lombok the nobility have already lost their traditional influence and a new type of leadership mainly recruited from the ranks of the common people has emerged.[32] At the same time, the ideology on which the nobility based their claim to privileges and special treatment, has also been replaced with an ideology based on orthodox Islamic concepts. In this new ideology, not only the privileges of the nobility are questioned, but the whole ranking system is attacked and finally abolished. In Suren, however, this change has barely begun, and the position of the nobility is largely uninfluenced by what has happened in the central parts of the island. This has been possible because of the isolated position of Suren north of the large Rinjani volcano which separates the village from the rest of the island.

In this essay, it has thus been shown how a traditional cosmology is expressed in the marriage system, and thereby manipulated by an élite that wishes to maintain its old positions. The ideology is thus used as a system-preserving factor by those who want to prevent radical changes of the system. But of course this is not a necessary function of all ideologies in all circumstances;[33] this is only how one aspect of the traditional ideology works in Suren today.

NOTES

1 The data on which this study is based were gathered during two periods of fieldwork, in 1972-3 and 1975-6, in a North Lombok village which I have called Suren. The fieldwork was financed by the Swedish Council for Humanistic Research and by the Scandinavian Institute of Asian Studies.

2 Cf. *Izikowitz, K.G.,* The Gotr Ceremony of the Boro Gadaba (in: Primitive Views of the World, ed. by I. Diamond, New York 1960, pp. 128-49). A hypothesis which will be further elaborated in a later essay is that surplus in this society traditionally should be invested in titles by staging a big feast at marriage, and/or in ancestors by staging equally big feasts 7 and 1,000 days after death.

3 Cf. *Polak, A.,* Some Aspects of a Process of Change in an Indonesian Community (in: Tropical Man, 4, 1971, pp. 108-16).

4 Each district nowadays has a religious office *(Kantor Urusan Agama)* and each village a *P3NTR (Pembantu, Penabat, Pendaftaran, Nikah, Talaq, Rudjuq).* The latter registers each marriage and reports to the religious office which issues a marriage licence.

5 *Adat* is defined by Moh Koesnoe as 'the whole body of teachings and their observance which governs the life of the Indonesian people and which has emerged from the people's conception of man and world'. *Koesnoe, M.,* Introduction into Indonesian Adat Law (Nijmegen 1971), p. 8.

6 *Nikah* is celebrated in order to make the marriage legally valid. Here the Arab language is used and not, as in marriages according to Surenese *adat*, a mixture of old Javanese and Sasak.

7 A *berugaq* is an elevated platform 1 metre above the ground, with a deeply overhanging grassroof, but without any walls. It is used as a meeting- and resting-place, and also, as in this case, for ritual purposes. Cf. also my article: *Cederroth, S.,* Symbols of a Sasak Community in Northern Lombok (in: Ethnos, 40, 1975).

8 There are five kinds of religious officials in this community: *Penghulu, Ketib, Lebe, Modin* and *Santri*, all collectively labelled *Kiyai*. They are a sort of Islamic priesthood, especially concerned with the transition to the hereafter. Cf. ibid.

9 Which place to be chosen depends on the status and wealth of the families contracting the marriage. If the ceremony takes place in the old mosque, the *Kiyai* has to be paid 10,000 Chinese coins, while the same

ceremony performed on any *berugaq* will cost only 444 coins. Usually, however, the *santren*, which is situated at the living place of the *Penghulu*, the highest-ranking of the religious officials, will be considered the most appropriate place for this ceremony and the costs will then be 1,700 coins. A *santren* is a small mosque, which in this community is used exclusively as a place for marriage ceremonies.

10 A *Pemangku* is a non-Islamic religious official, whose main duties concern the relations with the spirit world. Nowadays he is also responsible for the so-called *adat* ceremonies, i.e. all those traditional ceremonies which have no obvious connection with Islam. In Suren there exist more than 20 *Pemangku*, and Raden Sumbawali was the highest ranking of them all.

11 In *Echols, J.M. & Shadily, H.*, An Indonesian-English Dictionary (Ithaca 1975), *wali* is defined as 'male relative legally responsible for the bride under Moslem law, normally her father'. In marriage according to Surenese *adat*, *wali* is also used, with the difference that it is not the father who acts as *wali* but some of her brothers, or, if she has no brothers, any male patrilateral cousin.

12 Cf. *Geertz, C.*, Tihingan. A Balinese Village (in: Villages in Indonesia, ed. by Koentjaraningrat, Ithaca 1967), p. 222.

13 *Dumont, L.*, Homo Hierarchicus (London 1972), p. 57. The three characteristics are: separation in matters of marriage and contact, division of labour and hierarchy.

14 When I left Suren, there was an active headman functioning who came from the nobility, but in the elections he had to face several rivals for this attractive post. One of his rivals would probably be a Javanese policeman who had settled permanently in the village and succeeded in winning many adherents.

15 For instance the equivalent of *yes* in Suren can be four different words, depending on the situation. *Aoq* is used as every day language within the family, while *enggih* is used towards honoured guests or as the normal word of address to a person of higher title. Office holders belonging to the nobility can demand to be answered with the word *meran*, while the very few people who still can claim a right to use the title *Datu* are answered, also by other members of the nobility, with the extremely polite word *da*. This last mentioned word finally, is also used when visiting and addressing the ancestors in the different graveyards *(makam)* in Suren.

16 *A. Polak*, Some Conflicts over the Bride-Price in an Indonesian Peasant Community (in: Tropical Man, 4, 1971), p. 121.

17 *Notes and Queries on Anthropology*, (6th ed., 1964), p. 116.

18 *Goddy, J.*, Bridewealth and Dowry in Africa and Eurasia. Cambridge Papers in Social Anthropology, 7, 1973.

19 Many different kinds of breaches of *adat* can be considered if the family wants to obstruct the negotiations. Several of those breaches are so vaguely formulated that they can be applied in many different circumstances. There is for instance one paragraph which says that the bridegroom shall be fined 49,000 coins if he has said or done anything that offends the morality, and another paragraph obliges him to pay the same amount if he has pointed out himself and his own achievements in an untrue manner.

20 Patrilateral cousin marriages are considered somewhat more appropriate than matrilateral. *Saji gama* is for instance higher in marriages between matrilateral cousins than in marriages between patrilateral cousins.

21 Interviews were made in the following *kampung*: Suren Timur, Suren Barat, Karang Salah, Karang Badjo and Teres Genit. The three first mentioned *kampung* are inhabited by nobility, the two latter by commoners.

22 If twins of opposite sex are born, this is seen as a very dangerous event, since it is assumed that they have committed incest in the womb. They are brought up separately, but later forced to marry each other.

23 The Surenese themselves have an expression for this. They value endogamy in order that 'the thread connecting the living with the ancestors shall not be broken *(uah peget matan benang)*'.

24 The three *makam* are: *Makam Susuhunan, Makam Suren Barat* and *Makam Karang Salah*. Cf. *Cederroth, S.*, Symbols . . .

25 The three *kampu* are situated in Suren Timur, Suren Barat and Karang Badjo. There are historical reasons, upon which I shall not dwell here, for the non-existence of *kampu* among one of the nobility groups. When necessary for ritual of other purposes they unite with one of the other nobility groups, with which they have come to establish special relations.

26 *Inan Meni* is responsible for guarding and distributing the collected rice, and *Inan Pedangan* for cooking the rice.

27 Cf. *Boon, J.*, The Balinese Marriage Predicament: Individual, Strategical, Cultural (in: *American Ethnologist*, 3:2) pp. 199-201.

28 Cf. above note 20.

29 Cf. *Prins, M.J.*, Verspreide aanteekeningen over adatrecht en volksgebruiken in Midden-Lombok (in: Mededeelingen van de Kirtya, 6, 1939), pp. 67-70.

30 *Koesnoe, M.*, Receptie van de radjam straf in de adat Sasak van Bajan (in: Bijdragen tot de Taal-, Land- en Volkenkunde, 126, 1970, pp. 203-14).

31 Ibid., p. 203.

32 Cf. my article: *Cederroth, S.*, Religiösa reformrörelser på Lombok [Religious reform movements in Lombok] (in: Historisk Tidskrift, 1977, no. 3, pp. 350-73).

33 Cf. the discussion about counterpoints in *Werheim, W.F.*, East-West Parallels: Sociological Approaches to Modern Asia (The Hague 1964), Chapter 2.

BIBLIOGRAPHY

Baal, J. van, Het Alipfeest te Bayan (in: Djawa, 1941, pp. 1-41).

Boon, J., The Balinese Marriage Predicament: Individual, Strategical, Cultural (in: American Ethnologist, 3:2, pp. 191-214).

Cederroth, S., Symbols of a Sasak Community in Northern Lombok (in: Ethnos, 40, 1975, pp. 169-84).

Cederroth, S., Religiösa reformrörelser på Lombok [Religious reform movements in Lombok] (in: Historisk Tidskrift, 1977:3, pp. 350-73).

Dumont, L., Homo Hierarchicus. London 1972.

Echols, J.M. & Shadily, H., An Indonesian-English Dictionary. Ithaca 1975.

Geertz, C., Tihingan: A Balinese Village (in: Villages in Indonesia, ed. by Koentjaradiningrat, Ithaca 1967).

Goody, J., Bridewealth and Dowry in Africa and Eurasia. Cambridge Papers in Social Anthropology, 7, 1973.

Izikowitz, K.G., The Gotr Ceremony of the Boro Gadaba (in: Primitive Views of the World, ed. by I. Diamond, New York 1960, pp. 128-49).

Koesnoe, M., Receptie van de radjam straf in de adat Sasak van Bajan (in: Bijdragen tot de Taal-, Land- en Volkenkunde, 126, 1970, pp. 203-14).

Koesnoe, M., Introduction into Indonesian Adat Law. Nijmegen 1971.

Notes and Queries on Anthropology, 6th ed., 1964.

Polak, A., Some Aspects of a Process of Change in an Indonesian Community (in: Tropical Man, 4, 1971, pp. 108-16).

Polak, A., Some Conflicts over the Bride-Price in an Indonesian Peasant Community (in: Tropical Man, 4, 1971, pp. 118-48).

Prins, M.J., Eenige gegevens nopens Sasaksche volksgebruiken (in: Mededeelingen van de Kirtya, 6, 1939, pp. 34-54).

Prins, M.J., Verspreide aanteekeningen over adatrecht en volksgebruiken in Midden-Lombok (in: Mededeelingen van de Kirtya, 6, 1939, pp. 55-70).

Riel, A.C.J., Sasaksch huwelijksceremoniel in de Waktoe Tełoe-streken van Midden-Lombok (in: Djawa, 1941, pp. 81-8).

Wertheim, W.F., East-West Parallels: Sociological Approaches to Modern Asia. The Hague 1964.

NAMES, NAMING AND ADDRESS CUSTOMS IN MINAHASA

Wil Lundström-Burghoorn

INTRODUCTION

In this essay my intention is to give an ethnographic account of names, naming and address customs in Minahasa (N. Sulawesi). By this account I hope to emphasize the view that names and terms of address are much more than ethnographical details and curiosities of small value. They deserve the same attention as other ways of distinguishing and classifying persons and relationships. It is one way among many, to make an inquiry about categories of persons and relationships, which is the ultimate purpose of my study.

In naming and addressing a person what matters is what you want to emphasize and what is appropriate. Appropriateness is largely governed by general rules for conduct, which mainly reflect public values and ideas. What is selected for emphasis is more situational- and individual-bound. Different circumstances may require different emphases and consequently find different expressions. For example, utterances made in the domestic sphere are frequently unlike those made in the public sphere. The expressions may even be literally the same, but they have different meanings, dependent on the context they are used in. Take the term 'saudara' (Indonesian for relative). In daily speech it applies to relatives by blood, adoption and affines, while in oratory the term is used to address the audience. Apart from situational, the choice of emphasis when addressing a person, is individual-bound. It is related to the importance the speaker places on one of the applicable terms and the number of terms available to the addressed person. How do you want to conceive of him and how can he be conceived? There are many ways to conceive of a person and many modes in which to address him, but whatever form they have, 'they cannot help but communicate over and over again things about the self and self-other relationships'.[1] I will deal with the most common ones in Minahasa.

In Minahasa there are five sorts of labels which people can apply to one another in address and reference. These different sorts of labels are: personal names, surnames, kinship terms, teknonyms and public titles. The type of label used is conditioned by the following major sets of factors:

(a) ethnicity or 'Minahasancy'
(b) the different stages in the developmental cycle
(c) circumstances (situational in a pragmatic sense)
(d) prevailing fashions of address.

1. FACTORS CONDITIONING ADDRESS CUSTOMS

1.1 Ethnicity

In the day-to-day life, kin-terms are used in addressing kin as well as non-kin. This extra genealogical use of kin-terms is applicable to those persons who are considered to be 'kawanua', which broadly means: of the same place of origin, i.e. persons of Minahasan origin or married to Minahasans. Minahasans exclude persons of different origin by not using kin-terms towards them, though strangers may adopt this way of addressing Minahasans or themselves.

1.2 The different stages in the developmental cycle

Prevalent is the conception of a person in terms of generation, or put in another way, in terms of the stages of life. This is hardly surprising, as we know that things and ways to communicate the identity of an individual and his relations with others, are to a large degree patterned by the individual's position in the stages of life. This all pervasive notion influences proper conduct and consequently the modes of address.[2]

1.3 Circumstances

Under this heading I distinguish the infinite set of different contexts which require different expressions and what needs to be emphasized explicitly.

1.4 Prevailing fashions of address

This I consider to be a minor factor and first of more significance when the use seems to persist over time and become a convention.

These are the major factors that condition the type of label used in addressing people. Let me now examine the different sorts of labels, that is: personal names, surnames, kinship terms, teknonyms and public titles.

2. LABELS USED IN ADDRESSING

2.1 Personal names

A common view is to consider personal names in contrast with the other labels (surnames, kin-terms, teknonyms, public titles). The other labels are then grouped under the term titles, because they have the capacity to put the individuals into categories, while personal names leave the individual unclassified. A number of studies of names and naming have explored the classificatory and individualizing functions of names in different societies.[3] Roughly the postulation is, that personal names have the function to represent the individual, the uniqueness of a person, the association with self. In contrast titles function to classify a person, to put him into a category, to underline a relationship, to represent the individual in society.

I adopt here a somewhat different approach, viewing all these types of labels as having the capacity both to specify a human being individually and classify him. It is a matter of stronger or weaker capacity for either functions, rather than a question of having either one or the other function. One aspect can and often does overshadow the other. An individual's personal name identifies in most cases the unique individual but may also give the information about how the individual fits into society. For example, since an individual often shares one of his personal names with an ancestor, the aim is then to stress the relationship with that particular ancestor, which in its turn gives the information about membership in a constellation of people characterized by kinship ties.

Types of personal names. There is a luxuriant variety of personal names and it is often very entertaining to run through a list of Minahasan personal names. Each individual carries a set of personal names, which vary in degree of association with self and with the place of the individual in society. The names are given with respect to sex. Nearly everybody shares one of his names with another person, though never with a parent. The use of one of the names may shift several times during the course of a person's life. Moreover throughout his life, an individual continues to receive new labels, at his consociates, people who share a community of time and space[4] address him by alternative labels.

Minahasans do not hide their personal names, they overtly bear them and they are freely spoken. But it is considered improper to address a person of senior generation by his personal name. In that case it is only acceptable to use a personal name with a generational kin-term as a prefix. Minahasan personal names fall into eight broad categories: relationship names, celebrity names, circumstances of birth names, unanalysable names, pet names, nicknames, standard names, birth order names.

Relationship names. Relationship names refer to the bearer's or his name-giver's relationship with another person. These are baptismal names given to the new born child by his parents or some close relative. They are given to mark familial connections, usually ties of kinship but even ties of friendship. Often these ties of kinship are with someone in the ascending generations, but never the parent's name. It is now fashionable to use a combination of the parental names, thereby expressing their status as co-procreators. For example, if mother's name is Karla and father's name Olly, their child's name might be Karol. People tend to give their name and their ancestor's name to younger persons, to keep the names in use. Many of the names given to children are those of ancestors. The ancestor in question might have got the name from his ancestors or he might have had it as a private name.

In the latter case his private name turned into an open name when he became an ancestor. His descendents may take this name, though none of them has an exclusive right to that particular name. An individual is thus perceived in the context of who produced him, who one of his ancestors was.

Celebrity names. As well as relationship names these are baptismal names. These names are given to commemorate a personality. Personalities of very different characters, such as:

- biblical figures (e.g. David, Simon, Jozef)
- famous historical figures (Hannibal, Cleopatra)
- cultural heroes (e.g. Toar, Lumimuut both founding ancestors of Minahasa)
- famous actors and actresses (e.g. Olivia, Elvis)
- personally admired figures (e.g. someone admired a

successful farmer in the Philippines, whose surname was de la Cruz and he gave this as a personal name to his new born child).

Circumstances of birth names. These baptismal names are of two types; those referring to the time of birth such as 'Frida' (born on Friday) or 'Prokla' (born on the 17th of August, the day of proclamation of independence); and those referring to an unusual experience at the time of birth e.g. the singing of a bird, the mother's experience at that time.

Unanalysable names. These baptismal names have no explicit meaning. They do not indicate a relationship or membership in any sort of group. Often they are recent introductions.

Now we come to the group of additional names, names acquired in addition to baptismal names.

Pet names. Pet names are given when the child is still small. They are only used by close relatives in the domestic sphere. At the time the child reaches adulthood, the names are out of use. Public men may purposively bring into use again their pet name. A powerful man is on equal terms with you, when he encourages you to call him by his pet name. A man who was running for village headmanship, used to be known by the name Paul. During the campaign, he took the name 'Lollopop', his pet name at an early age.

Nicknames. There is very frequent use of nicknames. These are descriptive of the bearer in one or another way. For example:

- Physical appearance, such as 'telinga' (ear), for someone who had one of his ears shot off.
- Characteristic behaviour, such as 'doa' (pray), for a person who was said to pray a lot, even to the chickens.
- A special experience of the bearer, such as 'Lombok', for a man who was involved in the Lombok war of 1894.
- A person's formal roles, such as 'tete vacci', for the vaccinator of the village.

A number of the nicknames, those which refer to embarrassing incidents or physical peculiarities are very insulting. They are used by friends and relatives in joking, not in teasing. Nicknames may be given at any time from birth on.

Standard names. Name avoidance exists only in the case of addressing a person of higher generations and in case of serious illness during childhood. Serious illness not only causes name avoidance, but the child in question may not stay in the parental house and is brought up by other relatives in their dwelling groups. When they reach early adulthood, they return to the parental's dwelling group. These children get what seem to be standard names such as 'Purut', 'Utu','Mene', which may be coined as nonsense syllables. The bearers keep this name throughout life. Remarkably, these names often occur among a group of siblings. Any group of siblings may have an individual called 'Utu'. People give different explanations for their use, like: 'his name is Utu because he was sick during childhood' or 'because he is the youngest' or 'because he is so spoiled'. There is an inconsistency in the explanation and I can only note that there are a number of markers which qualify for the use of the name 'Utu'.

Birth-order names. A system of three labels is used to indicate the order of birth within a sibling group; 'tua' - 'tengah' - 'bungsuh': eldest - middle - youngest. 'Tua' is applied to the first born child, 'tengah' to someone falling by order of birth in the middle range of his sibling group, 'bungsuh' to the last-born child. The two last labels are not fixed to a person. Someone can be 'bungsuh', last-born child for that moment, but he by no means marks by this the end of the child-bearing period of the parents. The birth order names, with the exception of 'tua', indicate a relative rather than an absolute serial position. Their use is largely restricted to reference.

There are thus various types of personal names and an individual may have several names. The usage is mainly conditioned by circumstances and choice of emphasis. Minahasans themselves broadly class the circumstances into public and domestic. Public contexts are connected with 'fine' or 'school' names, domestic with 'daily' and 'home' names. The use of 'home' names is limited to a circle of close relatives and friends, while the use of 'fine' names is extended to the other villagers.

2.2 Surnames

The coming of Christianity has added the use of surnames. People take ancestral personal names, tribal names and mythological names as their surname. To a larger degree than personal names, this group of names has the capacity to stress an individual's place in society. However an individual's surname refers just to his potential place, not to his actual place in society. Each individual has one surname: his or her father's, while at marriage a woman takes her husband's surname. Without doubt, a surname refers to a kinship constellation of people, but does not necessarily refer to the group in which the individual wants to stress membership, or with which society identifies the bearer of the name.

Say a person's surname is 'lolong'. He shares this name with his fa., fafa, fafafa. The name is thus persistent in time. Still the person may emphasize that he belongs to the 'Supit' family (his fafawi was a 'Supit') and society recognizes him as a 'Supit'. One reason among many others may be that the 'Supit' family has been for generations an important family in that region. Respect, authority, bravery, wealth or influence is connected with that name. Descendants want to keep this up and be part of it, consequently they will stress that they are 'Supits', seeking for any possible link that can connect them with the 'Supits'. Of course the person cannot deny that he is a 'Lolong', but he may very well stress solidarity with the 'Supits', due to several conditions. We notice thus that a person's surname does not limit his association with the co-sharers of that name. Still a surname has the capacity to include and exclude individuals. What a surname does communicate is the following:

- Whether the bearer is a Minahasan or not.
- Being a real Minahasan, whether he belongs to the nobility or not.
- If the bearer is a Minahasan, whether he is a real Minahasan or a so-called 'borgo'. ('Borgo' are coastal people who since the sixteenth century lent the colonial government their services. These services were mainly in defending the coast, and in return they were treated by the government as 'strangers' and as such were freed from government services. Nowadays a great majority of them are fisherman.)
- And finally, to which traditional territorial grouping he belongs, since the name will be most frequent in the region where it originated.

In general, surnames are used in official contexts and very seldom in daily speech.

2.3 Kinship terms

Kin terms are used to address all persons of Minahasan origin or those married to Minahasans. All Minahasans, including the large number of Minahasans abroad, consider themselves 'kawanua', which broadly means: of the same place of origin ('wanua' - locality, village).

A stranger, that is a person from outside Minahasa can only be incorporated into the group of 'kawanua' by marriage. Settlement in itself does not qualify a person as a 'kawanua'. The terms in current use are derived from three different languages and traditions, namely: the indigenous language, Bahasa Indonesia and Dutch.

Two systems can be distinguished, one in the indigenous language, the other in the foreign languages (Indonesian and Dutch). Both systems have the same structure, terminological recognition of differences in genealogical generation, sex and relative age in the same generation. Their application is different; foreign terms are used in addressing remote relatives and non-relatives, while the indigenous terms are preferably used in referring to and addressing close relatives.

Thus beyond the limits of close relatives:

All females of ego's generation are called 'zus' (Dutch for sister).

All males of ego's generation are called 'broer' (Dutch for brother).

All females of the first ascending generation are called 'tanta' (Dutch for aunt).

All males of the first ascending generation are called 'oom' (Dutch for uncle).

All females of the second ascending generation are called 'nene' (Indonesian for grandmother) or 'oma' (Dutch for grandmother).

All males of the second ascending generation are called 'tete' (Indonesian for grandfather) or 'opa' (Dutch for grandfather).

Individuals in the first descending and second descending generation are called 'anak' (Indonesian for child) regardless of their sex.

All these terms should be avoided when referring to or addressing close relatives. For close relatives it is preferred to use the indigenous terms which fail to indicate the precise link between oneself and a close relative. We notice thus a very extended use of kin terms, a habituation which expresses familiarity in inter-personal relations.

2.4 Teknonymy

Teknonymy is the practice of defining one's identity by one's relation to another; to one's child in most cases. The name of the child, irrespective of sex, forms part of the teknonym, the other part refers to a kinship tie (father of . . . or mother of . . .). Teknonymy thus has to do with identification by a relation. In Minahasa it is the identity of parent or grandparent that is expressed in terms of the relation to their child or grandchild. After the birth of their first child, the couple start to be addressed by and referred to as father of and mother of so and so, whatever the name of the first born child happens to be. Only the first child marks the shift in status during adulthood. Through one's first child, one gets the status of parent, a very crucial status in society. But the teknonym expresses more than the status of parenthood of that first child, namely the jural responsibility for the welfare of not only that child but all one's children, as a result of parenthood. It classes one in the group of people who are characterized by parenthood or grandparenthood. These are admittedly broad categories, but significant ones, as the merging and distinguishing of persons according to the generation principle is very important and deserves priority over other forms (see kinship terms). In his article on teknonymy in Bali, Geertz recognizes as a feature of teknonymy the identification of man and wife as joint procreators.[5]

In the case of Minahasa I would consider this as a subordinate function. The identification of parenthood in itself is of greater significance. I would consider the following facts to support this assumption:

Teknonyms are applied to single parents, that is, widowed or divorced men and women or unmarried mothers.

Parents whose children are frequently sick do not use teknonyms. Their children address and refer to them as 'bo' (brother) and 'susi' (sister). It is considered contributive to the children's health when they avoid terms referring to the parental status. Instead they use terms that express siblingship, 'sameness' of generation. It is this stepping downwards in generation, rather than the dissolution of the husband-wife link that finds symbolic expression in the use of sibling terms. It is only a matter of a change in terms. Their jural responsibility of parenthood does not cease to exist. Of course, if one wants to continue considering the possible communicative aspects of terms, the use of sibling terms implies that they cannot be spouses. Isn't this a bit far-fetched? I am afraid that this way of reasoning will bring me too far from what people themselves signalize as communicative aspects, and perhaps too much weight would be put on the implications of the usage of terms.

There is a second change of name many years later when the couple become grandparents. Their names shift to grandfather of . . . and grandmother of . . . the inserted name being that of the first grandchild. Their children in turn are referred to as father of . . . and mother of . . . their own child. It is the first grandchild that makes you a grand-parent. It is in a way a signal that you can relax, that you can be sure that you will become an ancestor after your death, that you have got successors.[6] In the domestic domain the use of teknonyms is equal for everybody. In the politico-jural domain their use is restricted to public men. Thus there is a relationship between teknonymic usage and community status. Yet there are variations in mode of address to persons of the same status. The use of teknonyms is related to the emphasis the community wants to place on a person. In the public sphere the teknonyms join the category of public title. We notice for example that the rules for the usage of teknonyms, father of . . . name first child, grandfather of . . . name first grandchild, are not strictly followed. A man of political weight may be addressed by father of . . . a long time after the birth of a grandchild. There is also the possibility of using the names of favoured offspring. In general, then, teknonyms refer to generational status, but in the public domain they serve rather as status markers or titles.

2.5 Public titles

These are labels applied to strictly 'public men', often derived from a person's formal role. They are used in both reference and address. To give some examples: 'bapa pendeta' (father priest) - for the priest; 'bapa hukum tua' (father village elder) for the head of the village; 'njora pendeta' (njora from signora, priest) – the wife of the priest. Considering these very 'public men' there is a co-variation in terms of address for them. They can be addressed by their public title, a teknonym and, in official contexts their surnames, but even in official contexts and in oratory they may be addressed by their personal names. A well-known government official is often addressed by his personal name 'Jootje'. This name falls in the type of personal name I called unanalysable names, baptismal names which have no explicit meaning. The name 'Jootje' does not give you any information. The man who is addressed by this name in the public sphere is very active in village politics, he is married to a rich woman, he is a government officer, father of four children, adores movies and spends a lot of money for watching movies in the town. There are alternative labels for addressing him, but they seem to be so well known by the public that it seems unnecessary to point out his personal qualifications or relationships. Instead he is called 'Jootje'. Everybody knows immediately who the person is and that name which lacks explicit meaning seems to communicate all the alternative ways of addressing him.

3. CONCLUSION

The foregoing is the result of an investigation into the manner in which people are distinguished or grouped by the process of naming and addressing. There are many modes in which to address a person: personal names, surnames, kinship-terms, teknonyms, public titles. Decisive in addressing a person is what you want to emphasize and what is appropriate.[7]

My argument is, that the different types of labels have the capacity both to specify a human being as an individual and to classify him as a member of a category, i.e. to represent the individual in society.

NOTES

1 *Goodenough, W.*, Personal Names and Modes of Address in Two Oceanic Societies (in: Context and Meaning in Cultural Anthropology, ed. by M.E. Spiro, New York 1965), p. 275.

2 The close interdependency between conceptions of person, time and conduct is a general phenomenon, which has been subject for extensive discussion among anthropologists, see e.g. *Geertz, C.*, Person, Time and Conduct in Bali (in: Geertz, C., The Interpretations of Cultures, New York 1973); *Radcliffe-Brown, A.R.*, Introduction (in: African Systems of Kinship and Marriage, ed. by A.R. Radcliffe-Brown & D. Forde, London 1950); *Fortes, M.*, Names among the Tallensi of the Gold Coast (in: Afrikanistische Studien, 1955).

3 *Lévi-Strauss, C.*, La pensée sauvage. Paris 1962; *Goodenough, W.*, Personal . . .; *Needham, R.*, The System of Teknonyms and Death-Names of the Penan (in: South-Western Journal of Anthropology, 10, 1954).

4 *Geertz, C.*, Person . . ., p. 65.

5 *Geertz, C. & H.*, Teknonymy in Bali: Parenthood, Age-grading and Genealogical Amnesia (in: Journal of the Royal Anthropological Institute, 94, 1964), p. 104.

6 *Fortes, M.*, Names . . .

7 *Goodenough, W.*, Personal . . .

BIBLIOGRAPHY

Benjamin, G., Teminar Personal Names (in: Bijdragen tot de Taal-, Land- en Volkenkunde, 124, 1968).

Eder, J.F., Naming Practices and the Definition of Affines among the Batak of the Philippines (in: Ethnology, 14:1, 1975).

Feng, H.Y., Teknonymy as a Formative Factor in the Chinese Kinship System (in: American Anthropologist, 38, 1936).

Fortes, M., Names among the Tallensi of the Gold Coast (in: Afrikanistische Studien, 1955).

Geertz, C., Person, Time and Conduct in Bali (in: Geertz, C., The Interpretation of Cultures, New York 1973).

Geertz, C. & H., Teknonymy in Bali: Parenthood, Age-grading and Genealogical Amnesia (in: Journal of the Royal Anthropological Institute, 94, 1964).

Goodenough, W., Personal Names and Modes of Address in Two Oceanic Societies (in: Context and Meaning in Cultural Anthropology, ed. by M.E. Spiro, New York 1965).

Lévi-Strauss, C., La Pensée sauvage. Paris 1962.

Needham, R., The System of Teknonyms and Death-Names of the Penan (in: Southwestern Journal of Anthropology, 10, 1954).

Pollard, F.H. & Banks, E., Teknonymy and Other Customs among the Kayans, Kenyahs, Kelamantans and Others (in: Sarawak Museum Journal, 4:15, 1937).

Price, R. & S., Saramaka Onomastics: An Afro-American Naming System (in: Ethnology, 11:4, 1972).

Radcliffe-Brown, A.R., Introduction (in: African Systems of Kinship and Marriage, ed. by A.R. Radcliffe-Brown & D. Forde, London 1950).

CONTROVERSIAL RECIPROCITY: ON SOCIAL CHANGE AND ROLE NEGOTIATION IN A KELANTAN MALAY COMMUNITY

Ingrid Rudie

INTRODUCTION

This study represents an attempt to discuss some aspects of social change as it could be observed in a Malay village community in Kelantan about 1965. Empirically, it is a variation on the theme of how macro-level factors affect social structure in local communities. Analytically, I am interested in the nature of the social dynamic - the streams of interaction - that make changes materialize on the local level. The discussion will focus on a covert contest in words and deeds between neighbours who seem to differ in their handling and interpretation of institutionalized reciprocity. This contest can be seen as a striving to keep, or readjust, a working consensus on behaviour rules and mutual rights and duties in a situation where disturbing factors are brought into routinized relationships. This process has both an organizational and a cognitive side, sides which can be taken care of in a perspective of role negotiation

The gross trend of the change that takes place, is one of increasing market integration and urbanization. This implies that people in rural communities which are drawn into this process, change their positions relative to each other, and these changed relative positions necessitate a revision of habitual role relationships. In the empirical case which will be analysed below the neighbour role is under debate because increased social differentiation is about to make the inhabitants' opportunities and experiences more heterogeneous. An increasing number of the local people work in non-traditional occupations outside the locality. Their time is structured in new ways, and new orientations develop. This does not lead to a breach of relations, but to a discussion of the content of relations.

Underlying the present discussion is a kind of understanding of the interdependence between locality and wider society which is working its way into social anthropology.[1] Any locality must be seen as an aggregate of people who have face to face contact, but it is not necessarily corporate, or autonomous as a social unit in any respect. Each inhabitant takes part in a number of different activities which may be organized independently of each other, and some of which may take place outside, some inside, the locality. Every activity involves the participant in certain rights and duties, puts certain strictures on his use of time, and puts other strictures on, or opens new possibilities for, the way he can use his mind - in other words, trains him in the particular code that belongs to that particular activity. In a locality which is highly differentiated there are many fields of particular experience, many subcodes present in the inhabitants' repertoires, and only a fraction of this totality of repertoires need be shared by everybody. The amount of shared experience of course affects the ease with which people can reach a working concensus.[2] A role relationship is subject to a constant trial, and it functions at any point in time as a preliminary agreement dependent on the acknowledgement of rights and duties, possibilities for sanctioning each other, access to information. The neighbour role must be carved out between people who meet for the first time in the new residential area, and it must sometimes be changed, re-negotiated between old neighbours.

In a locality in which social differentiation is increasing, inhabitants have different part statuses, and play different roles, in different settings. The degree to which this is so affects the presentation of the neighbour role. A person's total experience furnishes him with material for presentation in the sense that he may draw directly on different role identities to prepare his presentation as a neighbour in a given situation. The counterparts may or may not support his presentation. They may share a large or a small amount of information with him - which is decisive for the degree of rapport between them, and the length of the process of reaching it.

1. SOME CHARACTERISTICS OF THE LOCALITY

At the time of fieldwork Kelantan was, as it still is today, characterized by a relatively low degree of industrialization. Malays constitute more than 90 per cent of the population, and Muslim morality is deeply ingrained in the Malay way of life.

The sub-district Alur Pinang[3] is situated in the middle of the densely populated Kelantan Plain. It is close to Kelantan's largest towns, which represent a market for labour and commodities. Our unit for this analysis is not the whole sub-district, but a smaller neighbourhood within it, a *kampong* called Simpang Pekan. The *kampong* is not an administrative unit, and I would prefer to translate it into 'neighbourhood' rather than 'local community', for it is neither well-bounded nor corporate politically, economically or ritually. The neighbourhood is vaguely separable from the environment on the basis of some ecological and social features. In social terms it can best be described as a relatively strongly interwoven patch on the network which stretches out in all directions. Within such local clusters people's relations to each other carry a variable amount of mutual obligations.

Alur Pinang belongs to that part of Kelantan's countryside which is most affected by economic complexity and differentiation. Within Alur Pinang our selected neighbourhood, Simpang Pekan, can be looked upon as a centre, comparatively more affected by occupational differentiation than the rest of the sub-district. Most of the inhabitants of Simpang Pekan manage by combining various sources of living. Most have some land, but few live exclusively by tilling their own land. Some combine agriculture with some craft; these have more freedom than others to decide on how to spend their own time. They can manage their own land, and are free to engage in various kinds of work arrangements. They are not dramatically in need, but will not decline a day's wage when they have the chance to earn one. Others combine agriculture with a permanent paid occupation as industrial or clerical worker. This group also counts a few civil servants whose high salaries enable them to invest in landed property. This group is subject to a strict timetable. They are mostly dependent on some kind of help to get their agricultural work done, or on letting land out on a sharecropping basis. Least privileged are those whose land is grossly insufficient, and who do not possess any particular skill, or have not managed to get a permanent job. These are dependent on taking land in sharecropping, or on working for a wage on other people's land.

All these groups differ in various ways. For one thing, they differ in the strictures put on their use of time. Further, they differ as regards economic success. Still further, they have different status repertoires and different repertoires of knowledge and experience. The clerical worker, the industrial worker, and the man who has always worked on his own farm are subject to different schemes of organization where different pragmatic rules apply. Even among those who are primarily farmers, different strategies for production and resources management prevail. While some stick mainly to the highly predictable routines of rice-growing, others get more and more involved in market gardening. This adds an element of new planning and calculation to their resource management - they must calculate with supply and demand and the prices on different products in the market, and with the labour requirements and growth cycle of a number of crops. This is more complicated than calculating with the amount of rice that one must produce for the family's consumption needs, which used to be the peasant's traditional measure of viability.

So far, we have mostly stressed the ways in which people in the locality differ from each other, and tried to point to socio-economic as well as cognitive sides of the differentiation. In another respect they are similar: they all share a need for obliging friendships, and a set of rules about how these friendships should be handled. This is generally in line with observations of several techniques from other peasant societies used by people to extend their obliging social network.[4] Friends are cultivated through ceremonial acknowledgements like feasts and gifts, and called upon for purposes of work exchange, to find jobs, write letters, offer hospitality and assistance to travellers. In Kelantan Malay society friendship and kinship have retained a great deal of their instrumentality. Direct striving for widening the network can be seen in the extensive use of the kinship idiom, in strategies behind the choice of a marriage partner, and in the strong motivation for investment in the 'ceremonial fund.'[5] On the local level it seems as if two counteracting tendencies are present: one disintegrating, which springs from increasing differentiation, and one integrating, which springs from a need for social resources in the form of many obliging relationships. To the individual local person this presents itself as a problem of reaching a compromise between the need for building oneself into a network of potential helpers, and the different restrictions to which he is subject on being able or willing, to afford participation in the system of reciprocity. Schematically - and cynically - this can be described as if each participant tries to use his friends maximally, at the same time as he himself often argues for being exempted from obligations that others try to put on him. Presented in a less cynical way, the striving for compromise shows itself in the different use, the different values, and the different understanding that people express when confronted with the demands for reciprocity that lie in the traditional system of labour exchange.

2. CONTROVERSIAL RECIPROCITY

In the widest meaning reciprocity comprises all the exchange of goods and services that fall outside regular market transactions. We can subsume a great deal of exchange of labour, as well as the ceremonial gift exchange which takes place both in ordinary daily visiting, and on more clearly ceremonial occasions. Work exchange can be regulated through an institution which is organized according to the principle of delayed exchange. It is labelled 'borrowing' *(pinyam)*. One person asks for help - asks to 'borrow' labour for a particular task. The helpers are not expected to work a full day, a good meal is served, and the expectation for reciprocation is open. This openness implies that the account can be left unclosed for an unlimited time, but in the long run every participant's normal expectation is that he will get as much help out of his reservoir of social relations as he invests in it. Nothing is specified as to which tasks can be solved with the help of labour exchange, but it seems more difficult to make people support tasks that can be defined as material production, and easier to solicit help for ceremonial work. We shall touch on this point at a later stage. A smooth functioning of this reciprocity probably necessitates a situation in which people are highly obliged to each other, and have basically predictable needs and opportunities. It seems to function well under one of two extreme kinds of circumstances: (1) when one person can solicit help on the basis of power, and (2) when participants are maximally equal and tied to each other in multiplex bonds, which also means that they are about equally good reciprocators and mutuality is guaranteed.[6]

The label *controversial reciprocity* does not imply that people question the principle of reciprocity, but rather that they debate ways of using it, or the legitimacy of some neighbours' requests for help. Individuals sometimes articulate the conflict between economic self-interest as this takes shape as a private problem of resource management, and the demand on helpfulness and neighbour loyalty which ideally applies in the local field of interaction. An informant expressed this precisely in the following statement: 'If people are kin, or close to us in some other respect, they can *borrow* (us for help). They serve food, but give no money. They say: "I have some work that needs to be done; I wonder if I can borrow you for a little while." If those who ask are close, we reckon that next time we can get help in return, for anything, housebuilding for instance. But if people are more remote we prefer being paid, hired. For then we can get money to buy things that our children need. But when people ask for help we are ashamed to refuse. Then what can we do to get away from it? We can say that we have a lot of work to do for ourselves; that we do not have the time.' The concepts *closeness* and *shame* stand for obligations in the social relations of kinship, friendship and neighbourhood, and for the fear of negative sanctions against those who refuse to fulfil moral obligations.

The wish for a *wage income* and the concern about being able to *buy things that one's children need* reflect the situation in which the household stands as an economic management unit, and uncertainties about other people's reciprocation is an element to contend with. It points to the fact that many neighbours cannot be trusted as reciprocators, and that in a local system of exchange there is no economic guarantee. The question 'what can we do to get away from it?' is really a question about finding an argument that is sufficiently acceptable so that it does not lead to negative sanctions in the form of broken relations, but at best changes the agreement about their content. The informant's statement reflects his conscious understanding of the strategies that are used to solve these problems.

We shall now proceed from this clear statement about a negotiation and look at a more complex course of interaction which makes up the negotiation in one particular case. The complicating factors are the very factors which give us more knowledge about the individual participants' different opportunity situations - which organizational and value circumstances structure his adaptation in the neighbourhood.

3. THREE EVENTS

The three events, which will now be described briefly, are all staged in one household, and one important factor can thus be kept constant. Two other factors vary. These are (a) the purpose of the event, and (b) the relations between the key persons and the other participants. Key persons are the married couple Yahya and Sadiah. Yahya used to be a *penggawa* - a local administrator - in Alur Pinang, and in that capacity had a great deal of local influence. At the period of field-work he had been promoted to a new administrative job in another district, but had kept his house at Simpang Pekan, and spent as much time as he could with his family there. Together he and Sadiah had a considerable amount of landed property which, as is typical in the local situation, was distributed on a number of small lots. They had little opportunity for working on the land themselves, so they partly let it out for share-cropping, partly hired labour, and partly - as we shall now see - tried to exploit the possibilities for 'borrowing' people. This family rarely reciprocated in kind, except for Sadiah's help with cooking at weddings and other celebrations. While Yahya was still in office in Alur Pinang his lack of reciprocation in kind seemed to have been substituted for by his administering services of a different order, by which he had, or was believed to have, considerable power of sanctioning others. An attitude to this effect often appeared in statements which, in short, had this content: 'When the penggawa asks for help no one dares refuse, for we think that next time *we* may need help from *him*.' As we shall soon see, people at Simpang Pekan eventually did dare to refuse.

Sadiah was an active business woman who sold batik and gold jewellery on a credit basis, and she was socially very visible in the neighbourhood, where she was the focal point in a circle of neighbour women who regularly helped each other cook for special occasions.

The first event was a working party held by Sadiah in order to prepare rice seedlings for transplanting. This party was a success. All the women who were asked turned up. Sadiah and her daughters took part in the work, and the sociable nature of the event was strongly underlined. Coffee and snacks served in the open, long breaks and bathing in the irrigation canal contributed to give the event a character of a picnic.

The second event was Yahya's attempt at calling a party to plant the rice on a piece of land near the house. It was getting late in the season, and it was urgent to get the rice started in order not to risk a reduced crop.

First some immediate neighbours were asked, but not one would come - they all excused themselves for lack of time. The members of Yahya's family did not fail to notice the contrast to the situation that had been predominant a couple of years earlier: 'Then it was always easy to get help, nobody ever said no. People around here have become so difficult now, they always have so much work for themselves.' At the second attempt Yahya succeeded in recruiting a gang from another neighbourhood, but by a different strategy this time. Helpers were called through a network of kinsmen and people who were tied in close and/or dependent relationships to these kinsmen. In other words, the factors *closeness* and *shame* were prominent. This event did not take on the same sociable nature that Sadiah's working party had a few days earlier. Neither Yahya nor the other men in his house (a son-in-law and two teenage sons) took part in the work and the excellent meal that was served to the helpers.

The third event took place when Yahya and Sadiah planned their daughter's wedding, and asked for help both for the preparations and the feast itself, to which about 3,000 guests had been invited. On this occasion help came abundantly. For more than one week before the wedding gangs turned up every day and cleared the garden, made fireplaces for outdoor cooking and built bamboo platforms for outdoor food serving. On the actual days of the wedding feast there was more than sufficient help for cooking and serving.

The help for this undertaking was recruited in two main ways. Most of the men were recruited with the help of the *penghulus* of the various local subdivisions of Alur Pinang. These penghulus are headmen - always of local origin, and mostly farmers - who were appointed as administrative assistants to the penggawa. Most of them had been working at the time when Yahya himself was in office in Alur Pinang, and were thus tied to him in old bonds of loyalty. Most of the women who helped with the cooking and food-serving were recruited directly by Sadiah herself. They belonged to her primary relations, and were mostly members of the local circle of mutual helpers.

These three events draw our attention to the contrast between reactions to 'productive' and 'ceremonial' undertakings. The third event is of a purely ceremonial nature. The two first have a productive purpose, but differ among themselves through qualities about the social relationships that are activated. Sadiah and the women who came to help her, also help each other at numerous large and small ceremonial undertakings, they are tied to each other in a network where exchange is quick and frequent, and the working party in Sadiah's rice nursery is an extension of this field. Yahya does not have the same resources to fall back upon in his partly unsuccessful attempts, and has to revert to paths where an element of power is present. The events are examples of request and response, of impression management and camouflaged criticisms. Failures do not disrupt the polite atmosphere of the locality, but they correct the way in which people can allow themselves to tie expectations to relationships.

In their daily encounters participants have to work on their material of experience. The roles of neighbour, busy worker, family provider, and penggawa are presented as arguments in a process of negotiation.

The *busy worker* has become a role stereotype, useful for all those who are tied to some activities involving a strict time schedule, and emphasizes a minimum of similarity between the senior civil servant and the streetworker. The farmer who is concerned with resource management against the background of market conditions and consumption needs, also adopts this role identity and presents it to others. *Family provider* is another stereotype that legitimizes, so to speak being a busy worker rather than a helpful neighbour. The use of these stereotypes convey the minimum necessary information about one's timetable. Before we go into the details of the negotiation we shall discuss some of the organizational and ideological conditions working behind it, and we shall also look into the differences between the role repertoires of men and women.

4. ORGANIZATIONAL CONDITIONS

The men in Yahya's family were all white-collar workers or schoolboys, and involved in duties which did not leave them free to work in the fields during morning hours. Many others in the neighbourhood were also workers or clerks in a similar situation as regards the opportunities for spending time. This means that many men must necessarily be poor reciprocators in a system of work exchange. The men who were asked for help, however, were primarily farmers, and thus in principle masters of their own timetable. But as we know, these also refused to give help to Yahya's rice planting. We have two points of departure for describing what we can call these neighbours' organizational situation, namely, their own schemes for self-employment, and the possibilities that the environment offers for engaging in co-operation of any kind.

For one thing, farmers are, like everybody else, dependent on a money economy. Money must be provided through the sale of products, or for those who have little land, by trying to earn small wages as often as there is an opportunity. Second, so many are already prevented from taking part in work exchange, that the purely demographic foundation for a smooth flow of help and counter-help may already have been destroyed. Hence farmers are in a social environment where fewer and fewer are masters of their own timetable, and their consumption needs as family providers draw them in the direction of 'market solutions' in their own resource management. People in this situation can, however, be pressed when the activated relationships contain sufficiently obliging elements. The present cases show several of these: Yahya's second attempt succeeded because he could draw on kinsmen and power relations.

The easiness with which he was said to obtain help only a couple of years previously was also based on power that he then had, but largely lost, in Alur Pinang when he was transferred to his new position. The common understanding of this power was that he could withhold important services from people if they did not concede his requests. Even the recruitment of help at the wedding was partly based on this: The penghulus had once been broken in to ties of loyalty to the pengawa, and he was still able to exert some formal political influence on them. They in their turn have some power in their own local subdivisions.

Sadiah's smooth recruitment to her working party presents a contrast to this. The division of tasks between the sexes enters here as a factor to be reckoned with. The women who took part also differ from each other in many respects, but they are similar in being responsible for housekeeping. In a Malay household there are frequent large and small occasions that involve preparing food for a number of guests. (Working parties are one such occasion, but most others are of a ceremonial kind - from large wedding feasts to small parties marking the end of Koranic studies, haircutting ceremonies, sending someone on a journey, etc.) All these occasions call for extra effort in cooking, and again, Malay cooking is quite time-consuming. Neighbour women summon each other for help, and this is a field of activity in which reciprocation flows easily. The responsibility for ceremonial cooking is an important part of women's responsibilities. Although most peasant women take direct part in the production and sale of goods, the domestic and ceremonial activities are not allowed to be pushed aside by market oriented activities. There are a few exceptions: travelling market traders and a handful of young women in salaried posts do not, as a rule, take part in the cooking round. However, these mostly share a household arrangement with another woman who is able to take care of such responsibilities, so most *households* are members of this circle of mutuality. Sadiah's working party - for a different purpose - was taken in and treated as an extension of the cooking round, and Sadiah's clever staging supported this understanding.

It was said in the informant's statement that was cited above, and it was seen in the discussion of Yahya's case, that closeness and shame - an extra element of obligation and power - could make a reluctant neighbour grant help. In the women's case there may also be power differentials, but they are made invisible because the high frequency of contact between persons who have similar needs for help seems to satisfy the egalitarian philosophy of work exchange. A predictable and short-term cycle of reciprocation emerges.

5. DIFFERENT INTERESTS AND CONCEPTS OF REALITY

The neighbours' refusal to come to Yahya's working party had an element of calculation and principal standpoint which can not be fully understood until we have looked into the cognitive sides of the interaction.

When they trust the listener, people do not hold back on their critical comments on Yahya's request for borrowing people. 'They always ask for help for they are always trying to take advantage, (they *want much*)' is a comment that reappears in slightly varying words. Seen in connection with the wish, strong in most people, for a wage income, this points to a view that the 'borrowing' transaction is close to a kind of exploitation of friendship in order to obtain profit. Seen from the point of view of the individual helper, a meal and a vague promise about future reciprocation - in which he believes less and less - is a poorer deal than a day's wage. If we look at the transaction from Yahya's point of view, another feature appears: there is little, practically no difference between the direct expense for food for the party, and the sum that he would have had to pay in wages to get the same amount of work done.[7] What he gains in the way of work by calling a party is quick planting at a point in the season when time has become scarce, and a reduced crop is risked. Yahya spends $10 to buy food. This food goes (a) to the work gang, (b) to the families of the women who helped with the cooking, and (c) to Yahya's own family who also raise the standard of their fare for a few days. The same amount of money could have paid almost three days' wage, sufficient to get the field planted. We are here faced with two different forms of investment - the one Yahya chooses, in keeping up wide ties of reciprocity of a universal nature, and the other - which some neighbours seem to consider 'right' - in an economic transaction which, in principle, can take place independently of additional social ties.

People's possible judgement of the working party as a kind of exploitation could have been reached through different lines of reasoning. First, the starting point could be a view of labour as a commodity that has a market price and should only be sold at that price. From this point of view a transaction can be regarded as unfair if one of the counterparts is able both to produce material goods for himself, and cultivate a wider network, for the same price that could have paid the worker a full wage. Another possible point of departure stresses morality and 'real' reciprocity rather than the rules of the market, and would imply that people who earn good money, should pay in money - in short, let this scarce good flow in their immediate social environment. This is perhaps an extension of the philosophy of reciprocity that lies behind the traditional system of work assistance and many other manifestations of non-market exchange. It should not be an aim of this discussion to try to decide which of these philosophies underlies people's choices, for that would be forcing the material unduly. Most people have certainly internalized parts of both 'market' and 'reciprocity' thinking, and will not, unless challenged, feel a need to sort the strands out in clean bundles.

6. NEGOTIATIONS AND READJUSTMENT

As suggested before, it is role identities that are thrown into the local forces of interaction and used as arguments. Various definitions can apply to the various roles. The man who asks for help, implies that he expects a good neighbour to be helpful. The one who refuses, probably holds that the good neighbour should not be demanding, or 'wanting much', as Yahya was secretly accused of doing. The man who 'wants much' may be seen as trying to exploit others. Particularly a man who earns money regularly risks this judgement - he can afford to pay, he should make his resources available to others. The man who refuses to help may well imply that the counterpart is a bad neighbour in this respect, but rules for polite face-work[8] forbid him to say so. Instead he expresses the role of busy worker or family provider. This legitimizes alternative use of time, and exempts him from co-operating.

But it must not be forgotten that role negotiation is a two-sided affair, and no ego ever has the full control of alter's interpretation and hence the results of his own presentation of self. The control diminishes when people stand apart as far as shared knowledge is concerned. To illustrate this we can have another look at the negotiation between Yahya and others over some time.

While Yahya was still in office in Alur Pinang, this situation probably applied: Yahya improvised the role of neighbour for himself and imputed the same role to others according to the morality of reciprocal exchange. They on their side imputed the role of penggawa to him in order to play safe with the realities of power. They were convinced that he would sanction them negatively if they did not concede to his requests, although this does not necessarily imply that he would have done so. What happened on the level of interaction was, anyway, that Yahya got support when he initiated interaction, and if he thought that he was supported as a neighbour rather than a powerholder, he was not necessarily corrected in this assumption.

At the time of fieldwork he was no longer in office, and no longer feared, at least not by those who were most informed about the administrative structure. He tried again to appeal to the good, helpful neighbours, and this time he was altercated in the neighbour, not the penggawa, role. He was judged as a demanding neighbour at that, a man who must be taught a lesson. So everybody in the neighbourhood responded by expressing roles which exempted them from engaging in the transaction. All the local farmers became busy workers and family providers.

Yahya's interpretation is to the effect that the neighbours have become 'difficult' - less helpful, no longer good neighbours.

When Yahya finally got hold of his helpers, he and the other men in the household stayed away from the work and the meal. This again, was subject to interpretation. They were busy, and presented themselves accordingly. They themselves knew that they lacked time to take part because of other important tasks. The work gang and the neighbours had another starting point: Yahya's relatively high rank sticks to him. He is still penggawa if not in Alur Pinang, he has money, a new car, and mixes with 'big people'. Besides, agricultural work is 'dirty', and it is only what one would expect that a man of high rank does not engage in it. Finally, considerable symbolic importance is tied to the sharing of food - it stands for equality, intimacy and confidence. The non-participation in work and non-sharing of food confirms certain expectations, strengthens assumptions about inequality, and they 'know' - or think they can conclude - that Yahya places himself at a distance from them. It is a part of the story that it is not Yahya's closest acquaintances who support this interpretation, for they know from frequent mixing that he is not 'really' superior. The slightly more distant neighbours draw their conclusions on a more meagre evidence, less shared knowledge, and the judgement about the counterpart becomes more schematic.[9]

Sadiah's impression management probably acts in the opposite direction within the neighbourhood. She and the neighbour women help each other with the cooking - an activity that is highly respected and associated with equality. The companionship is, so to speak, taken out into the field, Sadiah carefully clings to equality by taking part in the 'dirty' work - the others do not become *labourers* on *her* land. In this way the family's reputation becomes nuanced. Within one circle equality is accepted and stressed, while inequality is stressed in another circle. These are not to be looked upon as concentric circles in space, for there is room for both intimacy and estrangement within the near physical surroundings.

7. *SUMMARY AND CONCLUSION*

On one level this is a discussion of how change makes its way into the local subsystem through changes in the inhabitants' opportunities in wider society. Local social structure as a working consensus about rights and duties does not change until people challenge it with their new needs and interests. I have focused empirically on certain forms of reciprocity which are vulnerable to this challenge. The changed circumstances have brought about a situation in which many people become poor reciprocators because they are not available locally. Then the path is short to a situation in which some people always ask and others always help, and this is not to be tolerated despite the fact that the overt ideology of reciprocity does not specify anything about how the account should balance. To prevent the situation of intolerable imbalance from developing, it becomes necessary to teach demanding neighbours a lesson: that there are limits of exploitation of relationships which cannot be transgressed. This drawing of limits in fact implies a reduction of expectations tied to the neighbour role, perhaps we could say the removal of some rights and duties that used to be taken for granted. But the minimal communication sufficient to bring this result about, does not guarantee that there is a high degree of congruence in the ways in which people see each other. Small differences in social circumstances and style of living may easily lead to stereotyped assumptions and estrangement in neighbourhoods. We have looked in some detail at a case which underlines this point. Within Alur Pinang it is possible to find localities which differ considerably in the degree to which people have become estranged from each other, and this is directly correlated with the amount of occupational differentiation present.

Still, what we have observed earlier in this discussion about people's general eagerness to build up their social resources suggests that the principle of reciprocity is still a cause for great concern. For despite the thinning out of some kinds of reciprocity, the network of ceremonial exchange is extremely important. From our material it seems as though this network is to a large extent integrated through the ceremonial basework that women do in the domestic field. The direct exchange of services survive more easily in this field than anywhere else, and women also take care of the bulk of the ceremonial gift exchange, that takes place at small encounters, while men and women alike follow up at large celebrations. Reluctance to give of one's time to help a neighbour is not paired with any general parsimony in the ceremonial life. On the contrary, large resources of both time and money are spent. Most conspicuous are the celebrations that gather whole neighbourhoods and people from larger areas, and where attention, sympathy, money and services flow abundantly.

The ceremonial network has its losers and winners, but still more important, participants are tied together in mutual recognition so that the path is kept open for other forms of reciprocity. These other forms of co-operation are of a nature which can be labelled 'career assistance' or 'middleman services' of which some examples were mentioned early in this paper. These services present fewer problems to the balance of time and resources than the institution of 'borrowing' does. And they are more in demand than ever in a society which calls for increased mobility across social and physical distance. This is reflected in the shape of the ceremonial network, and the recognition that different people get in it. More distant friends are sometimes more important than immediate neighbours, and the winners in the ceremonial system of exchange - those who are sought most often and get most gifts - seem to be those who stand in the best position to mediate goods from the surrounding society. These are people whose network stretches across the local field of interaction and who take part in activities which make it possible for them to administer scarce goods available only outside the neighbourhood.

When certain people negotiate to get rid of some expectations in the neighbourhood, this does not mean a total giving-up on the idea of reciprocity, for they may only seek other network connections and other forms of exchange more in line with the challenges they meet in a wider sphere of society.

NOTES

1 *Bailey, F.G.,* Gifts and Poison. Oxford 1971; *Barth, F.,* Analytical Dimensions in the Comparison of Social Organizations (in: American Anthropologist, 74, 1972); *Grønhaug, R.,* Micro-Macro Relations: Social Organization in Antalya, Southern Turkey. Bergen: Dept. of Social Anthropology, University of Bergen 1974, mimeo; and others.

2 *McCall, G. & J.L. Simmons,* Identities and Interactions. New York 1966.

3 Names are fictitious.

4 E.g. *Wolf, E.,* Kinship, Friendship and Patron-Client Relations in Complex Societies. London 1966; *Foster, G.,* Interpersonal Relations in Peasant Societies (in: Human Organization, 1, 1960).

5 *Wolf, E.,* Peasants. Englewood Cliffs 1966.

6 *Rudie, I.,* Between Market and Neighbourhood. Oslo 1972, unpublished typescript.

7 Ibid.

8 *Goffman, E.,* Interactional Ritual. New York 1967.

9 *Bailey, F.G.,* Gifts and Poison.

BIBLIOGRAPHY

Bailey, F.G., Gifts and Poison, Oxford 1971.

Barth, F., Analytical Dimensions in the Comparison of Social Organizations (in: American Anthropologist, 74, 1972).

Foster, G., Interpersonal Relations in Peasant Societies (in: Human Organization, 1, 1960).

Goffman, E., Interactional Ritual. New York 1967.

Grønhaug, R., Micro-Macro Relations: Social Organization in Antalya, Southern Turkey. Bergen: Dept. of Social Anthropology, University of Bergen 1974, mimeo.

McCall, G. & J.L. Simmons., Identities and Interactions. New York 1966.

Rudie, I., Between Market and Neighbourhood. Oslo 1972, unpublished typescript.

Wolf, E., Kinship, Friendship and Patron-Client Relations in Complex Societies. London 1966.

Wolf, E., Peasants. Englewood Cliffs 1966.